Public or Private Goods?

Public or Private Goods?

Redefining Res Publica

Edited by

Brigitte Unger

Utrecht University School of Economics, the Netherlands and former Director, Institute of Economic and Social Research WSI in Dusseldorf, Germany

Daan van der Linde

Utrecht University School of Economics, the Netherlands

Michael Getzner

Center of Public Finance and Infrastructure Policy, Department of Spatial Planning, Vienna University of Technology, Austria

EE Edward Elgar PUBLISHING

Cheltenham, UK • Northampton, MA, USA

Published by
Edward Elgar Publishing Limited
The Lypiatts
15 Lansdown Road
Cheltenham
Glos GL50 2JA
UK

Edward Elgar Publishing, Inc.
William Pratt House
9 Dewey Court
Northampton
Massachusetts 01060
USA

A catalogue record for this book
is available from the British Library

Library of Congress Control Number: 2016957236

This book is available electronically in the **Elgar**online
Economics subject collection
DOI 10.4337/9781785369551

ISBN 978 1 78536 954 4 (cased)
ISBN 978 1 78536 955 1 (eBook)

Typeset by Servis Filmsetting Ltd, Stockport, Cheshire

Contents

PART III PUBLIC GOODS

Contributors

Florian Blank, Institute of Economic and Social Research (WSI), Hans Böckler Foundation, Germany.

Klaas van Egmond, Faculty of Geosciences, Utrecht University, the Netherlands.

Joras Ferwerda, Utrecht University School of Economics, Utrecht University, the Netherlands.

Michael Getzner, Centre of Public Finance and Infrastructure Policy, Department of Spatial Planning, Vienna University of Technology, Austria.

Loek Groot, Utrecht University School of Economics, Utrecht University, the Netherlands.

Gerlinde Gutheil-Knopp-Kirchwald, Centre of Public Finance and Infrastructure Policy, Department of Spatial Planning, Vienna University of Technology, Austria.

Justin Kadi, Institute for European Urban Studies, Bauhaus University Weimar, Germany.

Trudie Knijn, Utrecht University, the Netherlands and the University of Johannesburg, South Africa.

Ian Koetsier, Utrecht University School of Economics, Utrecht University, the Netherlands.

Jane Lewis, LSE, United Kingdom.

Daan van der Linde, Utrecht University School of Economics, Utrecht University, the Netherlands.

Brigitte Unger, Utrecht University School of Economics, Utrecht University, the Netherlands and former Director, Institute of Economic and Social Research (WSI), Germany.

Frans van Waarden, University College, Utrecht University, the Netherlands.

Grazia Withalm, Centre of Public Finance and Infrastructure Policy, Department of Spatial Planning, Vienna University of Technology, Austria.

Preface

The idea of this book emerged when an unpublished manuscript by Egon Matzner was discovered ten years after his untimely death (2003). Egon Matzner had been Professor of Public Sector Economics at Vienna University of Technology, and Director of the Wissenschaftszentrum Berlin für Sozialforschung (WZB). His latest thoughts centred around *res publica* in times of globalization. How can the public sphere be protected when nation states lose political ground? What should be the *res publica*, the public matter, in a changing world?

This book takes up these thoughts. It is the result of a joint research project, 'Res Publica', of the Wirtschafts- und Sozialwissenschaftliches Institut (WSI, the research institute of the German trade unions), and two international universities: Utrecht University School of Economics in the Netherlands, and the Vienna University of Technology's Center of Public Finance and Infrastructure Policy in Austria. This multidisciplinary and international project was financed by the Hans Böckler Foundation (HBS) in Düsseldorf.

The editors want to thank Michael Sommer (former head of the German Trade Union Confederation, DGB), and Dr Nikolaus Simon (former Executive Director of the Hans Böckler Foundation, HBS), for their encouragement and commitment in setting up this international project between the trade union research institute WSI and international academia. Dr Wolfgang Uellenberg-van Dawen from the managing board of the HBS gave many inspirations to this project. We want to thank the Hans Böckler Foundation, and indirectly all members of the DGB-related German trade unions, for the financial support which made this research project and the publication possible.

To prepare this book, several meetings took place at the WSI in Düsseldorf, at Vienna University of Technology and at Utrecht University in the Netherlands. We want to thank the participants of these meetings; notably, Florian Blank, Eric Seils and Dorothee Spannagel, from the WSI. Furthermore, the WSI was represented through its WSI–Eucos PhD students at Utrecht University. These were Swantje Falcke, Leydi Johana van den Braken, Ian Koetsier and Daan van der Linde. We want to thank Erik Stam, Jaap Bikker, Ioana Deleanu and Loek Groot from

Utrecht University School of Economics; Frans van Waarden, University College Utrecht; Hans Renes, Human Geography and Planning, Utrecht University; Stephan Leibfried from the University of Bremen; and Wolfgang Blaas, Wilfried Schönbäck, Gerlinde Gutheil-Knopp-Kirchwald, Grazia Withalm, Katharina Fischeneder and Leonhard Plank from Vienna University of Technology, for important input and presentations.

We thank all the authors for their contributions, and also many scholars who have discussed the chapters of this book on various occasions with us. Furthermore, we want to thank Douglas Deitemyer, Irene Popenberger and Iris Schneider for their help in editing the manuscript, and Matthew Pitman and Edward Elgar Publishing for their elegant style in publishing this book.

Our endeavour was a multidisciplinary one, bringing together scholars from various disciplines: economic research, sociology, political science, geography and spatial planning. This approach was both challenging and rewarding. When crossing disciplinary borders, we have to learn to speak each other's language and navigate across paradigms, yet we encounter new ideas which help us to understand, describe and justify the broad societal and political shifts we encounter in the world today. And this book is our attempt to share our insights on the matters of *res publica*.

Brigitte Unger, Daan van der Linde and Michael Getzner
Utrecht and Vienna, February 2017

1. Introduction

Brigitte Unger, Loek Groot and Daan van der Linde*

> The Settle-to-Carlisle line is the most celebrated obscure line in the world. British Rail has been wanting to close it down for years on the grounds that it doesn't pay its way, which is the most mad and preposterous line of argument imaginable. We've been hearing this warped reasoning for so long about so many things that it has become received wisdom, but when you think about it for even a nanosecond it is perfectly obvious that most worthwhile things don't begin to pay for themselves. If you followed this absurd logic any distance at all, you would have to get rid of traffic lights, lay-bys, schools, drains, national parks, museums, universities, old people and much else besides. So why on earth should something as useful as a railway line . . . have to demonstrate even the tiniest measure of economic viability to ensure its continued existence? This is a line of thinking that must be abandoned at once. (Bryson, 1995, p. 294)

This book on the *res publica* was inspired by a manuscript by Egon Matzner, former Director of the WZB (Wissenschaftszentrum Berlin für Sozialforschung) and founder of SASE Austria, who more than ten years ago shortly before his untimely death, in an article titled 'Redefining the public purpose: on the socio-economics of a global *res publica*' (Matzner, 2001) urged that one should rediscuss what has to be public (and what private) under the changed premises of globalization and Europeanization. Since the late 1980s waves of privatization of gas, electricity, coal and steel plants, of telecommunication and transport networks, of banks and post offices, have changed the role of the public sector. Today even core tasks of the *res publica* such as the provision of security are debated as to whether they should be provided or financed privately.

The term '*res publica*' goes back to Cicero's dialogue *De re publica*, in which he states that 'when all are subject to the rule of one tyrant, the state cannot be called a res publica'. It has been a recurrent theme ever since Paine (1791) defines it as 'RES-PUBLICA, the public affairs, or the public good; or literally translated, the public thing. It is a word of good original, referring to what ought to be the character and business of government'. In this book, we define the *res publica* as the realm of all matters which are decided upon in societal communications, and on a societal (often government) level with the aim to provide for a joint (public or societal) interest; contrary to 'private affairs' decided upon by private agents (households, firms).This book sets out to analyse shifts between the public and the private in different policy fields and to find out what the *res publica* has to be. What are the core functions in an economy and a society that have to remain public, and do these core functions change over time?

The book addresses two main questions which we want to introduce in this chapter:

1. What is public and why should something be in public responsibility? Which criteria, and theoretical and empirical arguments are relevant to determine whether the provision and financing of a good is a public or private responsibility, or a mixture of both? In sections 1 and 2, we discuss different models which aim to answer the question why something belongs to the *res publica*.
2. Who determines what is public and what is private? Which actors do what? And why are they doing this? How is the public intervention justified? How can one decide whether there is a role for public intervention, and given there is a role for public intervention, who intervenes and how?

This introduction to the *res publica* aims to provide a framework to address not only the normative question on what ought to be the character and business of government (or any other public authority), but also to positively evaluate shifts between private and public roles in recent history. As Van Waarden (2012) argues, historical evaluations of the balance between market, state and society may serve as an alternative for models arguing that the 'right' configuration exists: why did current tasks evolve the way they did, and what can be learned from the past? Changes in technology or in the economic environment (such as the emergence of the European Union and globalization) can be held responsible for shifts in the optimal allocation between the public and private sphere, but there might also be a major shift of preferences regarding what should be public or private. Van Waarden (2002, p. 44) refers to a study by Van Thiel (2000), who found that for many local projects the justification for privatization was shaky, and the main drivers were a general presumption against state involvement and herd behaviour among decision makers. This may lead to what Heath (2001, p. 296) calls 'ideological privatizations'. Although it is hard to claim that the pendulum in the division between public and private, or market and government, has begun to reverse its swing, we feel it is important to give an account of the public sector in order to better understand what is at stake.

1.1 WHAT IS PUBLIC?

In economics, a major concern is public versus private goods. Goods can be private, public and 'impure' public goods. The theory of public goods (henceforth: PGs) started with two seminal articles by Samuelson (1954, 1955), in which he gave a formal definition of a pure PG: a good both non-rival in consumption and non-excludable. His division thus runs along the lines of a strict dichotomy between private and public goods, the former being 'ordinary consumption goods which can be parceled out among different individuals', the latter 'collective consumption goods which all enjoy in common in the sense that each individual's consumption of such a good leads to no subtraction from any other individual's consumption of that good'. The main feature that distinguishes public from private goods is the fact that all receive the same quantity of the public good, whereas individuals may differ in the quantities consumed of private goods.[1] The Samuelson rule, which decides upon the allocation of funds regarding private consumption and public production, states that an optimal allocation is reached once the value of the total quantity of private goods individuals are willing to give up for one additional unit of public good equals the value of the inputs required to produce that additional unit of public good.

Building on this framework, the theory of PGs was extended along several lines, dependent upon which assumptions of the original Samuelson model were released. Not all goods satisfy Samuelson's strict definition: impure public goods lie between strictly non-rival and non-excludable public goods and private rival and excludable counterparts. These impure public goods may suffer from congestion or other externalities of consumption, while public goods in essence cannot. Tiebout (1956) for instance focused on non-excludability limited to localities, which gave rise to a theory of local PGs. In Buchanan's (1965) club good theory, the possibility of exclusion allows the good to be provided in the form of a club good (pay-per-view TV and subscription TV are good examples). Both theories claim that no market failures need to arise: by means of 'voting with their feet' in the case of local PGs, or by means of two-part tariffs with a membership and user fee in the case of club goods (a model applied by some European satellites), the market can provide optimal quantities and qualities of these impure PGs. For the provision of these types of impure public goods, it would imply that there is no or only a limited role to play for government.[2]

For the pure PG characterized by non-excludability, a free-rider problem arises, leading to a market failure, providing a *prima facie* case for government intervention. This in turn has led to the study of voting models in connection with optimal provision of PGs (see e.g. Bucovetsky, 1991).

Note that in Samuelson's original contribution, the government was simply assumed to expand the PG production, financed by means of lump sum taxation, up to the point where the sum of marginal benefits among citizens equals the price or marginal cost of the PG. The research question in the voting models is whether (and under which conditions and voting procedures) preferences are adequately aggregated and revealed in the political process (for example, the median voter theorem would predict that the provision level of the PG is determined by the preferences of the median voter only, which may diverge from the optimal provision level; see Hindriks and Myles, 2006, p. 113). In addition, a case for government intervention in providing PGs may only be given if the benefits (willingness to pay) of citizens is higher than the cost of providing PGs, and if the state itself provides the PGs efficiently; for example, marginal opportunity and transaction costs (including inefficiencies of the tax system) of providing PGs should be smaller than marginal benefits.

Following Samuelson, the two key characteristics of a pure PG give rise to the familiar cross table with private goods (rival and excludable), 'commons' (rival/congestible and non-excludable), collective (club) goods (non-rival and excludable) and PGs (non-rival and non-excludable). This two-way dichotomy may serve well to explain the basic theory of PGs to freshmen in economics, but as an adequate description the same dichotomy is far from complete to describe the rich variety of goods that do not squarely fall into one of these categories. Take the example of military defence, a paradigmatic example of a pure PG in economic textbooks (see e.g. Sandler and Hartley, 1995). The mere existence of military alliances shows that the PG military protection is at best only non-rival and non-excludable among members. Although at a national level military expenditures may be considered as PG outlays, on an international level they better fit the model of club goods, with military alliances in the role of clubs from which exclusion is possible. Taking defence as a non-rival but excludable club good, it follows that all friendly nations will be included in the alliance and that the alliance will have tight linkages to foster cooperation in order to neutralize the free-riding behaviour of small or poor allies (Sandler and Murdoch, 2000, p. 301). Another alternative for the pure PG model for defence is the joint product model, where military expenditure generates both private (within-ally) benefits and public (among-ally) benefits. For instance, defence spending on intelligence to reduce terrorist threats may give country-specific benefits as well as higher security among the allies. The joint product model allows the possibility that different categories of defence spending may vary in the degree to which they provide excludable and private benefits or alliance-wide benefits. Another example is given by medication to treat or cure AIDS or other contagious diseases (see e.g. Sonntag, 2010). As soon as these medications are invented, the knowledge acquired of how to make these substances can be considered as a global PG. However, the patent system temporarily transforms these goods into private goods. The Health Impact Fund initiated by Thomas Pogge and the Global Health Fund can be seen as attempts to recoup the welfare losses incurred by this transition from public to private goods and non-marginal cost pricing.[3]

These examples above show that subtle differences in the characteristics of different PGs may lead to entirely different outcomes with respect to actual and Pareto-optimal provision levels and feasible burden-sharing agreements. Any study of a PG should sort these features out in a systematic way. Bergstrom and Goodman (1973) are among the authors using econometric techniques to empirically estimate a degree of publicness for parks and recreation and police expenditures – both arguably impure public goods.

1.2 WHY SHOULD SOMETHING BE OF PUBLIC OR PRIVATE RESPONSIBILITY?

Modern-day economics textbooks argue the market is the default, and where government intends to intervene, the burden of proof is on the side of government. For the government to intervene, it must identify market failures and show that intervention will lead to improved outcomes. 'But according to which standard?', Heath (2011, p. 13) rightly asks, arguing that the normative standards used to show that intervention will lead to better outcomes must at the same time be able to explain the track record of the welfare state over the last century. We present three such models or approaches, labelled 'equality', 'community' and 'efficiency' by Heath (ibid., p. 14), which may both justify and explain public intervention.[4]

The redistributive or equality model claims that market economies arrive at generally unacceptable (that is, unequal) distributions of income and wealth and government intervenes to make the outcomes more equal (cf. Musgrave and Musgrave's 1989 'distribution function'). Streeck (2011), in his analysis of the tensions within 'democratic capitalism', suggests that the economy is:

> ruled by two conflicting principles, or regimes, of resource allocation: one operating according to marginal productivity, or what is revealed as merit by a 'free play of market forces,' and the other following social need, or entitlement, as certified by the collective choices of democratic politics. Governments under democratic capitalism are under pressure to honor both principles simultaneously although substantively the two almost never agree . . . Governments that

> fail to attend to democratic claims for protection and redistribution risk losing their majority while governments that disregard the claims for compensation from the owners of productive resources . . . cause economic dysfunctions and distortions that will be increasingly unsustainable and will thereby also undermine political support. (p. 3)

These concerns are echoes of De Tocqueville (1835), arguing that the scope of government depends on the extent of voting franchise and the distribution of wealth in society (see also Meltzer and Richard, 1981). The redistributive model suggests that the welfare state serves to limit the scope for exploitation of workers and argues that government should redistribute income and wealth to those both inside and outside the labour market (through, for example, unemployment insurance and welfare benefits). In this approach, the market stands for efficiency while government preserves equity, fairness and/or equality.

The community or morality model argues that the state should engage in activities that purposefully limit the scope of markets. Next to immaterial conditions such as human dignity and rights, freedom of thought and speech, proponents of this stream of thought argue that government must ensure the material conditions to exercise human rationality are met, which are necessary conditions for individual autonomy and democratic citizenship. Citizens (the civil society) have, of course, constantly to fight for and guarantee that the government (state institutions) provide these conditions, and that policy-makers truly fulfil the public interest. Authors such as Walzer (1983), Etzioni (1988) and, more recently, Sandel (1998) argue that 'needed' goods are not commodities, nor should they be treated as such (see also Boulding, 1969). In order to settle the question of whether a good should be provided publicly or privately, one should judge whether the commodification of that good is morally permissible, and if not, the free market exchange of that good should be blocked. Heralded examples of goods that should be provided publicly on moral grounds include water utilities, education, health care, military defence, police and court services; the latter, for instance, to provide equality of the law and equal legal certainty. For certain goods one may argue that everyone should have equal access (for example, primary education, basic health care, national statistics bureaus, cultural institutions, nature reserves). Certain goods, although in principle marketable, have specific properties in terms of safety and security, warranting public provision (for example, nuclear power plants or defence). This model rests on a presupposed 'public sector ethos' (Heath, 2011, p. 21), by which the public sector produces goods based on different motivations compared to the private sector, and policy-makers strive for the common good. While private corporations are driven by profit, the state, communitarians argue, is driven by the public interest and 'certain moral and civic goods are diminished or corrupted if bought and sold for money' (Sandel, 1998, p. 94, cited by Heath, 2011, p. 19).[5] According to this approach, one may even interpret a large part of the welfare state securing adequate food, housing, security and other basic necessities not so much by invoking redistributive concerns, but as the state protecting human dignity. It also explains why so many welfare benefits are provided in-kind, rather than as an equivalent cash payment (allowing for free exchange of these goods on the market). The reasoning is also manifest in case of merit goods, which justify public intervention based on paternalism. A recent example might be a system of mandatory pension savings, paternalistically merited as there may be a tendency for too-little savings due to too-high or hyperbolic discounting.

Finally, the efficiency model argues the state serves as just another way to reach production of certain goods, resolving issues of collective action. In those areas where the state outperforms markets – that is, in the case of natural monopolies, imperfect markets, externalities, production of public goods, incomplete markets and information failures (Stiglitz, 2000) – there is a clear argument from the perspective of efficiency for public intervention (allocation function of the government; cf. Musgrave and Musgrave, 1989). Matzner (2001), for instance, argues that growing population density and urbanization have led to increasing externalities from individual behaviour, calling for restraint of the pursuit of private interests which may negatively influence others.

According to this view, the state basically does the same as the market: providing goods and services; yet only does so where and when it can do so more efficiently. This line of reasoning is also used by Teulings et al. (2005), who argue that besides redistribution the main function of the state is to solve what they call 'complex externalities': externalities which the market is not able to overcome in spite of the Coase theorem. To explain the size of the welfare state, this approach must assume a kind of generality of market failures. These market failures are due to externalities, information asymmetries (giving rise to moral hazard, adverse selection and principal–agent problems), natural monopolies and the impracticability of concluding and enforcing contracts in some domains. Especially fruitful in this respect is to focus on transaction costs in market exchanges and in hierarchical organizations.[6] The comparative advantage of the state compared to corporations, co-operatives, civil organizations and not-for-profits is that the former can simply force citizens to cooperate, thereby reducing transaction costs, where the loss of freedom is to a large extent the freedom to free-ride (Heath, 2001, p. 174). The state therefore also acts as a coordinator of development (economic and social, urban and regional development) when the 'market' lacks the capacity for long-term (sustainable) and complex coordination of different aims and objectives, actors and driving forces.

The strength of this public efficiency approach is that it is able to provide an account of a widely heterogeneous set of government activities, and also how these may change over time due to technological changes or changes of circumstance (for example, emergence of the single European market). It can readily explain why the state is in the business of natural monopolies and correcting negative externalities (that is, by environmental taxes) and positive externalities (that is, in education, scientific research, nature preservation, vaccination or even weather forecasting). Krugman's definition of the state as an 'insurance company with an army' fits this approach, where all kinds of welfare programmes[7] are merely compulsory insurances solving adverse selection problems, while the army represents the state's role in providing public goods.[8]

Three Models of *Res Publica*

Heath (2011) argues that the efficiency model has the highest descriptive power, explaining the rise in government spending across the last century. For instance, the growth of government expenditure by the end of the nineteenth century was mainly due to the enormous public investment in rail and road infrastructures. For our purposes, however, what is important is to establish for any good or activity the right kind of justification for government intervention, whether be it out of a concern for equity, from moral concerns or for efficiency reasons. A too-narrow defence of the political left to defend the welfare state on fairness grounds runs the risk of viewing the welfare state as imposing a high economic cost (by deadweight losses and distortionary taxation), whereas it might in fact be more efficient than any feasible market solution for the goods and services provided (Heath, 2001, p. xvii). On the same footing, the presumption of market above government among the political right has the danger that where the government can deliver huge efficiency gains, in the name of liberty – in particular the unwillingness to pay taxes – these are forgone (ibid., p. 58).[9] The right justification also has implications for the trade-off between equity and efficiency:

> The left is willing to tolerate a lot of inefficiency in return for increased equality, and therefore wants an expanded role of the state. The right accuses the left of killing the goose that lays the golden eggs, and so demands deregulation of the economy and a rollback of the welfare state. The problem with both views is that their underlying assumption is totally mistaken. Far from serving as a drag on the economy, the state makes a huge contribution to the efficiency of the economy. It does so not only indirectly, by providing the background conditions

> needed for a flourishing market economy, but also directly by providing goods and services that are not available in the private sector. The state lays just as many golden eggs as the market. (Heath, 2001, pp. 200–201)

Thus, the activities of the state and the market are complementary and are undertaken to provide mutual benefits. A misplaced assessment of the welfare state in terms of delivering justice or fairness also runs the danger that if people care less about equity over time, then this may translate into a retrenchment of the welfare state.[10]

1.3 RELEVANT DIMENSIONS

In the above section we offered three general models for public intervention and suggested that the tasks of a *res publica* are: (1) redistributing, as market forces result in (democratically) unacceptable levels of income or wealth inequality; (2) producing goods which on moral grounds should not be treated as commodities on the market; and (3) producing those goods for which the public sector generally outperforms markets. In this section we offer three dimensions along which to organize the *res publica*: firstly, the production or the indirect provision of this good; secondly, public or private funding; and thirdly, regulation and standard setting. Along these dimensions we can understand shifts over time. For instance, are certain public tasks which previously were privately funded increasingly publicly funded? Or has the state moved from a role in the provision of specific goods or services to a role of a funder or regulator?

Barr (2012) firstly understands privatization in a simplified public–private dichotomy model as a move from public to private production and/or of financing. He adds, however, that the public sector might impose strict regulations and provisions. Taking the regulatory role into account, goods and services are located between the purely private, in which decisions about quantities to be produced and consumed are decentralized; and the purely public, where decisions on both production and finance are decided upon in the public domain by central planners. Privatization according to Barr is any move from public to private, yet noting that intermediary cases include those where although production and financing is purely private, the government may intervene by means of standards, regulations or competition law, and by securing property rights by means of public courts.

Dimension 1: Private or Public Production

The provision of public goods can be direct and indirect. Direct provision is public production and is important if market failures concentrate on the supply side of the market, that is, in the case of natural monopolies and adverse selection. The underlying normative implications of the decision between private or public production is given by De Beer (2004), who argues that a perfect market is only possible under very stringent conditions, such as perfect information and absence of transaction costs. The first theorem of welfare economics states that perfect markets produce efficient outcomes; or stated otherwise, that a competitive equilibrium is Pareto-efficient (Hindriks and Myles, 2006, p. 31). Proponents of privatization of publicly produced goods explicitly or implicitly tend to assume that any movement towards this (perhaps non-existent) perfect market will also improve efficiency. According to De Beer, this way of thinking is based on a fallacy. Even if for the sake of argument it is assumed that a purely private provision in a near-perfect market leads to a better performance than public provision, it does not necessarily imply that departing from public provision, all intermediary positions result in a better outcome. Outcomes may possibly be worse once former state-owned companies are partially privatized; often simultaneously lessening grip by government and lacking pressure from competitive forces, increasing prices and lowering quality. In addition, costs of (private) management, marketing and controlling add up to transaction costs which might not accrue in the case of public provision (for example, if consumption is mandatory in the case of publicly provided social insurance).

The trend of privatization in the last three decades with disappointing results at times is relevant here. It has manifested itself in different forms, ranging from transforming public organizations into agencies, deregulation and liberalization, to full privatization (especially the sale of state enterprises in formerly public utilities such as postal services, water and electricity, alongside the sale of publicly owned shares in private companies, such as airports). Against the potential efficiency effects of privatization, one must see the disadvantages. First, transaction costs increase, especially the legal costs to define and defend property rights (Van Waarden, 2001, p. 121). In case of patents and copyrights, the fragmentation of knowledge in private property may also inhibit the expansion of new knowledge (but might, on the other hand, form an incentive for research and development by companies). Second, privatization implies retrenchment of the public domain and expansion of the market, with a corresponding shift from political voice enacted by citizens to exit by consumers. Especially when privatization is not successful, the loss of voice is not compensated by the gain of exit, in the extreme leading to a situation of both no exit and no voice, as is the case in private monopolies.[11] Advocates of privatization will argue that privatizations sometimes fail because they fall short of full privatization. This may be the case, but it might also be the case that inherent market imperfections (the reason for public involvement in the first place) reappear after privatization. Van Waarden (2001, p. 126) hints at the danger that equal access to the political process is compromised by inequality (succinctly captured in the slogan 'One dollar, one vote') and suggests that ongoing privatization may cause a gradual decline in political participation, labelled '*Politikverdrossenheit*': why vote, if most is decided by the market and politics remains in charge of only a shrinking public domain? In the same vein, Judt (2010, p. 73) argues that one social cost of privatization often overlooked is that the more is privatized, the less we share in common:

> Any society, he [Edmund Burke] wrote in Reflections on the Revolution in France, which destroys the fabric of its state, must soon be 'disconnected into the dust and powder of individuality'. By eviscerating public services and reducing them to a network of farmed-out private providers, we have begun to dismantle the fabric of the state. As for the dust and powder of individuality. it resembles nothing so much as Hobbes's war of all against all, in which life for many people has once again become solitary, poor and more than a little nasty. One striking consequence of the disintegration of the public sector has been an increased difficulty in comprehending what we have in common with others. (p. 73)

> People who live in private spaces contribute actively to the dilution and corrosion of the public space. In other words, they exacerbate the circumstances which drove them to retreat in the first place. And by so doing, they pay a price. If public goods – public services, public spaces, public facilities – are devalued, diminished in the eyes of citizens and replaced by private services available against cash, then we lose the sense that common interests and common needs ought to trump private preferences and individual advantage. And once we cease to value the public over the private, surely we shall come in time to have difficulty seeing just why we should value law (the public good par excellence) over force. (p. 78)

Dimension 2: Private or Public Financing

Market defects may exist on both demand and supply sides of the market. Heath (2011) argues that public funding of goods (that is, through taxes) is in order when market failures are concentrated on the demand side, for instance due to non-excludability in consumption. Even though financed publicly, provision may still be private, for instance through contracting. Examples in which contracting is paramount are the construction and waste industries, often publicly funded yet provided by (competing) market parties. Theory regarding public funding often concentrates on methods of financing, exploring the progressivity or (distortionary) effects of taxation, for instance on labour supply or consumption decisions (Stiglitz, 2000).

In addition, increasingly governments have applied the benefit principle: services formerly for free and tax-funded are now subject to levies proportional to their use, together with a shift towards financing by demand, for example by means of vouchers (in the provision of care, education and reintegration services for the unemployed). On the one hand, such fees are levied on the basis that users should be aware that freely provided goods and services are costly, and that they should use these goods and services more deliberately. On the other hand, user fees form a barrier to using such goods which may have positive external effects, and to which all users should have access regardless of their income (for example, medicine).

Dimension 3: Regulation and Standard Setting

Government furthermore can intervene by law and regulation. Certain goods can be forbidden, others can be only produced if they fulfil certain standards. Environmentally friendly modes of production, a recreation zone for employees, health and safety regulations and food security regulations are public goods which are not set through market mechanisms but through law and order. There have likely been shifts towards more of this type of government intervention in various domains.

1.4 SOME FURTHER CONCERNS

The analysis so far presumes that the goods can be readily identified and measured, and if the government intervenes, the public clearly sees the benefits and costs involved. For some goods, however, it is far less clear how they can be produced, what the costs and benefits are, and how the public perceives government intervention. Specific goods and returns to these goods are often incommensurable, producing intangible benefits. When evaluating the benefits from education, for instance, one quickly runs into the problem of a large range of spillovers, the social benefits of which are not easily captured. Kindleberger (1983) extends Adam Smith's list of public goods as a necessary requirement for free trade with so-called 'elusive "goods"' among which are 'macroeconomic stability, redistribution of national income, the monetary system, and . . . standards of various sorts' (p. 1). The latter can all be catalogued under the rubric of so-called 'intangible' goods. The core public functions of Adam Smith (for example, security) may also be intangible, and it might be hard to imagine a situation where these goods and services are not provided.

While the lighthouse serves as the prototypical public good, goods such as cultural and natural heritage or economic stability are intangible (Frey and Steiner, 2011; Kaul et al., 1999). The market is extremely good at fulfilling our needs for 'medium-sized dry goods' (Heath, 2001, p. 129). The market economy serves well those people whose utility derives from cars, stereos or a house. 'If you happen to be the unlucky type of person whose needs are focused on more intangible goods', Heath (2001, p. 129) argues, 'such as going for a nature hike on a clear summer day – then the market will not serve you well. In fact, it will serve you quite poorly, since it will have a tendency to shift resources away from the production of the type of goods that you enjoy', and which are not traded on markets, for example owing to the lack of defined property rights.

Finally, different combinations of funding, provision or regulation are not necessarily neutral with regard to their political impact. In *The Submerged State*, Mettler (2011) claims that the way in which policy is being made has changed: new policy is by many perceived only as the freely functioning market economy at work. Her conclusion is that the impact of so-called 'visible governance' has diminished, while that of the 'submerged state' has grown (p. 16). Government increasingly operates indirectly and 'statelessly'. Today we may still benefit from many public services without even knowing it, Mettler (2011) claims; the underlying mechanisms including subsidized loans or guarantees by government, social benefits through tax breaks or incentives, and benefits and services provided by private third-party organizations and non-profits, either subsidized or 'contracted out' by government. Invisible government means less trust in the government and in government's effectiveness. Tax morale is lower with less visibility of government spending on social programmes. Judt (2010) argues along the same lines:

> What does it mean to those on the receiving end when everything from the local bus service to the regional parole officer are now part of some private company which measures their performance with exclusive reference to short-term profitability? In the first place, there is a negative welfare impact . . . The chief shortcoming of the old public services was the restrictive regulations and facilities – one-size-fits-all – with which they were notoriously associated: Swedish alcohol outlets, British Railways cafes, unionized French welfare offices and so forth. But at least their provision was universal, and for good and ill they were regarded as a public responsibility . . . a social service provided by a private company does not present itself as a collective good to which all citizens have a right. Unsurprisingly, there has been a sharp falling off in the number of people claiming benefits and services to which they are legally entitled. The result is an eviscerated society . . . seeking unemployment pay, medical attention, social

> benefits or other officially mandated services – it is no longer to the state, the administration or the government that he or she instinctively turns. The service or benefit in question is now often 'delivered' by a private intermediary. As a consequence, the thick mesh of social interactions and public goods has been reduced to a minimum, with nothing except authority and obedience binding the citizen to the state. (p. 73)

1.5 CONCLUSION

Section 1.2 has offered us three general approaches to public intervention, suggesting that government intervention is warranted to redistribute income as market forces result in (democratically) unacceptable levels of income or wealth inequality, in order to produce goods which on moral grounds should not be treated as commodities on the market, or to produce those goods for which the public sector generally outperforms markets. Section 1.1 has offered a classification of goods along the lines of public or private goods (or the intermediary impure good). Section 1.3 added public or private funding, public or private production. In addition, the role of regulation and standard setting has been addressed.

Table 1.1 allowed the contributors to this book to compare their specific subfields. Arguments for publicly funding pensions (Chapters 5 and 6) and unemployment insurance (Chapter 7), for instance, can run along the lines of each of the three models from section 1.2, treating public pensions as an (intergenerational) redistributive tool or treating unemployment insurance as a redistributive tool between those in and outside the labour market. From a moral point of view, one could argue that societies should ensure the material conditions for democratic citizenship and autonomy of the elderly after retirement or of the unemployed. Or from the perspective of efficiency, one could argue that public pension systems provide additional or even better hedging against risks compared to their privately funded counterparts, as do unemployment insurances, facing adverse selection problems when provided by the market. Chapters also focus on shifts

Table 1.1 A scheme to compare contributions

	Description (positive) Who are and were the actors?			Justification (normative) Why *should* the state intervene?		
	State	Civil Society	Market	Equality	Morality	Efficiency
Provision						
Funding						
Regulation						

among actors in the three dimensions given in section 1.3, shown in the descriptive panel of the table. Recent shifts away from public to private bodies are, for instance, found in the fight against money laundering (Chapter 3) or in social housing provision (Chapter 10).

NOTES

* With thanks to Michael Getzner and Frans van Waarden for helpful comments and additions.

1. Free disposal public goods, such as public television, allows that less is consumed than made available (Silvestre, 2012, p. 101).
2. In the case of television programmes, one might argue that the private provision of free programmes, financed by commercials and product placement, is merely driven by private profits, and thus probably leads to a lower quality of programmes. Quality programmes (for example, information, cultural affairs) may have to be publicly financed or provided.
3. For the Health Impact Fund, see: www.yale.edu/macmillan/igh/. For the Global Health Fund, see: www.theglobalfund.org/en/.
4. We leave out a third potentially significant function of the public sector, which is to stabilize the economy, and may be labelled 'stabilization function' according to Musgrave and Musgrave (1989).
5. This may even discourage state intervention in some fields of a private or civil society-based production of public goods if actors are intrinsically motivated, and if they consider their engagement to be corrupted by external incentives such as prices or government subsidies (they provide goods and services because these would be neither market- nor government-related).
6. Heath (2001, p. 167) states: 'there is no *a priori* reason to think that private-sector bureaucracies will be more efficient than public-sector bureaucracies. And in the absence of effective competition, they are likely to be very much less so. Thus the same forces that make it advantageous to form giant corporations also make it advantageous for the state to take on a strategic role in the economy. From an economic point of view, big business and big government are like fraternal twins.'
7. One can also argue that the risks of increasing labour specialization, requiring investments in highly specialized human capital and on-the-job training, are difficult to insure on private markets. Seen in this light, even the progressive income tax is an insurance device (see Sandmo, 1999, p. 146).
8. Heath (2011, p. 27) also identifies 'minority public goods': 'There are certain goods, however, which stand to benefit only a relatively small number of people, but where the group is difficult to identify and for various reasons is unlikely to self-identify . . . Examples would include hosting the Olympics and sponsoring athletes, having national parks, funding art galleries, and promoting cultural heritage events. Partisans of state involvement often try to posit subtle externality effects that enhance the welfare of those who are not the primary beneficiaries of these subsidies, in order to defend against the charge of rent-seeking. A more forthright defense would simply be to admit that the state is catering to a minority taste in these cases – a taste that would otherwise not be satisfied, because of contracting problems among private parties – but that because the state caters to a very wide range of such minority tastes over time, everyone is likely to benefit at some point from some such activity. Thus the overall activity of "providing minority public goods" can be seen as a public good.'
9. The reluctance among the right to accept Pigouvian taxes is described by Heath (2011, p. 117): 'ironically, it is often the most tough-minded, no-nonsense right-wingers who go all soft when it comes to economic competition. People who would never be so naïve to

suggest that athletes might "voluntarily" refrain from taking steroids will turn around and push for "industry self-regulation" over government intervention, as if corporations might just choose to stop polluting or refrain from producing false advertising'; and, 'the right simply doesn't want to admit that government is responsible for such massive improvements in our quality of life' (ibid., 169). One may say that Pigouvian taxes are part of the 'right' price, since they help to internalize externalities.

10. This may well be the case when social welfare systems are compared on the basis merely of efficiency: the United States (US) system of health care, for instance, is inefficient (with high transaction costs and low participation rates and coverage) compared to Canadian or European systems. One might argue that the majority of US citizens sacrifices efficiency for an abstract idea of liberty, possibly ignoring our second (community) function of providing a material basis for a dignified human life.
11. One example of publicly owned companies providing urban utilities highlights this problematic setting: the City of Vienna owns its holding providing, for example, transport services in the city. Formerly, members of the city council (and citizens) could ask for information regarding the efficiency of public provision of services. Nowadays, all details of the company organized as a limited liability company are considered to be a corporate secret. Democratic control is thus lost, and citizens are mere consumers of services.

REFERENCES

Barr, N. (2012). *The Economics of the Welfare State*, Oxford, UK and New York, USA: Oxford University Press.

Beer, P. de (2004). Beter Geen dan Halve Marktwerking. *Het Parool*, 28 February.

Bergstrom, T.C. and R.P. Goodman (1973). Private demands for public goods. *American Economic Review*, 63(3), 280–296.

Boulding, K.E. (1969). Economics as a moral science. *American Economic Review*, 59(1), 1–12.

Bryson, B. (1995). *Notes From a Small Island*, New York: Morrow.

Buchanan, J.M. (1965). An economic theory of clubs. *Economica*, 32(1), 1–14.

Bucovetsky, S. (1991). Choosing tax rates and expenditure levels using majority rule. *Journal of Public Economics*, 46, 113–131.

Etzioni, A. (1988). *The Moral Dimension: Toward a New Economics*, New York, UK and London, UK: Free Press and Collier Macmillan.

Frey, B. and L. Steiner (2011). World Heritage List: does it make sense? *International Journal of Cultural Policy*, 17(5), 555–573.

Heath, J. (2001). *The Efficient Society: Why Canada is as Close to Utopia as it Gets*, Toronto: Viking.

Heath, J. (2011). Three normative models of the welfare state. *Public Reason*, 3(2), 13–43.

Hindriks, J. and G.D. Myles (2006). *Intermediate Public Economics*, Cambridge, MA: MIT Press.

Judt, T. (2010). *Ill Fares the Land*, New York: Penguin Press.

Kaul, I., I. Grunberg and M.A. Stern (1999). *Global Public Goods*, New York: Oxford University Press.

Kindleberger, C.P. (1983). Standards as public, collective and private goods. *Kyklos*, 36(3), 377–396.

Matzner, E. (2001). Redefining the public purpose: on the socio-economics of a global *res publica*. Unpublished project proposal, Vienna.

Meltzer, A. and S. Richard (1981). A rational theory of the size of government. *Journal of Political Economy*, 89(5), 914–927.
Mettler, S. (2011). *The Submerged State: How Invisible Government Policies Undermine American Democracy*, Chicago, IL: University of Chicago Press.
Musgrave, R.A. and P.B. Musgrave (1989). *Public Finance in Theory and Practice*. New York: McGraw-Hill.
Paine, T. (1791). *Rights of Man*, London: J.S. Jordan.
Samuelson, P.A. (1954). The pure theory of public expenditure. *Review of Economics and Statistics*, 36(4), 387–389.
Samuelson, P.A. (1955). Diagrammatic exposition of a theory of public expenditure. *Review of Economics and Statistics*, 37(4), 350–356.
Sandel, M. (1998). *What Money Can't Buy: The Moral Limits of Markets, The Tanner Lectures on Human Values*, New York: Farrar, Straus & Giroux.
Sandler, T. and K. Hartley (1995). *The Economics of Defense*, Cambridge, UK and New York, USA: Cambridge University Press.
Sandler, T. and J.C. Murdoch (2000). On sharing NATO defence burdens in the 1990s and beyond. *Fiscal Studies*, 21(3), 297–327.
Sandmo, A. (1999). The public economics of redistribution and the welfare state. *Review of Population and Social Policy*, 8, 139–154.
Silvestre, J. (2012). *Public Microeconomics: Efficiency and Equity in Public Policy*, Cheltenham, UK and Northampton, MA, USA: Edward Elgar Publishing.
Sonntag, D. (2010). *AIDS and Aid: A Public Good Approach*, Heidelberg: Springer.
Stiglitz, J. (2000). *Economics of the Public Sector*, New York: W.W. Norton.
Streeck, W. (2011). The crises of democratic capitalism. *New Left Review*, 71, 5–29.
Teulings, C., A. Bovenberg and H. Dalen (2005). *De cirkel van Goede Intenties. De economie van het publieke belang*. Amsterdam: Amsterdam University Press.
Thiel, S. van (2000). Quango-cratization: trends, causes and consequences. Dissertation, Utrecht University.
Tiebout, C.M. (1956). A pure theory of local expenditures. *Journal of Political Economy*, 64, 416–424.
Tocqueville, A. de (1835). *Democracy in America*, Chicago, IL: University of Chicago.
Waarden, F. van (2001). Grenzen aan privatisering: een nieuwe tragedie van de commons? In J. Bussemaker and R. van der Ploeg, *Leven na Paars? Linkse visies op de derde weg*, Prometheus: Amsterdam.
Waarden, F. van (2002). De Tucht van de Economie. *S&D*, 59(1), 42–46.
Waarden, F. van (2012). Was Privatisering van het Publieke Domein wel in het Publieke Belang? Parlementaire Onderzoekscommissie 'Privatisering en Verzelfstandiging van Overheidsdiensten', Eerste Kamer der Staten-Generaal.
Walzer, M. (1983). Spheres of Justice: A Defense of Pluralism and Equality, New York: Basic Books.

on the horizontal axis represents the relation between specific groups of people and humankind as a whole, reflecting the contrast between regionalization and globalization. In both cases, the contrast on the horizontal axis goes back to the more fundamental contrast between the separate parts and the whole.

Emphasis on the separate parts leads to diversity, while emphasis on the whole will lead to uniformity. On the level of knowledge (beliefs), this contrast works out as the subjective versus the objective. Consequently, on the left-hand side of the proposed proxy for human nature it is assumed that there is one uniform, universal truth. However, on the right, universal truth does not exist; here, truth is multiform and highly subjective in nature.

The contrast on the vertical axis is between non-material and material values. Many philosophers and sociologists, such as Plato, Hegel, Steiner, Fromm and Sorokin, have discussed these opposing values, also in terms of mind versus matter, including the associated more spiritual-religious notions. Over the centuries, this contrast between mind versus matter also has fuelled the ongoing debate between institutional religion (upper left) and science (lower left), both claiming the 'one truth' as is typical for the values on the left-hand side of the figure.

2.4 MACROHISTORY

Before looking at how the value orientations constituting human nature relate to the demarcation between the public and the private domain, reference has to be made to the temporal changes in these value orientations. In a study on the privatization process in the Netherlands over recent decades, van Waarden (2012) suggests trying to understand the current equilibrium between market, state and society through a historical analysis. With respect to the significance of value orientations for this equilibrium, this translates into questioning the dynamical behaviour of these value orientations, in particular the question of which values dominate when, and why. Being aware of the higher level of abstraction in case of dominating value orientations rather than the decisions resulting from the policy process, the overall dynamics of value orientations will be discussed from a macro perspective and will require a macrohistoric approach. Thus the initial assumption is that history can be understood as a rather predictable journey through the pattern of value orientations underlying human nature (as presented in Figure 2.2). Omitting smaller-scale fluctuations, the overall pattern of dominating orientations over the last two millennia is given in Figure 2.3. Projected onto the two-dimensional plane of the pattern of 'human nature', historical developments form a telling connection.

2. Value-based demarcation between the public and the private domain

Klaas van Egmond

2.1 INTRODUCTION

The fall of the Berlin Wall in 1989 manifested the failure of the Eastern European, collectivistic economies. In the antagonist camp of laissez-faire capitalism, euphoria was great. Fukuyama (1992) heralded 'the end of history'; the liberal democracies of the West had proven to be superior. In the wake of this euphoria, well-functioning public organizations were suddenly framed as Eastern European relics that were said to have lost their legitimacy. In the following years, many governmental organizations were privatized, and much infrastructure, supported by the rule: markets whenever possible, the state whenever necessary. The latter was only relevant in cases of proven market failure. Privatization was generally motivated by qualitative expectations with respect to the increase in efficiency.

In the Netherlands, for example, privatization of public tasks was effectuated for energy production, the (social) housing sector, the railway system, telecommunications and the financial sector. Privatization of drinking water infrastructure was dropped in 1999 in the wake of an outbreak of Legionnaires' disease at a flower exhibition, killing 28 people. Opposing arguments with respect to the effectiveness of the democratic system and the trade-off between the bureaucracy of the public system and transaction costs in the private system were not taken into account. Two decades later many of the disadvantages mentioned at the time did, in fact, materialize:

- In the energy system competition did increase, but the transition to a less fossil fuel-intensive energy production can now only be enforced indirectly via licences and a (non-functioning) market for carbon dioxide (CO_2) emission rights.
- The railway system has been split into a publicly owned rail system infrastructure and a private train transport organization. Lack of

coordination between the two has led to a performance level below the original, non-privatized system.

- Liberalization of the financial sector led to the 2007–2008 financial crisis, initiating an economic stagnation that is still felt. After a long period of high profits in the financial sector, the government had to bail out the banks which implied that the loss of many tens of billions of euros was to be paid by the taxpayer. More important is the structural failure in the financial system with respect to money creation. In a physically growing society (more cars, houses, and so on), more money has to be brought into circulation to maintain price stability. As argued by Aristotle, and since then by many philosophers and economists through the centuries, it is the fundamental prerogative of the community (state) to create this money, receive the social benefits thereof and give direction to social development. However, private banks have acquired this right to money creation and they appropriate the enormous benefits (Van Egmond and de Vries, 2016). This means that huge public interests are appropriated by a small private elite, which by definition brings society back to a feudal state.

Privatization and liberalization have led to more power in the hands of corporate business at the cost of democratic abilities to produce public goods, both on the national and on the European level. For example, no effective policy was set in place to combat climate change by decreasing CO_2 emissions, to a large extent as the result of lobbying activities by parties with commercial interests. A further consequence of the increasing private sector domination is increasing inequality in wealth and income in the society at large, putting social stability at risk.

2.2 THE MYTH OF VALUE-NEUTRAL CRITERIA FOR THE PUBLIC–PRIVATE DEMARCATION

The privatization trend in the 1990s was motivated by criteria which were claimed to be value-neutral. However, on closer inspection, this claim of value-neutrality cannot be maintained. All criteria appear to be value-laden:

- Efficiency and effectiveness make sense only in relation to well-articulated ends that are to be pursued. In the absence of a clear notion of societal ends, bookkeeping qualities such as gross domestic product (GDP) or employment are considered meaningful objectives. But they are very one-sided choices and cannot be considered to be value-neutral. For example, environmental degradation and the costs of physical and social disruption are contributing positively to GDP.

- Criteria for a more equal wealth and income distribution are based on moral considerations. Moral limits, such as the rejection of child labour, might reduce the efficiency at which GDP growth is realized, and it goes without saying that they are value-laden.
- Utilitarianism, as proposed by Hume, Bentham and Mill in the nineteenth century, is also value-laden, notwithstanding its claim of value-neutrality. The goal of 'the greatest happiness for the greatest number' refers to happiness, which is evidently value-laden. It relates to the extent to which human ends are realized. These ends emerge from underlying value orientations. As a consequence, utilitarianism cannot be of help in finding a rational demarcation between the public and the private domain.

It can be concluded that criteria for the public–private demarcation are far from value-neutral. Apparently, underlying value orientations play an important role. It might be argued that in the free market these value orientations are revealed as preferences. The more goods become private goods that can be traded as commodities on the markets, the more they become subject to market prices depending on these preferences. This implies that these preferences would result in proper allocation of the 'needed' goods.

However, it is the above-mentioned correspondence between property and underlying value orientation that results in the fact that not all needed goods are tradable commodities. Equal access to education, health care, nature, and so on might correspond to more fundamental, underlying values as well.

Human Nature

Property, be it private or public, appears to have a bearing on the values of the individual. Referring to Hegel, Munzer (1990) points to the significance of private property to 'personality'. Property protects certain rights of the individual. Apart for their significance to privacy, these rights also enable the owner to bring about changes in the world as a moral and political agent. It might be argued that property would enhance self-awareness, as more property creates more possibilities to express one's individual values, thus creating a specific, individual identity. In that case, the individual identifies themself by means of property, for example the identification with their car (nowadays still the underlying psychology of many

these lines of thought, an indication and a legitimization of the public–private demarcation might be found in an overall notion of 'human nature' with its diversity of values and its (complex) harmony of virtues. Herein the virtues emerge from many contrasting vices. Against this background an attempt will be made to find an empirical proxy for Aristotle's 'human nature', in the expectation of obtaining some meaningful guidance for the public–private demarcation and, if possible in any way, its subsequent legitimization.

2.3 HUMAN VALUE ORIENTATIONS CONSTITUTING HUMAN NATURE

Freedom is the ability to prioritize and realize some values above others. Value orientations thus may vary widely both within and between societies, reflecting Aristotle's diversity. In the attempt to find a common denominator that might represent the total diversity of values as 'human nature' and herein the 'unity of the virtues', several sources of human value orientations were studied and compared (Van Egmond and de Vries, 2011).

Social Surveys

The most direct (empirical) way of obtaining an idea of what people value in life and how they think the world functions is to ask them, such as by means of a survey (Aalbers, 2006). More than 10000 (Dutch) people were questioned on the basis of the so-called Rokeach values (Rokeach, 1973). Value orientations of respondents can be deduced by both ranking and rating these Rokeach values. As shown in Figure 2.1, the results of such a survey can be condensed in a statistically meaningful way (principal component analysis) into two main dimensions: the contrast of giving (upper) versus taking (lower) and the contrast of small world (right) versus big world (left). The first component, along the vertical axis, is very close to the contrast of religious versus worldly and non-material versus material. The second component, on the horizontal axis, can be associated with an orientation toward one's own local community versus the world as a whole or, from a more individual stance, as the contrast between self and other and between individual and collective.

Within this framework, eight clusters were identified, the main characteristics of which – followed by the percentage of people in this category – are: Caring (14 per cent), Conservative (15 per cent), Hedonist (10 per cent), Luxury-seeking (10 per cent), Businesslike (8 per cent), Cosmopolitan (9 per cent), Engaged (13 per cent), and the middle group containing those

commercials). In doing so, there is an immediate link to moral character, given the fact that the pursuit of certain values is more worthwhile than that of others. This pursuit might be conceived by the person themself or by others as a virtue or a vice.

Those who are by definition excluded from somebody else's private property, of course, do not have these benefits with respect to self-expression. Given the subsequent distribution problem, the demarcation between public and private property thus has an impact on the abilities of people's individuation in the society at large.

In the psychological conception of 'personality' there is an additional need to integrate one's personal thoughts and attitudes, including such identifications, which then form the personality as a whole (ibid., p. 85). The integration of the many property-based identifications reflects the overall underlying value orientation. Given the integration of all these aspects into 'personality', it would make sense to look at the mutual relations between all those single, underlying values, the ranking of these values and the implication of this choice for moral character: virtue or vice.

In his *After Virtue*, Alasdair MacIntyre (1981) demonstrates that there is no 'rational' solution to the problem of virtue versus vice: 'moral judgements, being expressions of attitude or feeling, are neither true or false and agreement in moral judgement is not to be secured by any rational method, for there is none'.

As a further consequence MacIntyre considers the Enlightenment to be a failure, as it did not succeed in its attempts 'to find a rational basis for [the philosophers'] moral beliefs. They inherited incoherent fragments of a once coherent scheme of thought and action and, since they did not recognize their own peculiar historical and cultural situation, they could not recognize the impossible and quixotic character of their self-appointed task'. This is demonstrated, for example, by the fact that, as MacIntyre points out, in his later work Kant acknowledged 'that without a teleological framework the whole project of morality becomes unintelligible'. That teleological framework presupposes an ultimate end to human existence in which man can realize his essential human nature.

And herewith MacIntyre concludes that we have to return to the Aristotelian tradition as a central functional concept of man as having an essential nature and an essential purpose and function. In his *Nicomachean Ethics*, Aristotle (1925) recognizes the diversity of values and the unity of virtues, which are all in harmony with each other. He considers a virtue as the quality that enables people to realize their specific human objective (*telos*), which only becomes clear during the process. The core of Aristotle's reasoning is that virtue is a 'middle way' between two vices. Virtue therefore may be pursued only by following the middle way. Along

Figure 2.1 Value orientations in the population (RIVM, TNS-NIPO)

who are Balanced (21 per cent). Caring people value non-material aspects of life, whereas the Luxury-seekers value the material ones. Conservatives may share a non-material-oriented lifestyle with the Caring people, but tend to focus more on their own local situation. On the opposite side there are the Cosmopolitan and Businesslike people, for whom the monetary and material aspects of the 'big world' make up quality of life. On the lower right-hand side of Figure 2.1, Hedonists are small-scale and ego-oriented, in combination with a material, worldly attitude. The Engaged people are their opposites, on the upper left, with a focus on large, global issues and non-material aspects. The group of Balanced people in the centre award more or less equal weight to matters along the two axes or represent indifferent attitudes.

The characteristics of the individual segments of the diagram represent the value orientations of individual people. The eight clusters are groups of people with more or less homogeneous value orientations who therefore largely share a specific value orientation. Together these orientations constitute the proxy for 'human nature', thus defined as the totality of human value orientations and related understanding of the world. As such, Figure 2.1, which represents the eight clusters of shared orientations, is the first approximation of this human nature. Herein, from a statistical point of view, the structure of these orientations can best be explained by the vertical relation (axis) that describes the contrast between a more non-materialist/mind attitude and a more materialist/matter one, and the horizontal relation (axis) that describes the contrast between the part and the whole, between the individual and the collective.

Psychological and Philosophical Understanding

Subsequently, this initial proxy for human nature is enhanced with the relevant insights of psychology and philosophy. The presentation in Figure 2.1 of the clusters or individual value orientations arranged as opposites in opposing quadrants is in keeping with findings by the psychologist Jung (1960). He stated that the human psyche consists of processes of which the energy is generated by the reconciliation of several kinds of opposites. Indeed, there is ample evidence that the human mind tends to operate by thinking in opposites. When the empirical results from the value surveys are enriched with the many psychological and philosophical insights, a next and more robust version of the pattern representing human nature is obtained, as presented in Figure 2.2 (Van Egmond, 2014).

Here, the horizontal axis represents the mutual relation between people. Based on the philosophical insights of Kant, Levinas, Jung and Pauli, these relations are interpreted as the contrast between the individual and the collective, between self and other. On a higher, social level, the contrast

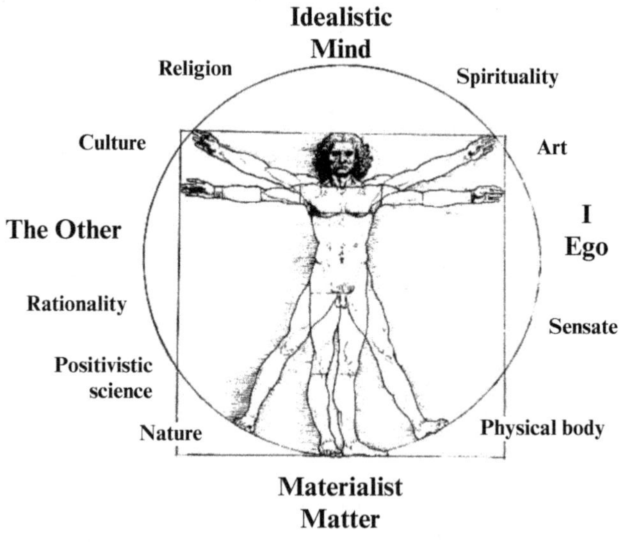

Figure 2.2 Enriched approximation of 'human nature'

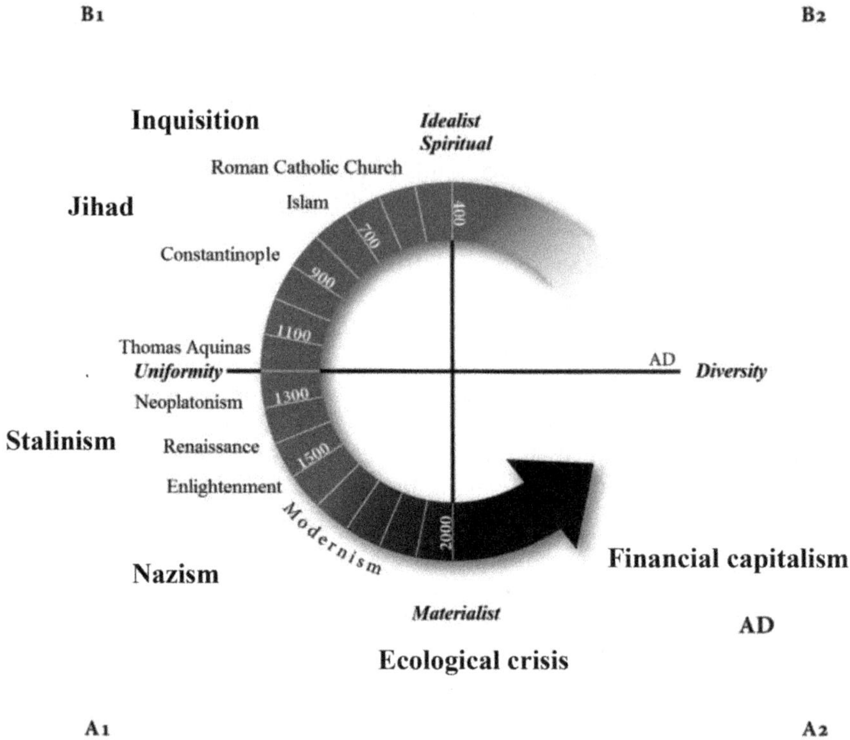

Figure 2.3 Dominating value orientations over the last two millennia and their corresponding catastrophes

Over the past 2000 years, the great social discontinuities such as religious wars, totalitarian ideologies (for example, communism and fascism) and the ecological, financial and economic crises are understood to be caused by the increasing one-sidedness of the prevailing value orientations. This process consists of a series of different mechanisms, starting with the loss of respect for opposing values and followed by the reversal of ends and means. At a later stage, the value orientation becomes ideological and fundamentalist; society has become its own caricature.

After the initial phase of early Christianity with its multiform, individual belief system (Figure 2.3; upper right), the need for uniformity finally set the stage for the 'one truth' Catholic ('universal') church, which subsequently turned into its own caricature in the Inquisition and religious wars (upper left). The subsequent battle between church and science about the single truth was won by (materialist) science, paving the way for the Enlightenment and the Industrial Revolution. Nineteenth-century Romanticism was a temporary (upper right) reaction to the extreme material and conformist values of modern (lower left) industrialism. Resuming the original course in the direction of collectivism and (secular) materialism, Marxism resulted in collectivistic communism. Here, catastrophe resulted from the extreme one-sidedness of collectivistic values, leaving no room at all for individualist values and the expression thereof.

Darwinism, as an expression of modernistic science, was also turned into a caricature of itself with a time lag of about 100 years, finally enabling Nazism with a still collectivistic orientation (*Ein Volk, ein Reich, ein Führer*). The increasingly dominant materialist value orientation gave rise to the current ecological crisis (bottom). While still dominated by materialist values, the already-started movement at the right-hand individualist side of the pattern shifts societal power to the private sector, in particular to the financial system. This then became an end in itself and a means for individual material gain, denying the earlier orientations on more collective values. This process was triggered by the previously mentioned fall of the Berlin Wall in 1989; the collectivist values were exhausted and in an antagonist ('action is reaction') scheme; history ends (for the time being) in the lower right quadrant, in which individualist and materialist values dominate (iPhone, iMac, increasing inequality, and so on). In collectivism there was no room left for individualism; in absolute individualism, there is no room left for collective values; 'there is no such thing as society' (UK Prime Minister Margaret Thatcher). History thus tends toward either public or private one-sidedness and associated catastrophes.

It can be concluded that in history the demarcation between the public and the private domain has been directly dependent on the underlying value orientations. As suggested by van Waarden, the rationale for the demarcation then is likely to be found in these value orientations and their dynamics. Thus the tendency to one-sidedness and subsequent catastrophe has to be avoided. Maintaining (dynamic) equilibrium in the human nature value pattern evidently contributes to social quality and stability.

2.5 CAPABILITIES

Moving now from value orientations and their dynamics to the question of the demarcation between the public and the private domain, there appears to be a strong correspondence between value orientations, 'capabilities' and economic goods.

According to Sen and Nussbaum (see Sen, 1993), the above-discussed human values are realized by means of 'capabilities'. They provide the

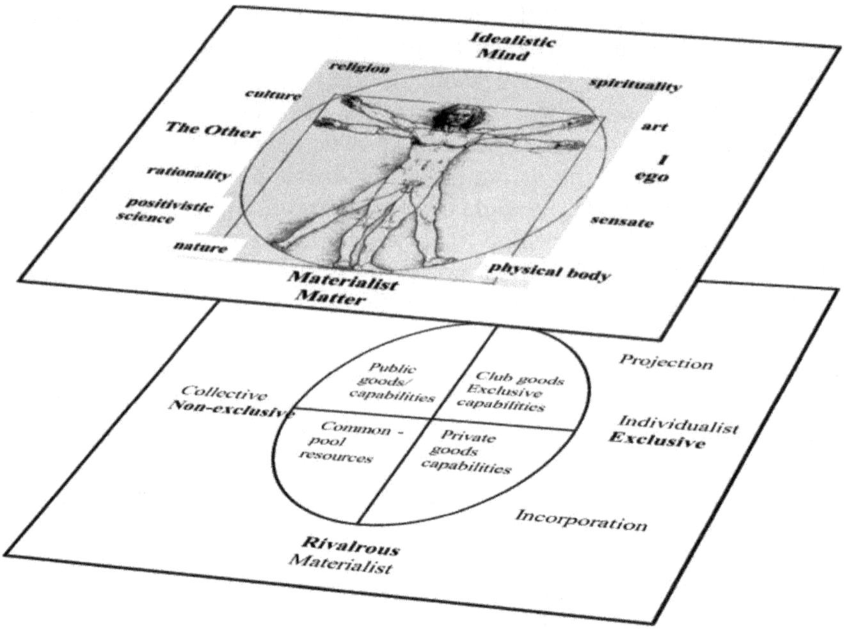

Figure 2.4 Economic goods as capabilities (lower level) support the realization of human values (upper level)

potential to realize what is valued. Examples of capabilities are skills, material possessions, money, knowledge and insight. They are coupled more or less 1:1 to the value orientations. The availability of capabilities is more important to the quality of life than is the actual realization of the corresponding values. Having the ability to do something is more important than actually doing it. These capabilities in turn relate to a large extent to economic goods, including skills and knowledge. So there is also a strong correspondence between the value orientations and the economic goods, as depicted in Figure 2.4.

2.6 PUBLIC AND PRIVATE GOODS

Economic goods are usually categorized by two criteria: excludability, as the extent to which people other than the owner can be excluded from the use of the economic good; and rivalrousness, as the extent to which there is competition about the good. Combining these two criteria results in the scheme presented in Figures 2.4 and 2.5.

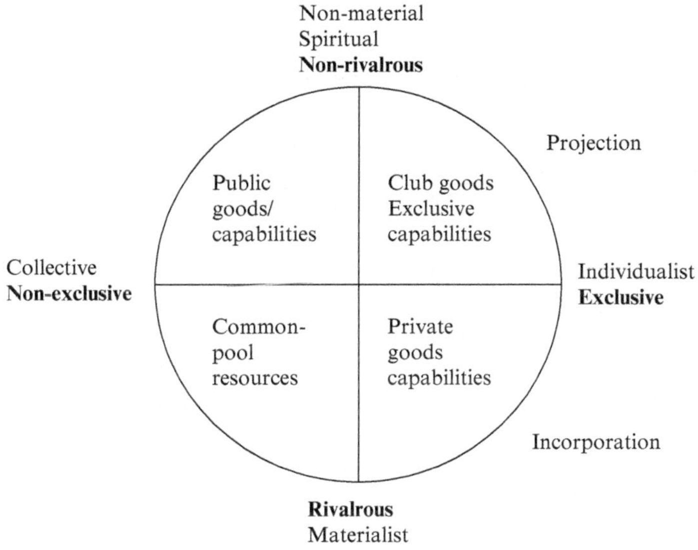

Figure 2.5 Economic goods, in relation to value orientations

The vertical axis represents the contrast of rivalrous/non-rivalrous, as (more or less) coinciding with the contrast of materialist/non-materialist. Non-materialist goods are normally less rivalrous; many people can be the owner of an idea or (cultural) ability; there is no restriction on the availability and it is available in endless amounts. For material goods this is not (or seldom) the case. If too many people have a claim on a material good, it will ultimately no longer be available.

In the horizontal direction, goods are distinguished between goods which are collectively available to everybody on the left-hand side and goods which are exclusively available to the respective private owners on the right-hand side. The latter are categorized as private goods, the former as physical common-pool resources, which are available to the community as a whole, such as water, air and atmosphere, nature reserves and physical, mineable resources like oil or gas. The non-material counterpart of these physical resources is the public goods (upper left), for example public institutions, cultural, educational and scientific infrastructure, and so on. An example of non-rivalrous but exclusive goods (upper right) is intellectual property, such as a patent.

Appropriation

Usual reasoning with respect to the divide between public (including common-pool resources) and private property is based on the theories of incorporation and projection (Munzer, 1990). Under incorporation the appropriation of a good is motivated or legitimized by its literal consumption (as in the case of food). But it can also be an extension of the owner's body. For example, a car might be seen as a 'prosthesis' of the owner's legs. In this way a house and a car can be argued to be private, while infrastructure of energy, mobility, money and education should be considered to be a public good. The same holds for nature reserves and resources. The ownership of production facilities can be substantiated in this way as well.

In case of projection, the good is appropriated by the 'projection' of the owner in terms of (physical or mental) labour, for example in food gathering. John Locke viewed this as mixing one's labour with unowned things and thus converting them into property. Hegel, as well, sees property as an embodiment or projection of the individual, or of their self-actualization: the previously discussed 'personality'. His analysis supports the idea that persons/personality, bodies and property are strongly connected (ibid., p. 67). To a large extent these theories on incorporation and projection are thus based on the above considerations with respect to (the realization of) values. They already make clear that appropriation has to be motivated by means of a rather direct relation with one's labour or with the functioning of one's body; shelter (housing), for example, can be seen as something which can be appropriated as it can be considered an extension or direct protection of the body. In this way a legitimization for having property is found in the functional relation between someone's body or labour and the appropriated object.

In theory (Munzer, 1990) the appropriation of commons and public goods is bounded by the limits of projection and incorporation. This limits private goods to goods which are directly related to (extensions of) body or mind.

Under the domination of the lower-right individualist and materialist value orientations, an important mechanism of appropriation is money. In the Western world, the creation of money, which according to Aristotle is a social construct and thus the prerogative of the public and government, has been privatized and taken over by commercial banks. Most likely this is the most fundamental error in the public–private balance in Western civilization. The money which governments have to borrow from these banks is created 'out of nothing'. By indebting governments in this way, private institutions force governments to sell their public goods and commons to these private organizations. This has been and still is an important driver for private appropriation of public goods. But apart from these theories, additional legitimization for a more balanced public–private demarcation can be deduced from the correspondence between the above-mentioned nature of economic goods and human nature as the overarching pattern of value orientations.

2.7 PUBLIC OR PRIVATE

The macrohistory as presented in Figure 2.3 demonstrates that in history the dominating value orientations are time and again shifted to the one-sided and catastrophic periphery of the human value pattern by 'centrifugal' forces, such as the need for identification. This centrifugal movement can be judged as bad (vice), while centripetal movement away from the periphery to the centre can be interpreted as good (virtue). Returning to Aristotle, this brings about the unity of virtues, amidst the diversity of values. It shapes an Aristotelian ethical framework, in which the virtue is the middle way between two (opposing, one-sided) vices.

This suggests that legitimization for a more balanced public–private demarcation can be deduced from the correspondence between the nature of economic goods and human nature as the overarching pattern of value orientations. Given the substantiated correspondence between human nature and its counterpart in capabilities and economic goods (Figure 2.4), the demarcation between public and private goods thus can also be interpreted as good, as long as the divide tends to the centre, both for the physical rivalrous goods and the non-material non-rivalrous goods. Conversely, more one-sided orientations into the periphery can be seen as bad. An important failure of these one-sided value orientations is that such orientations erroneously claim to coincide with the human nature value pattern as a whole, resulting in thinking that 'there is no alternative'. This means that the far-reaching appropriation claims from the private, lower-right orientation are erroneously experienced as legitimate. They just fail to see the alternative, given by human nature itself, as they lose human nature from sight in their euphoric one-sided thinking.

In the first place this would mean that orientations either on the collectivist–public or on the individualist–private side of the spectrum cannot be substantiated, thus obliterating the principle of 'markets whenever possible, the state whenever necessary'. The background of this reasoning is that the public ownership of common-pool resources and public goods is equally legitimized by underlying value orientations as the private ownership of private goods, as can be seen in the lower-right quadrant.

For example, nature reserves or the admission to nature areas directly correspond to values in the lower-left part of the human value orientation. Referring to Sen, the (potential) ability to visit nature at any time is an important value as such. No further legitimization is necessary to consider nature reserves as commons. Nevertheless, there is a strong tendency (at least in the Netherlands and the European Union) to privatize nature areas, which earlier were part of the national commons. This tendency toward private appropriation can be understood as the shift of the dominating value orientation to the lower-right quadrant, with individualism and materialism as its main features.

Changing Role of Labour

The above considerations are partly based on the projection of one's labour onto goods, in doing so legitimizing the appropriation of such goods. However, the role of labour in the economic process is expected to change rapidly. Robotization might mitigate labour, especially in physical production processes. This will further erode projection as a legitimization for appropriation; who owns the robots? It stresses the conclusion that the public–private demarcation of property and ownership should be based on underlying value orientations, rather than on considerations with respect to labour.

2.8 DISCUSSION AND CONCLUSION

Privatization and private appropriation of goods which relate to public values cannot be substantiated. The privatization trend in the 1990s was motivated by one-sided arguments such as 'markets whenever possible, the state whenever necessary'. Given their one-sidedness, these arguments can be considered as ideologies. The now dominant one-sided individualist–materialist part of the overall value pattern of 'human nature' arrogates to be the whole pattern, with the subsequent appropriation of significant areas of the public domain. History has proven this one-sidedness to be very threatening. Partial reasoning on the basis of fragments of the overall pattern of human nature, such as rationality (Kant) and efficiency (economics) has failed. In both political development and with respect to the public–private demarcation, the notion of societal ends has to be articulated. Returning to the Aristotelian worldview, the ultimate sustainable societal end, which will become clear during the process, has to be found in the realization of human nature as a whole, not of its pathological parts.

REFERENCES

Aalbers, T. (2006). *Waardeoriëntaties, wereldbeelden en maatschappelijke vraagstukken*, MNP rapport 550031002, Bilthoven, Netherlands: MNP / PBL Institute. www.pbl.nl (in Dutch).

Aristotle (1925). *The Nicomachean Ethics*, translated by W.D. Ross, Oxford: Clarendon Press. https://socserv2.socsci.mcmaster.ca/econ/ugcm/3ll3/aristotle/Ethics.pdf.

Fukuyama, F. (1992). *The End of History and the Last Man*, New York: Free Press.

Jung, C.G. (1960). *The Nature of the Psyche*, Princeton, NJ: Princeton University Press.

MacIntyre, A. (1981). *After Virtue: A Study in Moral Theory*, London: Gerald Duckworth & Co..

Munzer, S.R. (1990). *A Theory on Property*, Cambridge: Cambridge University Press.

Rokeach, M. (1973). *The Nature of Human Values*, New York: Free Press.

Sen, A. (1993). Capability and well-being. In M. Nussbaum and A. Sen (eds), *The Quality of Life*, Oxford: Clarendon Press, pp. 30–53.

Van Egmond, N.D. (2014). *Sustainable Civilization*. London: Palgrave Macmillan.

Van Egmond, N.D. and H.J.M. de Vries (2011). Sustainability: the search for the integral worldview. *Futures*, 43, 853–867.

Van Egmond, N.D. and B.J.M. de Vries (2016). Dynamics of a sustainable financial-economic system. Working Paper, Sustainable Finance Lab. www.sustainablefinancelab.nl.

Van Waarden, F. (2012). *Was Privatisering van het Publieke Domein wel in het Publieke Belang?* Een kritische beschouwing over het Nederlandse privatiseringsbeleid van de afgelopen decennia. Working Paper, Utrecht University.

PART I

Traditional core tasks of the state: security

3. The fight against money laundering: a public task?

Joras Ferwerda

3.1 INTRODUCTION

Should the provision of security be a task reserved for the public sector? Adam Smith, the father of economics, identified security as a core duty of the state (Smith, 1776). Since security is a rather broad concept, this chapter will focus on the financial side of providing security. Nowadays criminals are caught not only as a result of their criminal behaviour, but also when they channel their ill-gotten gains through the financial sector or when they invest them in other economic sectors. This is done with so-called anti-money laundering regulations. This book attempts to show that private parties regularly assist in or take over formerly public tasks in terms of provision of services. However, in the fight against money laundering, not only is the provision partly shifted to the private sector, but the private sector also has to provide the funding.[1] This leads to specific problems that are addressed in this chapter.

The current anti-money laundering policies around the world resemble the regulation strategy of nodal governance. Nodal governance basically means that the government is the policy maker, but that the execution of the policy is (partly) carried out by other parties: the nodes. A common reference point within contemporary governance literature is the nautical analogy where the state is performing steering functions while leaving the rowing to others (Osborne and Gaebler, 1992). Nodal governance is advocated currently as a policy model for security, in which it displaces the state effectively and self-consciously from its longstanding privileged position as exclusive provider of security (see Wood and Dupont, 2006). Loader and Walker (2005) argue, however, that in the model of nodal governance the state is not simply one among many equal nodes, but is a privileged entity, best able to foster democratic conditions and equitable forms of security. Loader and Walker (2001) see policing – guaranteeing security – as a public good and refute the pejorative connection between policing and the state. Crawford (2006) also argues that it would be foolish to 'throw out the state' with the governance bath water in the field of security and policing.

In the 1980s and 1990s in many Western economies the size of the government (at least in terms of budget) was reduced by privatizing formerly public functions, such as public transport, telecommunications and energy provision. Braithwaite (2000, 2005) argues that the regulatory control directly spawned by the privatization programmes of the 1980s and 1990s did not lead to deregulation, but to new forms of regulation that do not fit the customary command-and-control model and the traditional divide between public and private. So the clear picture with the public sector on the one side and the private on the other might have become somewhat blurred. This also applies to the fight against money laundering.

Many of the conclusions in this chapter also apply to the detection of terrorism financing. The policies against money laundering and financing terrorism have many similarities and are often coupled at the regulatory level; see, for example, the European Union (EU) anti-money laundering (AML) and counter-terrorism (CTF) financing directive and the 40 recommendations of the Financial Action Task Force (FATF). However, the actual behaviour that is fought with these policies differs vastly: 'While money laundering tries to give a legitimate source to the proceeds of crime ("making black money white"), terrorist financing is about using both legitimate and illegitimate money to commit a crime ("making grey money black")' (Ferwerda, 2012, p. 10). For consistency and readability, this chapter focuses on the detection of money laundering only. Although the analysis in this chapter takes the policies in the United States of America (USA) as a starting point, the analysis basically applies to all countries in the world, since standards in anti-money laundering policies have been spread (and 'pushed') all over the world.

3.2 THE EMERGENCE OF THE FIGHT AGAINST MONEY LAUNDERING

Money laundering as a crime is not that old. It became a regulatory issue only in the late 1990s (Unger, 2013). The activity of money laundering, however, is much older. The term 'money laundering' was coined in connection with the gangster Al Capone, who channelled his unlawful gains through launderettes to make them appear legal (Van Duyne, 2003, p. 73). Launderettes were a flourishing, cash-intensive business in the 1930s, when hardly any private households owned a washing machine. For Al Capone, this was an ideal business sector to slip money from illegal alcohol sales into the cash register (Unger, 2013, p. 19). However, disguising the origin of illegal money is even older. One of the oldest techniques to circumvent government scrutiny was the use of international trade to move money undetected from one country to the other using fake invoices or falsely declared merchandise (Zdanowicz, 2009).

Even though Al Capone was labelled Public Enemy No. 1, the police were not able to detain him for his illegal sale of alcohol. Eventually they did find a way to jail Al Capone. The Internal Revenue Service (IRS) caught him for tax evasion instead of the predicate crime (the illegal sale of alcohol), a novel method in those days. In 1931 Capone was eventually sentenced to 11 years in prison, fined $57 692, and held liable for $215 000 plus interest due on his back taxes (Bergreen, 1996, p. 484). In this highly publicized case it is clear to see who was responsible for the detection and prosecution of this criminal: the public sector. Nowadays, the tactic of catching criminals not for the predicate crime that generates the wealth, but for the handling of the proceeds, is much more common, especially in countries where this can simplify a court case, such as in the Netherlands (see Unger et al., 2014).

The money laundering regulations that appeared on the world stage as a serious issue in the 1990s were mainly the result of a failed war on drugs in the United States (Unger, 2013, p. 19). Organized crime, foreign and domestic, was making a lot of money trafficking and dealing drugs, while the anti-drug policies were not able to control the issue. Simple economics tells us that drugs confiscated at the border limits supply, which means that at the same level of demand prices will increase. If people are still willing to buy the drugs at the increased price, the higher price makes it even more attractive to smuggle drugs. This in turn increases the supply and can bring price and consumption back to the original level. In the long run, this leaves repressive anti-drug policies completely ineffective in the sense that the problem is not reduced a single bit (Reuter and Kleiman, 1986). The USA – already committed to the war on drugs – had no signs that it was going to win this war in the 1990s. This might have sparked the idea to transform the war on drugs into a war on drug money, so to speak. Anti-money laundering policies can help to detect and eventually confiscate the ill-gotten gains from drug-related crimes. The events of 9/11 made money laundering regulations almost overnight an even more prominent issue. Suddenly money laundering became a top concern for national and international safety and was put on the agenda of international organizations (Unger, 2013). The grip on the financial system was needed to prevent money laundering and financing terrorism.

Getting Al Capone locked behind bars was due to the actions of public entities that were ultimately responsible to do so. The police used to be the only actor charged with the task of detecting and catching criminals.

However, in the first 'money laundering case', Al Capone was caught by the IRS, not the police. With financial and economic crimes, public bodies apart from the police were involved in detecting and catching criminals, but it was still a public task to do so. The next section shows how this public task was shifted partly to the private sector, mainly the 'gatekeepers of the financial sector'.

3.3 THE CONTEMPORARY FIGHT AGAINST MONEY LAUNDERING

> Money laundering is typically a transnational crime. The reason for cross-border activity in money laundering operations is probably because this can add a layer of disguise and because the attitude towards money laundering could be more tolerant in other countries. The fight against money laundering therefore needs an international approach. (Ferwerda, 2012, p. 9)

The current international anti-money laundering framework started with the publication of the 40 recommendations of the Financial Action Task Force (FATF) developed in 1990. With these recommendations the FATF – an intergovernmental body established by the G-7 countries in 1989 – takes the lead in the international fight against money laundering, setting anti-money laundering policy standards and incentivizing all countries around the world to comply with them. Although these recommendations are not 'hard law', the FATF managed to get basically all countries involved. This is done by evaluating each country to what extent they comply with the recommendations using bilateral evaluations and by putting the countries that do not comply sufficiently with the recommendations on a 'blacklist' (see Unger and Ferwerda, 2008). Today, almost all countries in the world are members of the FATF or a FATF regional style body.[2] Countries around the world have transposed the 40 recommendations of the FATF into their respective national laws. Nowadays the anti-money laundering policies are no longer targeted towards drug-related crimes alone, but are applied to target a broad range of wealth-generating crimes, such as (tax) fraud, extortion, illegal trade in firearms, corruption and insider trading.

The approach of the contemporary fight against money laundering resembles that of 'nodal governance' (see e.g. Burris et al., 2005; Shearing and Wood, 2003). It is not the public sector that executes all the policing – thus guaranteeing security. The fight is assisted by private parties, in this case the so-called 'gatekeepers of the financial sector' such as banks, notaries and insurance agents. Also other private actors that might observe (indications of) money laundering are involved, such as lawyers, dealers in precious stones and metals, casinos, and so on. The idea is that all these private parties might be in a better position to observe money laundering than the police or other law enforcement agencies. The current framework is as follows. Private parties are given all kinds of guidelines and instructions to enable them to observe possible money laundering actions. These can be anything: trying to open a bank account anonymously or in the name of someone else, large cash deposits at the bank, strange purchase behaviour (such as a paying real estate with cash) or any other irregular behaviour. Countries developed lists of objective and subjective criteria to determine which behaviour could indicate money laundering practices. Since these private parties are dealing constantly with regular customers in their business, the idea is that they should also be able to determine which behaviour is deviant and could indicate an act of money laundering. These so-called reporting entities (types of institutions that are obliged by law to assist in the fight against money laundering) have to report all money laundering suspicions to the Financial Intelligence Unit. Each country has set up a Financial Intelligence Unit to receive all the suspicious transaction reports.[3] This Financial Intelligence Unit screens the incoming reports and forwards the relevant cases to the police or other law enforcement agencies, so that they can eventually use these to investigate and hopefully catch the money launderer. Although law enforcement agencies also have autonomous powers to track and detect money laundering, the duties of the private sector are a significant part of the contemporary fight against money laundering. So the international fight against money laundering, initiated with the 40 recommendations of the FATF, led to a shift in responsibility. While it was originally the governments' concern to make sure money laundering is detected and prosecuted, it is now also a responsibility of private actors.

The incentives for banks and other reporting entities to report money laundering are twofold. On the one hand it enables them to keep the sector or business clean. If money laundering became rampant in a certain sector or business this would damage their reputation, which in turn could damage business activities. On the other hand, the reporting institutions are punished when a supervisor finds out that they did not report a money laundering suspicion. These punishments range from warnings or monetary fines, to imprisonment for the responsible actor or revocation of the licence to operate in the sector.

Although there are these two clear incentives for reporting entities to fight money laundering, there is a clear disincentive to do so: the reporting entities themselves bear the full costs for their anti-money laundering efforts. This naturally raises the question to what extent these regulations are effective.

3.4 HOW SUCCESSFUL IS THE CURRENT FIGHT AGAINST MONEY LAUNDERING?

The application of nodal governance in the fight against money laundering seems logical – the gatekeepers of the financial sector might know their customers and their regular behaviour better than public bodies – but has a fundamental problem: the incentive structure of the nodes. The reporting entities extend the reach of the public bodies involved, but their eventual goal is making money, not serving the public task. The reporting entities have to bear private costs for a public task with shared benefit. Optimal behaviour for profit-driven companies is therefore to minimize their costs for the public task in order to maximize own profits.[4]

Takáts (2011) describes the behaviour of reporting entities towards their public task in his theory of 'Crying Wolf'. The 'Crying Wolf Theory' states that when entities are asked to report suspicious behaviour and are fined when they fail to do so, increasing the fine can lead to excessive reporting which dilutes information and reduces overall effectiveness. The analogy here is the children's story, 'The boy who cried wolf', where a boy cried 'Wolf!' so often for fun that his cries became meaningless. So when there actually was a wolf that attacked the sheep, nobody would listen any more. Takáts (2011) shows empirically with US data that there is an inverse U-shaped relation between the effectiveness of the reporting system and the height of the fines. When fines increase, the amount of suspicious transaction reports increases, but this does not necessarily improve the overall effectiveness of the reporting system. Once the fines become too high, banks will report each and every transaction to make sure that they cannot be charged for not reporting a suspicious transaction. When all transactions are reported, the institution that receives these reports (the Financial Intelligence Unit) will drown in information and no longer be able to filter adequately, thus crippling the effectiveness of the reporting system. In this theoretical model with empirical underpinning, reporting entities do not aim to serve the public good, but they act as rational individualistic profit maximizers.

When setting up their theoretical model, Dalla Pellegrina and Masciandaro (2009) start with the observation that anti-money laundering regulations are designed on the assumption that the reporting entities have a self-interest in fighting money laundering. They doubt that this assumption is true, and analyse what needs to be done when reporting entities are not self-interested in fighting money laundering. Starting from the principal–agent problem between the policy maker and the reporting entity, they come to the conclusion that a supervisor would be more effective (reducing the information asymmetry between the policy maker and the reporting entity) than fines in stimulating the reporting entity to do what it is supposed to do in the first place.

Ferwerda et al. (forthcoming) also see a principal–agent problem in the anti-money laundering framework, but they concentrate on the relationship between the international policy maker (the FATF) and the nation states that are responsible for the responsiveness of the public and private parties involved in the fight against money laundering. The focus lies on the reporting entities and their incentive structure that does not align with the public bodies involved. Ferwerda et al. (forthcoming) conclude that the current incentive-inducing framework with punishments for non-compliance is ineffective, and give several policy recommendations on how to improve this.

The current nodal governance framework of anti-money laundering policy is ineffective due to the deviant incentive structure of the nodes. Why would the private parties minimize their efforts on such important aspects as fighting international crime and terrorism? The support from business and society for a regulatory policy towards money laundering is weak, because it is a global phenomenon which is not directly harmful and has no direct negative effects on society and business, nor is its scale known (Unger, 2013, p. 19).

3.5 CONCLUSION

The fight against money laundering shifted the traditional responsibility for security partly away from the public bodies. While traditionally only the law enforcement agencies were responsible for detecting and catching criminals, new forms of crime involved further public bodies in the fight against money laundering, especially tax authorities. The big change, however, came when the global anti-money laundering policies requested private parties to assist. In the spirit of nodal governance, commercial entities such as banks were asked to monitor their customers and detect money launderers and terrorist financiers. This move is not illogical: the gatekeepers of the financial system might be much better suited to distinguish regular financial behaviour from irregular. These gatekeepers know the customs in the sector and, moreover, they know their clients. By requesting the participation of private parties a knowledge gap has been bridged.

The involvement of private parties in the fight against money laundering has not been an undisputed success however. The main problem is that compliance to anti-money laundering policies does not come as naturally to commercial entities as it does to public bodies. These entities are serving the public good at their own expense. The private parties have been pushed into compliance with threats of sentences for non-compliance. This external motivation is vulnerable to strategic behaviour. Just to prevent any claims of non-compliance, banks and other entities might start reporting way too much, eventually crippling the overall effectiveness of the policy. The nodal governance concept can be beneficial in these modern times, but without the right incentive structure for the parties involved, its success cannot be guaranteed.

3.6 POLICY IMPLICATIONS

A clear policy option is to rewind the whole involvement of private parties in the fight against money laundering and put the responsibility completely back to the state. This would take away the deviant incentive structure, but could also bring back the knowledge gap that was bridged by the involvement of private parties: law enforcement agencies know less about the customers of, for example, banks and their behaviour, especially when it comes to evaluate client behaviour as common or unusual. Moreover, we might not want law enforcement agencies looking through the personal financial behaviour of innocent people. Therefore, an intermediate solution could be interesting.

Reporting institutions could be supervised regarding compliance with anti-money laundering regulations by supervisory institutions, which are either public bodies (like the central bank) or professional bodies (such as a bar association). These supervisors can serve as intermediate between the private and the public sector: an independent administrative agency funded for the purpose of serving the public good without the powers of a law enforcement agency. The supervisors would be supposed to be close to the sector they supervise and should therefore be better informed about the sector than a law enforcement agency. Moreover, these supervisors already have access to the files and knowledge of the reporting institutions, which is necessary to properly supervise them. They go through the data of the reporting entity to check whether no clues were missed – no transactions that had to be reported. The supervisors of reporting entities could therefore do the reporting of unusual/suspicious transactions with less incentive problems and without the knowledge gap the law enforcement agency would have. The FIU can stay as a buffer and filter between the supervisors sending the reports and the law enforcement agencies that follow up on the most serious threats.

Of course such a shift would need serious scrutiny and thought before it can be applied. Some points of concern are for instance whether this

Table 3.1 Res publica: table to jointly compare projects

	Description (positive) Who are and were the actors?			Justification (normative) Why should the public intervene?		
	State	Community	Market	Equality	Morality	Efficiency
Provision	X	⟶	X		X	X
Funding	X	⟶	X		X	X
Regulation	X				X	

would not give the supervisors too much power, whether this framework has sufficient checks and balances and how it affects privacy.

3.7 *RES PUBLICA*

Catching criminals used to be the main responsibility of the state, in terms of provision, funding and regulation. Although the regulation is still largely[5] done by the state, the provision and funding is now also done by the market (Table 3.1). In particular, the fact that the private parties have to bear the costs for their execution of a public task is problematic here, because this creates a deviant incentive structure. Due to these deviant incentive structures in the market, the involvement of commercial market parties in the fight against money laundering seems ineffective. We can also question whether it is fair to let market parties pay for the policies of the government. Moreover, it might be morally wrong to give market parties, that have a purely commercial interest, the ability to confiscate (though temporarily) the property of civilians.

NOTES

1. Even some policy making shifted to private bodies, with the risk-based approach initiated in 2012.
2. The countries that do not seem to be members or observers of the FATF or a FATF-regional style body are: Burundi, Iran, Israel, Jersey, Madagascar and North Korea (http://www.fatf-gafi.org/countries/, retrieved on 16 June 2016).
3. Some countries have somewhat different names for more or less the same thing: unusual transaction reports, suspicious activity reports, and so on (see e.g. Unger et al., 2014).
4. Net costs are being talked about here, since the private benefit from fighting money laundering is subtracted: when you comply with the regulations, you do not face the probability of being sanctioned for neglecting your task.
5. Some policy making shifted to the private parties with the risk-based approach initiated in 2012.

REFERENCES

Bergreen, L. (1996). *Capone: The Man and the Era*. Simon & Schuster. Retrieved from https://books.google.nl/books?hl=en&lr=&id=MI6MH4u7oCwC&oi=fnd&pg=PA15&dq=Capone:+The+Man+and+the+Era,+by+Laurence+Bergreen&ots=YUsxrLHcYC&sig=gVh4iae9uJ_gP01CH81NC_ao5Rw.

Braithwaite, J. (2000). The new regulatory state and the transformation of criminology. *British Journal of Criminology*, 40(2), 222–238.

Braithwaite, J.B. (2005). Neoliberalism or regulatory capitalism. RegNet Occasional Paper, 5. Retrieved from http://papers.ssrn.com/sol3/papers.cfm?abstract_id=875789.

Burris, S., P. Drahos and C. Shearing (2005). Nodal governance. *Australian Journal of Legal Philosophy*, 30. Retrieved from http://papers.ssrn.com/sol3/papers.cfm?abstract_id=760928.

Crawford, A. (2006). Networked governance and the post-regulatory state? Steering, rowing and anchoring the provision of policing and security. *Theoretical Criminology*, 10(4), 449–479.

Dalla Pellegrina, L. and D. Masciandaro (2009). The risk-based approach in the new European anti-money laundering legislation: a law and economics view. *Review of Law and Economics*, 5(2), 931–952.

Ferwerda, J. (2012). *The Multidisciplinary Economics of Money Laundering*. Utrecht University. Retrieved from http://dspace.library.uu.nl/handle/1874/257920.

Ferwerda, J., I. Deleanu, M. van de Broek and B. Unger (forthcoming). Performing in the books to pass evaluations – strategic behavior to untruthfully reporting money laundering. *Crime Law and Social Change.*

Loader, I. and N. Walker (2001). Policing as a public good: reconstituting the connections between policing and the state. *Theoretical Criminology*, 5(1), 9–35.

Loader, I. and N. Walker (2005). Necessary virtues: the legitimate place of the state in the production of security. In B. Dupont and J. Wood (eds), *Democracy, Society and the Governance of Security*, Cambridge: Cambridge University Press, pp. 165–195.

Osborne, D. and T. Gaebler (1992). *Reinventing Government: How the Entrepreneurial Spirit is Transforming Government*. Reading, MA: Addison Wesley.

Reuter, P. and M.A. Kleiman (1986). Risks and prices: an economic analysis of drug enforcement. *Crime and Justice*, 7, 289–340.

Shearing, C. and J. Wood (2003). Nodal governance, democracy, and the new 'denizens'. *Journal of Law and Society*, 30(3), 400–419.

Smith, A. (1776). *An Inquiry into the Wealth of Nations*, London: Strahan & Cadell.

Takáts, E. (2011). A theory of 'crying wolf': the economics of money laundering enforcement. *Journal of Law, Economics, and Organization*, 27(1), 32–78.

Unger, B. (2013). Money laundering regulation: from Al Capone to Al Qaeda. In B. Unger and D. van der Linde (eds), *Research Handbook on Money Laundering*, Cheltenham, UK and Northampton, MA, USA: Edward Elgar Publishing, pp. 19–34.

Unger, B. and J. Ferwerda (2008). Regulating money laundering and tax havens: the role of blacklisting. Discussion Paper Series, Tjalling C. Koopmans Research Institute, 08(12). Retrieved from http://dspace.library.uu.nl/handle/1874/309681.

Unger, B., J. Ferwerda, M. van den Broek and I. Deleanu (2014). *The Economic and Legal Effectiveness of the European Union's Anti-Money Laundering Policy*, Cheltenham, UK and Northampton, MA, USA: Edward Elgar Publishing.

Van Duyne, P.C. (2003). Money laundering policy, fears and facts. In P.C. van Duyne, K. von Lampe and J.L. Newell (eds), *Criminal Finances and Organizing Crime in Europe*, Nijmegen: Wolf Legal Publishers, pp. 67–104. Retrieved from http://www.petrusvanduyne.nl/files/Witwassen%20Fears%20and%20Facts.pdf.

Wood, J. and B. Dupont (2006). *Democracy, Society, and the Governance of Security*, Cambridge University Press. Retrieved from http://journals.cambridge.org/production/action/cjoGetFulltext?fulltextid=1438924.

Zdanowicz, J.S. (2009). Trade-based money laundering and terrorist financing. *Review of Law and Economics*, *5*, 855–878.

4. Natural disasters and (future) government debt

Ian Koetsier

4.1 INTRODUCTION

Natural disasters are becoming ever more frequent (see Figure 4.1). Major disasters have struck all around the globe, leading to major disruptions, even in major economies. Recent examples are hurricanes Katrina and Sandy. Extreme weather events have happened in the past, and they will happen in the future (Banholzer et al., 2014). Several scientific sources suggest that anthropogenic climate change increases the frequency of

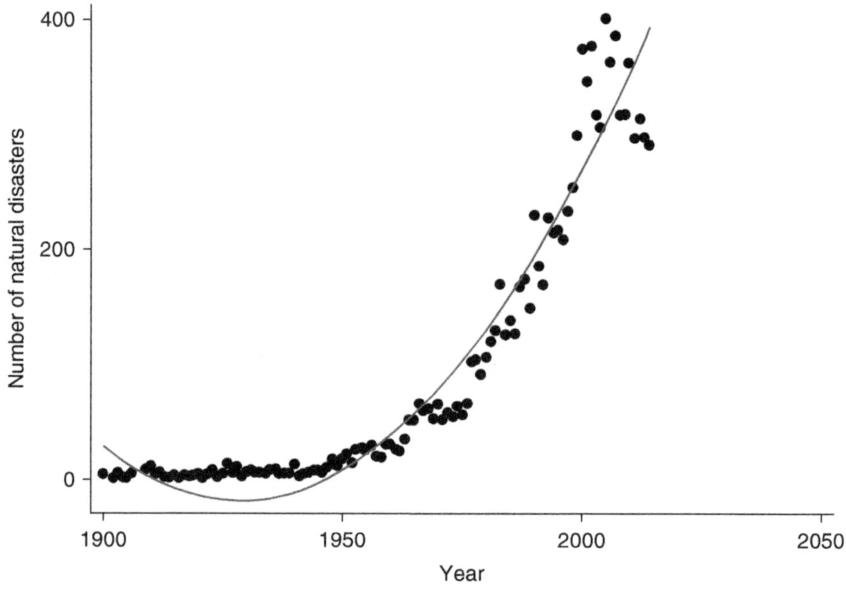

Source: Based on data from the Emergency Events Database (EM-DAT, 2016a).

Figure 4.1 The occurrence of natural disasters, 1900–2015

extreme weather events and has a substantial impact on the climate in certain regions (Raschky, 2008). According to the 2015 Global Assessment Report on Disaster Risk Reduction, expected annual average losses from earthquakes, tsunamis, tropical cyclones and river flooding are now estimated at US$314 billion in the built environment alone (CRED/UNISDR, 2015). The brunt of these direct costs is often borne by the government for two main reasons: first, governments consider disaster relief to be their moral obligation; second, they are deemed to be the most efficient providers of disaster assistance.

This chapter focuses on the *ex post* costs of natural disasters, which are not limited to direct costs but also include secondary costs, such as production disruptions, additional government expenses, and so on. There are several ways in which natural disasters affect a government's fiscal position. First of all, the direct relief and reconstruction costs will lead to higher spending (for example, rebuilding houses, schools, hospitals and infrastructure) and possibly crowd-out other, more productive spending (for example, educational spending). Thus the effects of a disaster are not necessarily limited to short-term consequences for the financial position of the government. Furthermore, disasters can have an effect on tax collection (capabilities) as production disruptions lead to lower tax revenues. Other aspects include a worsening of the current account as the country's exports decline and imports for reconstruction surge (Borensztein et al., 2009). In relation to this, the exchange rate may deteriorate. In particular, countries with foreign currency-denominated debt will face debt sustainability issues. Hence, there is some evidence that the interest rate on government bonds and the sovereign default premium might increase after a (large) disaster. In addition, inflation might spike due to a lack of supply and increased transport costs as well as the demand for reconstruction after a natural disaster. In this chapter I try to capture a comprehensive view of these different effects on the government's fiscal position. Therefore, the main focus is on government debt, as the separate effects on government revenue, government expenditure, the interest rate and the exchange rate are ultimately absorbed into the government debt position.

There have been some attempts to investigate the macroeconomic effects of natural disasters. While most of these studies concentrate on the effects on output (for a comprehensive survey of the literature, see Cavallo and Noy, 2010), only a limited number of studies are available on the effects of disasters on the government's fiscal position (Rasmussen, 2004; Noy and Nualsri, 2011; Acevedo, 2014). These studies often focus only on a very limited set of countries, especially Caribbean countries. Although all of them have contributed to the understanding of the fiscal costs of natural disasters, I aim to draw more generalizable conclusions due to my large sample of countries. Contrary to other studies, I also take a forward-looking approach. This chapter attempts to approximate the development of government liabilities from future natural disasters, so-called implicit government debt, which consists of future (non-contract) liabilities for the government which it deems a government's (moral) obligation to fulfil. In the present case, this moral obligation is future spending on natural disaster relief and reconstruction. My main research question is: how do past and future natural disasters affect government debt? I look at the short- and long-run effects because I study the trajectory of government debt in the post-disaster period.

The chapter contributes to the understanding of the government's fiscal position. To my knowledge, this chapter is the most comprehensive attempt to estimate the effect of natural disasters on government debt. I employ multiple controls, such as the pre-disaster goodness of fit, sovereign defaults, the occurrence of multiple disasters and so on. My disaster data are obtained from the Emergency Events Database (EM-DAT), and I include a large and diverse set of 69 countries in the analysis.[1] The merit of this approach is that it allows to derive general patterns for the development of government debt after a natural disaster. This chapter also aims to make a methodological contribution by employing the synthetic control method, which creates a counterfactual that closely resembles the characteristics of the country under investigation.[2] In addition, I try to make some predictions on the effect of climate change on the government's implicit liabilities from natural disasters.

The chapter is structured as follows. Section 4.2 discusses different forms of provision for natural disaster relief and reconstruction, and section 4.3 looks at the natural disaster literature. In section 4.4, I discuss methodology and data, and section 4.5 highlights the results. Section 4.6 shows the consequences of climate change on the occurrence of natural disasters and the associated future possible increase in fiscal costs. I discuss policy recommendations in section 4.7, and section 4.8 concludes.

4.2 PRIVATE OR PUBLIC PROVISION

The classical theory of public goods introduced by Samuelson (1954) uses a strict dichotomy between private and public goods, but this dichotomy is hard to apply to disaster relief and reconstruction. While a home that needs to be rebuilt qualifies as a private good,[3] this black-and-white approach is hard to maintain when people endure incredible hardship due to a natural disaster, which is sometimes even seen as the 'wrath of

God'. As a consequence, we move beyond the classical dichotomy. Heath (2011, p. 14) identifies other reasons for government intervention. Natural disaster relief and reconstruction evidently relate to public provision as described in the morality model. According to the introduction of this book, this model applies to both immaterial conditions, like human dignity and rights, and material conditions. Disaster relief and reconstruction aim to restore immaterial conditions (such as human dignity) and meet basic material needs (such as clothes, housing and food). Therefore, disaster relief and reconstruction both qualify as core public tasks. In general, the government performs the majority of these tasks; it is best positioned to acquire the necessary funds and prioritize the needs of the population.[4] While civil society is involved in providing disaster aid and reconstruction, its role is more modest, and the government is often involved in funding and directing these activities.

Although government intervention is deemed essential in the aftermath of natural disasters, this does not by itself explain why people do not buy insurance in the private market. After all, it is often private property which is destroyed. The simple answer is that the private disaster insurance market is either non-existent or incomplete. In other words, there is no alternative to public provision. This phenomenon is called the 'disaster syndrome'.

The natural disaster insurance market is characterized by distorted demand and insufficient supply. The distorted demand comes from two factors: irrational behaviour and bail-out expectations. First, the characteristics of natural disasters lead people to behave in an economically irrational manner. People are often unable to assess the risk of a natural disaster, which is unsurprising given the high level of uncertainty associated with natural disasters (for example, the place of occurrence, the severity of the disaster etc.). To make things worse, this uncertainty will continue to grow for weather-related disasters due to the unpredictability of climate change. Moreover, people tend to underinsure because they underestimate the risk of low-probability high-loss events (Raschky, 2008). As these problems are an integral part of natural disasters themselves, it is unlikely that they will be solved in the near future. Second, the expected bail-out by the government or a charity also leads to different behaviour on the demand side. In a similar vein as, for example, banks, individuals tend to underinsure in expectation of a bail-out (for example, disaster relief, the reconstruction of homes, and so on). This is called 'charity hazard'. Even in the United States, there is a very strong belief that the government will and should take action in the event of a natural disaster. A recent survey[5] by the Pew Research Center, which asked Americans about their view on the role of government, revealed that 88 per cent of Americans agree that responding to a natural disaster is a task for the government. Disaster relief and reconstruction came second on the list of the most important government tasks, only after keeping the country safe from terrorism.

The supply side of natural disaster insurance is equally distorted. There is a clear case of missing markets (a classical market failure). Actual coverage for some types of natural disasters is limited, even in countries with highly developed insurance markets (Skidmore and Toya, 2002). People are just unable to insure themselves against natural disasters, or some disasters, due to lack of supply. It is no surprise according to Borensztein et al. (2009) that insurance companies do not step into this market. According to the authors:

> a company providing car insurance can achieve a good diversification if it has many clients because in that case the volume of claims would be predictable with a high level of accuracy. In contrast, natural disasters are low-probability events that cause extremely large losses when they occur and thus not easily diversifiable in the same way as car insurance. (Borensztein et al., 2009, p. 279)

Put differently, the missing market is the result of correlated risks. In addition, the natural disaster risk might be too big to insure for insurance companies. Since the recent financial crisis, it has been clear that even insurance companies can run into trouble (for instance, AIG). In the event of a major natural disaster, funds might prove insufficient, and disaster insurance companies might turn out to be a contingent government liability.

From a macroeconomic perspective, it may be wise for a government to intervene. Governments try to limit output volatilities by conducting countercyclical policies. Stable macroeconomic circumstances are deemed essential. These might be disrupted by a natural disaster. Barro (2009) shows that the welfare costs of the usual economic fluctuations (that is, the business cycle) are equivalent to a decline in gross domestic product (GDP) by about 1.5 per cent per year, whereas calibrations indicate that society would willingly reduce GDP by around 20 per cent each year to eliminate rare disasters. The welfare loss from natural disasters is unacceptable to society and government. Dealing with its macroeconomic consequences should be in the hands of the government: the welfare consequences for the country's citizens are too big to leave to the private sector.

Disaster relief is clearly a core public task (see Table 4.1). Due to the supply and demand characteristics of the market, the government is the most effective provider of this type of insurance,[6] as other forms of provision for high-impact, low but increasing probability risks are regarded as insufficient or ineffective. The goals of public invention are only achievable, however, if the government has the necessary resources to deal with

Table 4.1 Res publica: table to jointly compare projects

	Description (positive) Who are and were the actors?			Justification (normative) Why *should* the public intervene?		
	State	Community	Market	Equality	Community/ Morality	Efficiency
Provision	XXXXXX				XXXXXX	
Funding	XXXXXX				XXXXXX	
Regulation						

the costs of a natural disaster. Therefore, this chapter focuses on the fiscal costs of natural disasters. Accurate estimates of the likely fiscal costs of a disaster are useful in that they enable a better cost–benefit evaluation of various mitigation programmes (Cavallo and Noy, 2010). In addition, disaster prevention is also a public task, as it has all the attributes of a public good. The government must be able to reap the benefits of its own efforts to improve preparedness. Privatization of disaster relief can lead to a decline in prevention efforts, as the direct benefits are not reaped by the government. Another motivation to estimate the fiscal cost of disasters is to better enable governments to insure: (1) directly against disaster losses; (2) indirectly through the issuance of catastrophe bonds (cat bonds); or (3) through precautionary savings (Cavallo and Noy, 2010).

4.3 EMPIRICAL EVIDENCE

Most of the macroeconomic literature on the costs of natural disasters focuses on the consequences for output. The evidence here is mixed. Some studies rely on a Schumpeterian creative destruction argument and find positive effects on economic growth (see e.g. Skidmore and Toya, 2002). When a natural disaster destroys part of a country's capital stock, this will lead to growth in the reconstruction phase. However, most studies find a negative effect on output (see e.g. Rasmussen, 2004; Noy, 2009; Raddatz, 2009; Noy and Nualsri, 2011; Acevedo, 2014). According to Cavallo and Noy (2010), taking into account the severity of a disaster might bridge the contradiction in the findings on output growth above. In general, the severity of the natural disaster and the country's level of development are deemed important for the impact on output.[7]

In methodological terms, this chapter follows Cavallo et al. (2013), who investigate the effect of a large natural disaster on output and compute the counterfactual using a synthetic control method. Contrary to other studies, the authors do not find a decline in output for large natural disaster when they control for political changes. However, they study only a very limited number of natural disasters. In this chapter, I use the synthetic control method to determine the effect of a natural disaster on government finances. Although economic growth is one of the channels by which a natural disaster could influence the size of government debt, it is not the main focus of my research. Still, the discussion of the output effect gives some insights into the possible effects on government debt, and which aspects partly determine the costs of a natural disaster. There have been a few attempts to quantify the impact of natural disasters on the government's fiscal position, which have focused mostly on the disaster-prone region of the Caribbean.

Rasmussen (2004) investigates the macroeconomic implications of natural disasters in the Caribbean for the period 1970 to 2002. His analysis includes the effect on the fiscal balance. It should be noted that his study focuses on small island states which are members of the Eastern Caribbean Currency Union. He stresses that there is a large variation in outcomes for the fiscal balance. However, he finds that median public debt will increase by a cumulative 6.5 percentage points over three years as a result of a small reduction in revenue and an increase in spending, a median reduction in real GDP growth by 2.2 percentage points and a median increase of the current account deficit by 10.8 per cent of GDP in the year of the disaster.[8]

Heger et al. (2008), who investigate the macroeconomic costs of a natural disaster for the Caribbean, find a strong decline in GDP per capita but a subsequent recovery in the following years. Their finding on external debt is counterintuitive, though.[9] External debt decreases in the year following a natural disaster. This may, however, be explained by flows of aid to the afflicted country and the subsequent external debt relief that is granted in the course of reconstruction (Heger et al., 2008). External debt relief may be insufficient to lower government debt as whole, though. In this way, their results can be reconciled with the findings of Rasmussen (2004).

In a more recent paper, Acevedo (2014) investigates the effect of storms and floods on GDP per capita and public debt using a panel vector autoregression (VAR) model for the Caribbean[10] in the period 1970 to 2009. He finds a negative effect on GDP per capita growth for both types of disasters, but the evidence on public debt is mixed. According to the author, debt only increases with floods. Another notable finding is the effect of debt relief. He finds weak evidence that debt relief contributes to easing the negative effects of storms on debt.

Noy and Nualsri (2011) estimate the fiscal consequences of a natural disaster for a broader set of countries. They obtain their disaster data from the EM-DAT database, and their dataset includes 22 developed and 20 developing countries. Contrary to most studies, they use quarterly data employing a panel VAR framework.[11] Their main finding is that fiscal policy is countercyclical in developed economies and procyclical in developing economies (reducing spending and increasing revenues). The fiscal consequences are also split along these lines. For developed countries, the authors find that government debt increases following a shock (1.07 per cent of GDP) and rises to more than 8 per cent of GDP over one year and a half (Noy and Nualsri, 2011). This is the consequence of higher spending and lower revenues, which translates into an increase in borrowing. In contrast, developing economies pursue procyclical policies that result in a decline in government debt.

Melecky and Raddatz (2011) investigate the economic and fiscal consequences of a natural disaster for middle- and high-income countries over the period 1975 through 2008. They divide disasters into three broad categories: geological disasters, climatic disasters and a residual group (for example, famines, industrial accidents). The authors find that, on average, budget deficits increase only after climatic disasters, but the increase in deficits is widespread across all events for lower-middle-income countries. They confirm the finding reported by Raddatz (2009) that higher initial government debt has no effect on the size of the deficit and the development of output. In addition, financial development shields an economy from the consequences of disasters. However, these lower costs go hand in hand with expanding budget deficits. Melecky and Raddatz (2011) also find that insurance penetration influences the costs of a natural disaster. High insurance penetration lowers the output and deficit consequences.

In summary, there is some evidence that government debt increases after a natural disaster. However, whether the evidence is generalizable beyond the Caribbean region, or holds for both the short as well as the long run, remains open for discussion.

4.4 METHODOLOGY AND DATA

My disaster dataset obtained from the EM-DAT database includes extreme temperature, storm, wildfire, drought, mass movement (dry), volcanic activity, earthquake, landslide and flood events for the period 1900–2015 (see Figure 4.2). To prevent the inclusion of natural hazards, disasters have to meet at least one of the following criteria specified in the EM-DAT guidelines (EM-DAT, 2016b): ten or more deaths, 100 or more people affected, injured or homeless, or the declaration of a state of emergency or an appeal for international assistance.[12] The dataset provides information

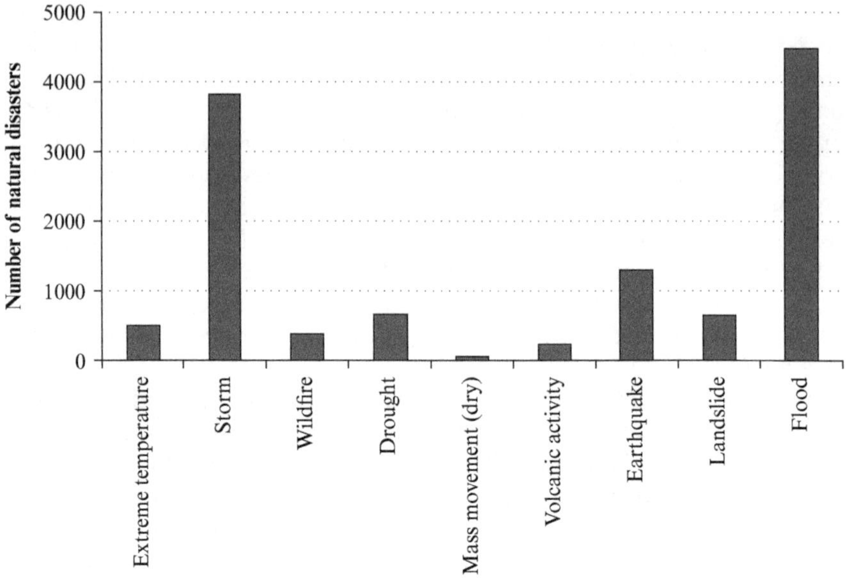

Source: Based on data from the Emergency Events Database (EM-DAT, 2016a).

Figure 4.2 Natural disasters by category, 1900–2015

on the type of disaster, the frequency of occurrence, total deaths, the number of those injured, homeless or otherwise affected, and total damage per country-year. Total damage includes only direct damage, whereas I am also interested in the secondary effects of a disaster, especially the effect on government debt. This study uses EM-DAT data from 1900–2015 for an analysis of climate change, because climate change is a long-term climatological process. For the synthetic control method, I take the period from 1971 to 2012 due to data limitations for macroeconomic variables. The macroeconomic data are obtained from multiple sources, among them the United Nations and the World Bank.

Some studies voice some concerns about the EM-DAT dataset. My main reason for choosing it is that it is the most comprehensive disaster dataset available. It includes data from 1900 onwards, and covers the entire world. However, I am aware of some drawbacks. First, the dataset is compiled from multiple sources, which leads to differences in definitions and there is no common methodology. Furthermore, the outcome cannot always be verified, which makes it hard to check the credibility of the sources. However, this chapter focuses on large disasters, which are often recorded by multiple sources. In addition, the use of multiple sources also prevents a bias from overestimation of total damages by developing country governments. Moreover, there are also cases where governments conceal the occurrence of a specific disaster. In this respect, the variety of sources of the EM-DAT database is an advantage, as it minimizes the chances that an event goes completely unrecorded, even if no official report is filed by the affected country (Jaramillo, 2007). Second, improvements in disaster reporting might lead to bias over time. This effect is less likely to influence the results because I focus on large natural disasters. Furthermore, I check for improved reporting in the climate change analysis. Third, some climate events occur in a specific period in the year, such as hurricanes. Ideally I would like to control for this by correcting for the month of occurrence, but I cannot do so due to data limitations. However, the focus of the chapter is on the entire post-disaster trajectory, and correcting for the month of occurrence is more important when a study focuses on the short-term effects of natural disasters. Furthermore, the unpredictability of natural disasters is sometimes not in their occurrence but in their timing and severity. Fourth, the EM-DAT dataset does not provide all information for all natural disasters in the dataset. As a consequence, I decided to focus on deaths. I am aware that different disaster types will have different consequences in terms of direct costs, the total number of people affected and deaths. However, I choose to show deaths because the number of deaths is most widely available in the EM-DAT database (see Koetsier, forthcoming for the other measures).

I do not test for alternative theories of natural disaster costs, as this chapter is primarily interested in the fiscal costs of natural disasters. I use the synthetic control groups developed by Abadie et al. (2010), which allows to track fiscal costs in the pre- and post-disaster period. In doing so, I impose a stricter threshold than the EM-DAT database, whose relatively low threshold would result in the inclusion of a large number of small disasters. My threshold is a minimum of five deaths per 100,000 inhabitants.[13] This is also more in line with the general perception of natural disasters. Another reason for imposing a threshold is a consequence of my estimation method. The synthetic control method requires that some countries remain unaffected by natural disasters. When a natural disaster occurs, I want to compare the non-disaster and disaster developments at the country-level. For the construction of the non-disaster counterfactual, I need a group of non-disaster countries. The synthetic control group is composed of multiple countries that are assigned specific weights which add up to 1, that is, the weighted countries create a synthetic country as if the disaster country was not affected by a natural disaster. The counterfactual is based on the countries' similarities in the period before the natural disaster based on a selection of controls. I use the ten-year pre-disaster period to ensure that the synthetic control group closely resembles the disaster country in the years before the disaster. This is important because it assures a good match between the disaster country and the synthetic country. My sample period stretches from 1971 to 2012. The goal is to check the difference between disaster country A and the respective synthetic control group, that is, the non-disaster country A (the constructed counterfactual). This estimation gives an indication of the costs of a natural disaster.

I focus on the fiscal consequences of natural disasters, which are macroeconomic in nature. The selection of controls is obtained from the economic growth literature (see Barro and Sala-i-Martin, 2003). Following Abadie et al. (2010), I also include pre-intervention outcomes of the variable of interest for the first half of the pre-disaster period ($DEBT_{t-10}, \ldots, DEBT_{t-6}$). As additional variables, I use GDP growth, openness, population growth, general government expenditure growth, GDP per capita, the GDP share of agriculture, hunting and minerals,[14] gross capital formation (as a percentage of GDP), the average latitude,[15] the years of education, and major episodes of political violence in the estimation. Another reason why I include these controls is the impact of preparedness on disaster severity. Therefore, I include numerous controls for the level of development, as this results in a better match between the synthetic control group and the disaster country in the pre-disaster period.

4.5 RESULTS

I start by conducting the synthetic control analysis. Others studies have applied a 'hard' threshold for the classification of disaster and non-disaster countries: a country either suffers a natural disaster in the sample period or it does not. My preferred specification does not apply a hard threshold for the identification of a natural disaster, though. I introduce a second, stricter threshold for non-disaster countries. To qualify as a non-disaster country, a country may not experience a natural disaster with more than one death per 100,000 inhabitants. This serves to exclude countries that did experience a sizeable disaster but were not classified as such using the 'hard' threshold. In addition, I also address the issue of large idiosyncratic shocks in the variable of interest. Huge fluctuations of the level of government debt in the control group could prove problematic, especially in the post-disaster period. Therefore, I exclude those countries from the non-disaster country group whose year-on-year fluctuations in absolute terms are among the top 1 per cent of the non-disaster countries included in the analysis. These countries are eliminated from the pool of possible synthetic

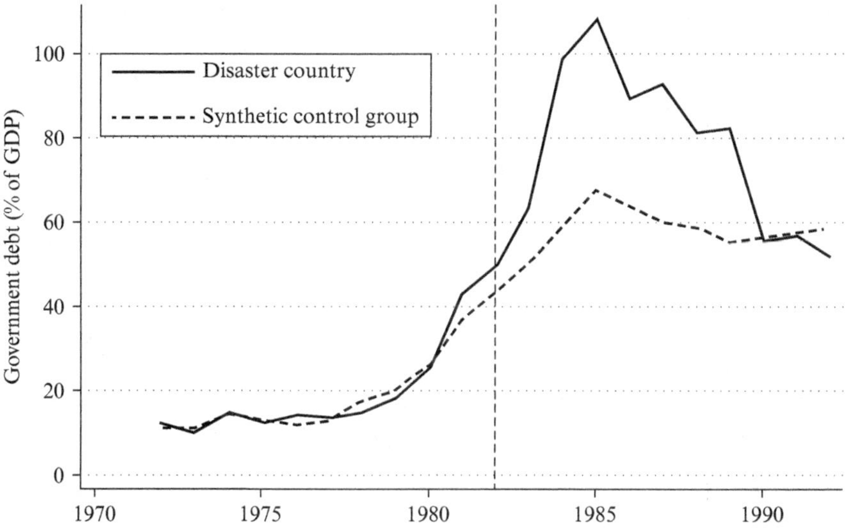

Figure 4.3 Graphical representation of the synthetic control method for El Salvador, 1982

control countries, no matter why the fluctuations occur. This is also irrelevant as this chapter focuses not on the non-disaster countries but on those affected by a natural disaster.

In the first step of the analysis, I estimate the synthetic control group per country. Figure 4.3 shows the country-level estimations for El Salvador. In the pre-disaster period, the disaster country and the synthetic control group lines are more or less identical, which gives credibility to the estimated effect for the post-disaster period because the synthetic control group is a good predictor of developments in El Salvador. I utilize the difference between the synthetic control group and El Salvador in the post-disaster period to approximate the treatment effect ($\hat{\alpha}_g$). In this case, it is the effect of a natural disaster on government debt. Even though a country-by-country exercise is interesting and has its merits, I am primarily interested in the overall effect of natural disasters on government debt. In other words, the aim is to draw general conclusions about the effect of a natural disaster on government debt.

Therefore, in a second step, I average the country-specific effects illustrated in Figure 4.3 in the following way:

$$\bar{\alpha} = (\bar{\alpha}_{T_0+1}, \ldots, \bar{\alpha}_T) = \frac{1}{G}\sum_{g=1}^{G} (\hat{\alpha}_{g,T_0+1}, \ldots, \hat{\alpha}_{g,T}) \tag{4.1}$$

where $\hat{\alpha}$ represents the country-specific treatment effects from the disaster ($T_0 + 1$) until the end of the post-disaster period (T). I calculate all these country-specific effects and average them for the post-disaster period over the number of natural disasters (G). Notice that we can observe the entire post-disaster trajectory of government debt ($\overline{\alpha}_{T_0+1},\ldots,\overline{\alpha}_T$).

In the third step of the analysis, I control for some additional features to improve and check the robustness of the average treatment effect. There are several ways to deal with the level of government debt after a natural disaster. Defaulting on your obligations is one option. This study uses the data provided by Reinhart and Rogoff (2009) and their updates to identify domestic and external default,[16] which allows me to check whether domestic and/or external default play a role in the costs of a natural disaster.

The results reveal that natural disasters can have a sizable effect on government debt.[17] I present the results of the preferred specification. This specification controls for idiosyncratic shocks of the dependent variable in the control group and it does not use countries that face a medium-sized disaster in the control group. It is found that government debt increases substantially in the short and long term. Figure 4.4 shows this result graphically. The estimated increase in government debt is in a range from approximately 23 percentage points to 37 percentage points. The reader should note that the effect can potentially continue beyond the period studied. Figure 4.4 still shows an upward trend compared to the synthetic control group. Of course, it is necessary to be cautious in interpreting this result as a golden rule for all countries around the world. The heterogeneity in the post-disaster period is relatively large even though the different models give relatively similar estimates of the effect. Thus, in general, my findings prove to be very robust. Furthermore, the increase of government debt is found for the average and median effects in the sample. In other words, the effect is not driven by outliers, so the estimates seem to be generally applicable. Several reasons can be given why the effect is still sizable in the long run. The reconstruction phase after a major disaster takes a long time, even in developed countries (a notable example is New Orleans after Hurricane Katrina). Other factors might also play a role. For instance, the tax base and/or taxation ability might be hurt in the long term as well. In addition, development assistance and aid might stop after some time when the public loses interest.

The results indicate a larger increase in government debt than previous studies do, which may be due to the fact that these studies mostly focus on the short-term effect. In addition, I provide median and average results for a large sample of countries, whereas other studies do not provide evidence on both. However, the different findings mostly result from different estimation periods. My results come close to the short-term effects reported in

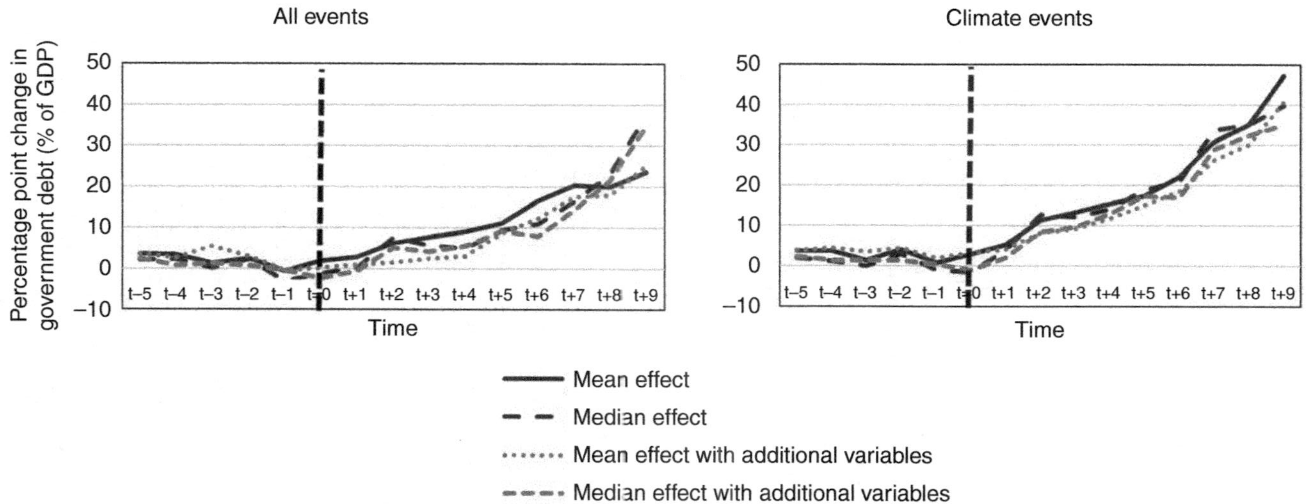

Figure 4.4 The mean and median effects of natural disasters controlling for sovereign default

Rasmussen (2004) and Noy and Nualsri (2011). Rasmussen (2004) finds a median increase in public debt of 6.5 percentage points after three years, while Noy and Nualsri (2011) find an increase of 8 percentage points for developed countries after one and a half years. My results point to a rise between 2 per cent of GDP and 8 per cent of GDP vis-à-vis the synthetic control group after approximately two and a half years after the disaster. The close match with those estimates increases confidence in my findings on the short- and the long-term effect.

To limit possible interference, I estimate the results again using only the first disaster on record in a specific country. Dealing with multiple disasters in quick succession might be different from encountering only one major disaster. I re-estimate the effect on the size of government debt and find roughly similar results; the increase ranges from 15 percentage points to 37 percentage points. The fact that the findings are quite similar may be due to the relatively high disaster threshold (as mentioned earlier, a disaster must be sizable to classify as a natural disaster). As a consequence, the effect on government debt tends to be sizable too, even without a second disaster.

The pre-disaster fit of the synthetic control group is of critical importance for the credibility of the treatment effect found. Abadie et al. (2010) use the root mean square percentage error (RMSPE)[18] to investigate the goodness of fit in the placebo procedure. Here it is used to assess the credibility of the results for the disaster countries. A better match between the disaster country and the synthetic control group in the pre-disaster period gives greater confidence in the predicted treatment effect in the post-disaster period. Therefore, I rate estimates with a lower RMSPE in the pre-disaster period higher than estimates with a high pre-disaster period RMSPE. Accordingly, I rank natural disasters based on their RMSPE (a high ranking means a low RMSPE). I decided against a weighting scheme as this turned out to put too much emphasis on one observation (the simple weighting scheme I did apply put a weight of over 80 per cent on one observation in some specifications). Although I deem the fit of the RMSPE important, I prefer to exploit all information in the panel. Therefore, I use a ranking mechanism to utilize all natural disasters in the sample and still put more weight on the synthetic control groups with a better fit. It is found that natural disasters lead to an increase in government debt by between 11 per cent of GDP and 37 per cent of GDP vis-à-vis the synthetic control group. While the average effect (11 per cent to 15 per cent of GDP) is somewhat lower than the earlier results (23 per cent to 25 per cent of GDP), it is still a sizable effect. The effect on government debt seems to level out after six and a half years. That means that, from that time on, the development in government debt is similar for disaster countries and non-disaster countries.

The evidence on anthropological climate change shows that the frequency and intensity of climate disasters will increase in the future (see IPCC, 2014; CRED/UNISDR, 2015). Therefore, we want to provide indicative evidence on the future costs of climate change. Most importantly, implicit government debt is a future obligation, and climate change is likely to have an impact on it. As a consequence, it is of the utmost importance to look at the effect of climate events on government debt. Climate events are defined as natural disasters whose frequency and intensity can be influenced by climate change.[19] I define extreme temperature, storms, droughts and floods as climate events, and volcanic activity and earthquakes as non-climate events. Note that I exclude wildfires as they might be caused by humans and not per se by a higher occurrence of thunderstorms. Furthermore, mass movements (dry) and landslides are also excluded because they are relatively local phenomena and, as such, do not meet the threshold in this study. Figure 4.4 illustrates that the effect of a climate event is larger than that of an average natural disaster, so that climate events cause government debt to increase to a higher level than non-climate events do. This corresponds to the findings of Melecky and Raddatz (2011) who obtain a similar result for the budget deficit. Furthermore, it is interesting to see that this effect is unlikely to be driven by outliers. The median and average values lie relatively close together for both specifications. The effect on government debt, between 34 per cent of GDP and 47 per cent of GDP, is very substantial. Therefore, climate change has the potential to lead to a substantial increase in implicit government debt now and in the future. In the next section, I will isolate the climate change effect from the regular climate effects to estimate the contribution of climate change to implicit government debt.[20]

There are several reasons why I regard my results as relatively conservative estimates. For example, I do not take net development assistance into account. High inflows of development aid could function as a substitute of government spending, and ultimately these flows could mask part of the effect of a natural disaster on government debt. Furthermore, I ignore countries that default on their sovereign debt obligations. The reader should note that the results above only represent countries which managed to honour their debt obligations over the pre- and post-disaster period. In other words, the worst-off countries in terms of increases in government debt may not even be included.

Some issues are addressed in a separate paper (Koetsier, forthcoming). For example, I did not explicitly differentiate between developing and developed countries.[21] It seems probable that developing countries face different borrowing constraints than developed countries. Moreover, the type of natural disaster can have an effect on the level of government debt. As a consequence, pooling disasters might lead to an over- or underestimation for some disaster types. Furthermore, in Koetsier (forthcoming), I correct for the possible endogeneity of natural disasters by using exogenous measures to define a large natural disaster (for example, the magnitude of an earthquake). However, these issues are beyond the scope of this chapter.

4.6 THE CLIMATE CHANGE EFFECT

One of the major drawbacks of this study is that it uses historical data to estimate the costs of natural disasters. For a policymaker, a forward-looking perspective is of the utmost importance. Implicit public debt is a future liability – in this case, the obligation to pay for disaster reconstruction and relief. Even though I use historical data, my estimates of the fiscal costs of natural disasters provide policymakers with some guidance on the future fiscal cost.

Climate change is likely to increase the intensity and frequency of climate events. Policymakers should be aware that weather-related disasters are becoming more frequent (CRED/UNISDR, 2015). Despite the wide variation in the scenarios on the development of climate events, there is very compelling evidence that the frequency and intensity of such events is increasing and will continue to do so in the future (Banholzer et al., 2014; IPCC, 2014; CRED/UNISDR, 2015). An extensive discussion on climate change itself is obviously beyond the scope of this chapter. Still, climate change may already have an effect on the occurrence of natural disasters. In recent decades, changes in climate have had an impact on natural and human systems on all continents and across the oceans (IPCC, 2014). While Figure 4.1 shows that the number of reported disasters has clearly increased over time, this change is not necessarily attributed to climate change. Two other factors may also play a role: first, improved reporting and technological change may have led to the increase in reporting; second, the world population has increased more than fourfold since 1900 according to United Nations data. To fall under the definition of a natural disaster, a natural hazard has to destroy property or affect the population, which has become more likely in light of the population increase. As a result, more natural hazards will become natural disasters and will be classified accordingly in the EM-DAT database.

The first step is to determine the change in the occurrence of climate events. Peduzzi (2005) uses earthquakes to distinguish the influence of improved access to information from the influence of climate change. I follow his approach and distinguish between climate and non-climate events (see Figure 4.5). My assumption is that improved reporting will hold

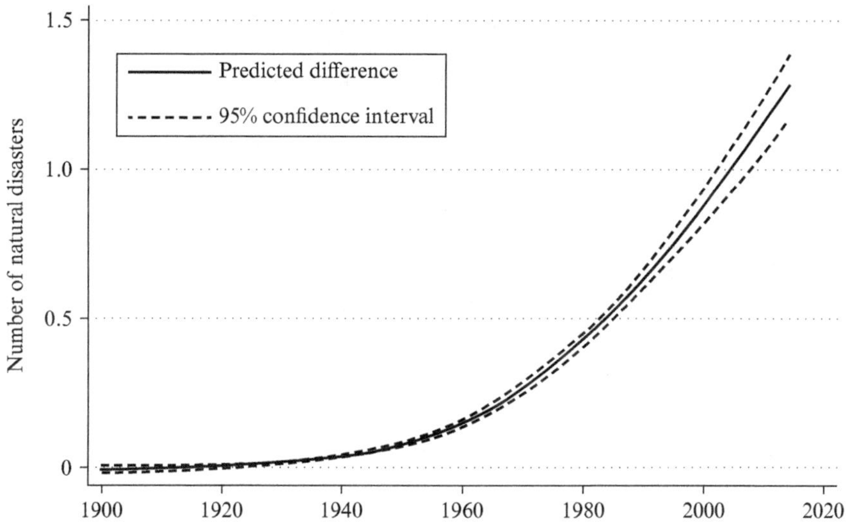

Figure 4.5 The difference between climate events and non-climate events

for both categories. In other words, climate and non-climate events benefit equally from easier reporting due to improved technology, such as the Internet. My analysis uses the difference between climate and non-climate events to investigate whether the mix of disasters has changed. If there is a change in the mix of disasters, I will attribute it to climate change if the difference is positive. A positive sign means that there are more climate events than non-climate events, and I am particularly interested in the trend.

It is found that the number of climate events as compared with non-climate events has increased rapidly from 1900 onwards. In 1900, the number of climate and non-climate events was approximately equal on a country basis. However, in 2014, a country would be hit by almost one and a half more climate events every year than non-climate events. I find the same positive relation for different degrees of severity (a minimum of one, five or ten deaths per 100,000 inhabitants). The difference is of course smaller for (rare) severe disasters. However, the positive trend is undisputable. According to Jaramillo (2007), a word of caution is in order. A country that is regularly hit by earthquakes is likely to build its infrastructure accordingly, so that the relation shown above may simply reflect better preparedness. However, the same reasoning holds for, for example, floods and storms.

Climate change has altered the severity and frequency of disasters, even over the past 115 years. If the past trend has any predictive value for the future, the trend is highly likely to be upward sloping, which also seems to be in line with the scientific evidence on climate change. As a consequence, implicit government liabilities are likely to grow over time. In this regard, the high cost of climate events is especially worrisome. These costs will probably not be equally spread across the globe. The Notre Dame Global Adaptation Index (ND-GAIN, 2015) reveals great variation in the vulnerability of countries (see Figure 4.6). Therefore, the fiscal costs will probably be distributed more unevenly than a single estimate suggests. In general, the brunt of these costs is likely to fall on developing countries. This finding is reinforced when the countries' preparedness is investigated. Those believed to be the most vulnerable to climate change are also the ones least prepared.

4.7 POLICY RECOMMENDATIONS

The increasing frequency of natural disasters should prompt policy action. There are two undisputed measures available for lowering the cost of natural disasters. First, we have to fight climate change, which will be particularly beneficial for future government finances. Emissions of carbon dioxide and most other greenhouse gases remain in the atmosphere for decades if not centuries, and the accumulated stock of such emissions is what leads to environmental problems (Newell et al., 2013). Even if we stop emitting today, the process of climate change will not stop in an instant. Second, prevention measures are also essential. To estimate the effectiveness of government expenditure on prevention, it is necessary to provide estimates of the potential costs of natural disasters. This study provides these estimates in particular for large natural disasters. Even though prevention measures and the fight against climate change will mitigate some disaster and disaster effects. The government should also prepare itself for the consequences of a natural disaster for its finances.

There are four main options available to cover the immediate costs of a natural disaster: private insurance, *ex ante* disaster funds, catastrophe bonds and international assistance. Let us look at these options in greater detail. The first, private insurance (see section 4.2), is not a viable option. As mentioned earlier, the market for natural disaster insurance is not well developed overall and is virtually non-existent in many developing countries (Rasmussen, 2004). Thus private insurance can only marginally reduce the cost of natural disasters for the government.

The second option, creating an *ex ante* disaster fund, is highly inefficient for governments and households alike. In particular, a large natural disaster may deplete a household's entire precautionary savings. In a

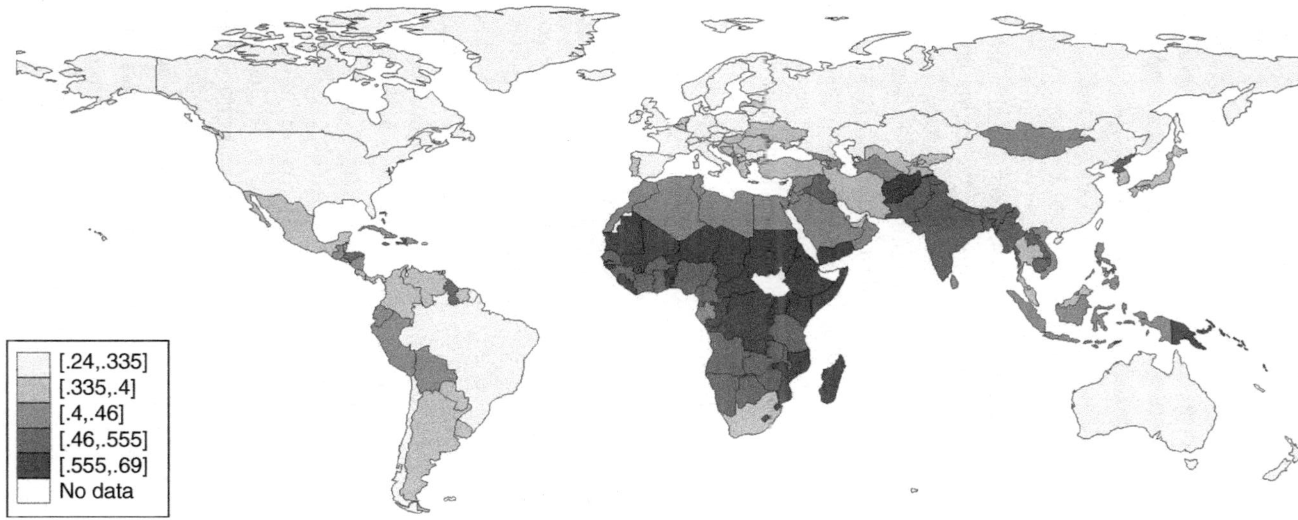

Source: ND-GAIN (2015).

Figure 4.6 ND-GAIN vulnerability index, 2014

similar vein, governments can self-insure by setting aside funds, but these are also limited in size. Mexico's Fondo Nacional de Desastres Naturales (FONDEN) is the most prominent example of this type of self-insurance. However, the opportunity costs may be high when the government's borrowing costs are high. In addition, the government must be willing to incur upfront costs in the first place.[22] Furthermore, political opportunism can lead to misuse of the disaster funds for other purposes.

The third solution, catastrophe bonds (cat bonds), can be implemented by any country. It is relatively easy to implement because no international cooperation is necessary. The decision can be taken unilaterally or with some assistance from the International Monetary Fund. Cat bonds help insulate government finances from the impact of a major disaster. There are three parties involved: a distinct special purpose vehicle (SPV), investors, and the insured country or pool of countries.[23] Investors buy a safe sovereign bond, like a US Treasury bond or a German Bund, and transfer it to an SPV. When no natural disaster occurs, the investors receive an insurance premium plus the interest rate on the safe government bond. The situation is different when a disaster strikes. The natural disaster must meet the factual trigger of the cat bond, which is an objective measure of disaster severity such as the Richter scale, flood height or wind speed.[24] If the trigger is met, the investor's claim is lost. The SPV sells the safe government bond and transfers the proceeds to the affected country.[25]

The first capital market instrument linked to catastrophe risk was introduced in 1994 as a means for reinsurers to transfer some of their own risks to capital markets (Cavallo and Noy, 2010). Since then, some governments have exploited the opportunity to insure themselves against disasters. In 2015, the outstanding value of cat bonds was US$25 billion. Using cat bonds for disaster insurance offers a number of advantages. First of all, they guarantee an immediate payout without conditions. Numerous studies note that it takes a long time for aid pledges to materialize, and that the funds come with strings attached (see Borensztein et al., 2009). A cat bond can be paid out almost instantaneously, which can be attributed to the factual trigger. A quick payout limits the macroeconomic consequences of a natural disaster, and it limits human suffering. Second, the issuance of cat bonds has a positive impact on the sustainability of government finances, because there is no sizable upfront payment required (as in the case of an *ex ante* fund). In addition, cat bonds make the other (non-cat) government bonds more secure and lead to lower interest rates on this type of government debt. Moreover, cat bonds allow spreading disaster risk to institutional and other international investors (that is, transferring disaster risk to private parties). Overall, this could help to stabilize the macroeconomic environment before and after a natural disaster. Third, demand for this type of securities is high and increasing rapidly, especially in the current low interest rate environment. Institutional investors are searching for investment opportunities. In addition, the risk inherent in cat bonds is not correlated to that of other investment categories, like bonds and shares. Investors' growing interest is reflected in the growth of the cat bond market over the last decade. The value of outstanding cat bonds has increased by more than fivefold (Artemis, 2016). Fourth, the usage of cat bonds contributes to government prevention efforts. Better preparedness leads to lower insurance costs, and lower costs directly benefit the incumbent politicians. Thus they directly reap the benefits of improving building regulation, investing in flood protection and so on. Furthermore, there is no moral hazard in this type of disaster insurance. Overall, there are great opportunities for governments and investors alike to further develop the cat bond market.[26]

As a fourth main option, fiscal assistance from developed countries to developing countries is needed in the event of a natural disaster. The Paris Agreement offers some opportunity for a funding mechanism to help developing countries which experience a natural disaster. In accordance with Article 53 of the United Nations Framework Convention on Climate Change's Proposal by the President, 'financial resources provided to developing countries should enhance the implementation of their policies, strategies, regulations and action plans and their climate change actions with respect to both mitigation and adaptation' (United Nations Framework Convention on Climate Change, 2015, p. 8). Under the Agreement, developed countries have a collective quantified goal from a floor of US$100 billion per year to meet the obligations specified above. This leaves some room for the provision of funds to developing countries in the aftermath of a climate event. There are several reasons to justify the usage of these funds to provide post-disaster relief. First of all, developing countries suffer from developed countries' past and current behaviour – developing countries have contributed only marginally to climate change. Second, there seems to be some relation between climate change and conflict (and migration as a consequence of climate events or the resulting conflicts). Barnett and Adger (2007), for example, argue that 'in certain circumstances these direct and indirect impacts of climate change on human security may in turn increase the risk of violent conflict' (ibid., p. 639).

The usage of funds linked to the Paris Agreement does not diminish the importance of cat bonds. Most importantly, developed countries cannot use the funds from the Paris Agreement. For developing countries, cat bonds could complement the funds from the Paris Agreement because they allow for additional insurance and insurance of non-climate events. Hence, requests for international assistance prove to be quite time-consuming. Cat bonds can provide immediate relief for developing countries, and international funds can take over in the long run. In addition, cat bonds can be issued on a unilateral basis, which makes it possible for policymakers to tailor their policies to country-specific climate risks.

4.8 CONCLUSIONS

This chapter investigates the influence of a natural disaster on a government's fiscal position. It uses synthetic control groups to track the consequences. The control group is constructed to resemble the disaster country, but without the disaster. The main finding is that natural disasters significantly increase government debt. This increase ranges from 23 per cent of GDP to 37 per cent of GDP. Other checks confirm the robustness of this finding. Most importantly, the increase in government debt is even more pronounced for climate events. It is found that a climate event will cause an increase in government debt by between 34 per cent and 47 per cent of GDP.

The chapter also explores the effects of anthropogenic climate change on the occurrence of natural disasters. Unsurprisingly, it is found that climate change increases the frequency of climate events (extreme temperatures, storms, droughts or floods). This implies that the estimates of the fiscal impact of natural disasters are probably too low with regard to the government's future obligations. The number of climate events is found to increase consistently over all levels of disaster severity, in line with the notion that disasters become more frequent and more severe. In addition, climate events have a larger impact on government debt than non-climate events. As a result, I expect implicit government debt to grow in the future. However, the future fiscal costs of climate change are likely to be distributed very unevenly. Developing countries are especially vulnerable, so they will have to bear the brunt of the costs associated with climate change.

Disaster insurance and reconstruction are core government tasks and will remain so in the future. My results highlight the urgent need to deal with climate change and increase preparedness. However, this will not be sufficient, as climate change is an ongoing process which does not stop at once. Therefore, it is also of the utmost importance to give governments the tools they need to cover the rising cost of natural disasters. Government must insure their fiscal position on the international bond market. I propose the issuance of cat bonds to spread the disaster risk over international investors. This limits the (future) fiscal costs and economic disruptions due to a natural disaster. In this way, governments can transfer part of the natural disaster risk to the private sector. The recent growth in cat bonds demonstrates that this is a viable option. For developing countries, I propose to complement the issuance of cat bonds with funds obtained under the Paris Agreement (which aims to raise US$100 billion per year prior to 2025). Part of these funds can be used to provide post-disaster relief to developing economies. In the short term, cat bonds can alleviate fiscal constraints, whereas in the long term, international assistance can take over this role.

NOTES

1. Algeria, Argentina, Australia, Austria, Bolivia, Burundi, Cameroon, Canada, Central African Republic, Chad, Chile, Colombia, Costa Rica, Cote d'Ivoire, Denmark, Dominican Republic, Ecuador, Egypt, El Salvador, Fiji, Finland, France, Gabon, Ghana, Greece, Guatemala, Guyana, Haiti, Honduras, Iceland, India, Ireland, Italy, Japan, Kenya, Malaysia, Mali, Mauritius, Mexico, Morocco, Nepal, Netherlands, New Zealand, Nicaragua, Niger, Nigeria, Norway, Pakistan, Panama, Paraguay, Peru, Philippines, Portugal, Rwanda, Sierra Leone, Singapore, South Africa, South Korea, Spain, Sri Lanka, Sweden, Switzerland, Thailand, Turkey, United Kingdom, United States, Uruguay, Venezuela and Zambia.
2. The method identifies the optimal synthetic control from a pool of non-disaster countries.
3. There might be positive externalities for the neighbours if a destroyed home is rebuilt. However, I choose to disregard these externalities because they are believed to be relatively small compared to the costs of reconstruction.
4. Government failure can lead to suboptimal prioritization of people's needs, for example, as a result of corruption.
5. The numbers are based on a national survey by the Pew Research Center, based on more than 6,000 interviews conducted between 27 August and 4 October 2015 (Pew Research Center, 2015).
6. Government failure is a problem in some countries, though.
7. Other factors, like the state of the business cycle, may also play a role. However, I focus only on the main factors.
8. These very large same-year effects are all the more striking when one considers that all the events occurred in the second half of the year (Rasmussen, 2004).
9. Raddatz (2009) actually focuses on the growth effects of natural disasters but also touches briefly on the external debt position. He finds that the debt position before the disaster does not affect the output loss incurred.
10. Antigua and Barbuda, Bahamas, Barbados, Dominica, Dominican Republic, Grenada, Haiti, Jamaica, St Kitts and Nevis, St Lucia, St Vincent and the Grenadines, and Trinidad and Tobago.
11. Their panel VAR framework also controls for the business cycle.
12. See EM-DAT (2016b).
13. I also investigate the number of deaths, the total number of those affected and damage as a per cent of GDP for the other thresholds (for details, see Koetsier, forthcoming).
14. Some sectors, such as agriculture, tourism, and water, are affected more than others by extreme climate events (IPCC, 2012).
15. I include the average latitude to account for climate circumstances.
16. Notice that all countries in the sample are independent, so they make autonomous decisions with regard to a default. In addition, due to their independence, it is less likely that they have some kind of implicit guarantee of their debt because there is no colonizing country.
17. For more results, see Koetsier (forthcoming).

18. The RMSPE is calculated as $RMSPE = \sqrt{\frac{1}{n}\Sigma_{i=1}^{n}\left(\frac{y_i - \hat{y}_i}{y_i}\right)^2}$.
19. I am aware that there have always been climate events. However, the first step to assessing the costs is to look into the historical costs of such events.
20. I do not show my placebo analysis. In this analysis, the non-disaster countries are used to determine whether the post-disaster outcome is not simply the result of random chance.
21. I implicitly took the differences into account through my selection of control variables (for example, GDP per capita).
22. Politicians are usually judged based on their performance in the aftermath of a natural disaster, and not blamed for its occurrence in the first place.
23. One example of risk pooling is the Caribbean Catastrophe Risk Insurance Facility (CCRIF), a multi-country risk pool that allows for immediate diversification of disaster risk.
24. Notice that no estimation of the potential costs is required, which saves precious time and funds. Most importantly, it allows for immediate access to the funds.
25. For instance, in May 2006 and again in October 2009, the Mexican government obtained earthquake and hurricane insurance by means of cat bonds and a direct purchase of coverage from international reinsurers (Cavallo and Noy, 2010).
26. Even though cat bonds provide a good method of shielding government finances from the effects of a natural disaster, there are some possible drawbacks. Cat bonds are relatively new financial instruments which might suffer from illiquid markets and high risk premia. Moreover, the extent of financial markets development matters for the functioning of the cat bond market. In addition, after the recent financial crisis, new financial instruments might be perceived as risky. However, the structure of a cat bond is easy to understand, and it has a clear trigger. Another drawback is that the volume of cat bonds might be insufficient when a major disaster strikes. Still, the positive effect of more secure government finances and instantaneous payout allows the government to deal with a disaster more effectively. Moreover, it makes sovereign default less likely or the haircut less severe, even when a very large natural disaster strikes.

REFERENCES

Abadie, A., A. Diamond and J. Hainmueller (2010). Synthetic control methods for comparative case studies: estimating the effect of California's tobacco control program. *Journal of American Statistical Association*, 105(490), 493–505.

Acevedo, S. (2014). Debt, growth and natural disasters: a Caribbean trilogy. IMF Working Paper, WP/14/125.

Artemis (2016). Catastrophe bonds & ILS issued and outstanding by year. *Artemis Catastrophe Bond and Insurance-Linked Securities Deal Directory*. Accessed 30 March 2016 at http://www.artemis.bm/deal_directory/cat_bonds_ils_issued_outstanding.html.

Banholzer, S., J. Kossin and S. Donner (2014). The impact of climate change on natural disasters. In A. Singh and Z. Zommers (eds), *Reducing Disaster: Early Warning Systems For Climate Change*, Dordrecht: Springer, pp. 21–49.

Barnett, J. and W.N. Adger (2007). Climate change, human security and violent conflict. *Political Geography*, 26, 639–655.

Barro, R. (2009). Rare disasters, asset prices, and welfare costs. *American Economic Review*, 99(1), 243–264.

Barro, R. and X. Sala-i-Martin (2003). *Economic Growth*, 2nd edition, Cambridge, MA: MIT Press.

Borensztein, E., E. Cavallo and P. Valenzuela (2009). Debt sustainability under

catastrophic risk: the case for government budget insurance. *Risk Management and Insurance Review*, 12(2), 273–294.
Cavallo, E., S. Galiani, I. Noy and J. Pantano (2013). Catastrophic natural disasters and economic growth. *Review of Economics and Statistics*, 95(5), 1549–1561.
Cavallo, E. and I. Noy (2010). The economics of natural disasters: a survey. Inter-American Development Bank Working Paper Series, IDB-WP-124.
Centre for Research on the Epidemiology of Disasters, United Nations Office for Disaster Risk Reduction (CRED/UNISDR) (2015). *The Human Cost of Weather Related Disasters, 1995–2015*. Accessed 30 March 2016 at https://www.unisdr.org/2015/docs/climatechange/COP21_WeatherDisastersReport_2015_FINAL.pdf.
EM-DAT (2016a). *The CRED/OFDA International Disaster Database*, D. Guha-Sapir, R. Below, P. Hoyois, Université Catholique de Louvain, Brussels. www.emdat.be.
EM-DAT (2016b). EM-DAT guidelines. Accessed 30 March 2016 at http://www.emdat.be/guidelines.
Heath, J. (2011). Three normative models of the welfare state. *Public Reasons*, 3(2), 13–43.
Heger, M., A. Julca and O. Paddison (2008). Analysing the impact of natural hazards in small economies: the Caribbean case. UNU-WIDER Research Paper, 2008/25.
Intergovernmental Panel on Climate Change (IPCC) (2012). *Managing the Risks of Extreme Events and Disasters to Advance Climate Change Adaptation*, New York: Cambridge University Press.
Intergovernmental Panel on Climate Change (IPCC) (2014). Summary for policymakers. In C.B. Field, V.R. Barros, D.J. Dokken, K.J. Mach, M.D. Mastrandrea, et al. (eds), *Climate Change 2014: Impacts, Adaptation, and Vulnerability*. Cambridge, UK and New York, USA: Cambridge University Press, pp. 1–32.
Jaramillo, C.R. (2007). Natural disasters and growth: evidence using a wide panel of countries. Documento CEDE, 2007–14.
Koetsier, I. (forthcoming). The fiscal impact of natural disasters. Tjalling C. Koopmans Research Institute Discussion Paper Series.
Melecky, M. and C. Raddatz (2011). How do governments respond after catastrophes? Natural-disaster shocks and the fiscal stance. World Bank Policy Research Working Paper, 5564.
Newell, R., W. Pizer and D. Raimi (2013). Carbon markets 15 years after Kyoto: lessons learned, new challenges. *Journal of Economic Perspectives*, 27(1), 123–146.
Notre Dame Global Adaptation Index (ND-GAIN) (2015). Country rankings. Accessed 30 March 2016 at http://index.gain.org/ranking.
Noy, I. (2009). The macroeconomic consequences of disasters. *Journal of Development Economics*, 88, 221–231.
Noy, I. and A. Nualsri (2011). Fiscal storms: public spending and revenues in the aftermath of natural disasters. *Environment and Development Economics*, 16(1), 113–128.
Peduzzi, P. (2005). Is climate change increasing the frequency of hazardous events?. *Environment and Poverty Times*, 2005(3), 7.
Pew Research Center (2015). Beyond Distrust: How Americans View Their

Government. Washington: Pew Research Center. Accessed 30 March 2016 at http://www.people-press.org/files/2015/11/11-23-2015-Governance-release.pdf.
Raddatz, C. (2009). The wrath of God: macroeconomic costs of natural disasters. World Bank Policy Research Working Paper, 5039.
Raschky, P. (2008). Institutions and the losses from natural disasters. *Natural Hazards and Earth System Sciences*, 8, 627–634.
Rasmussen, T.N. (2004). Macroeconomic implications of natural disasters in the Caribbean. IMF Working Paper, WP/04/224.
Reinhart, Carmen M. and Kenneth S. Rogoff (2009). *This Time is Different: Eight Centuries of Financial Folly*, Princeton, NJ: Princeton University Press.
Samuelson, P. (1954). The pure theory of public expenditure. *Review of Economics and Statistics*, 36(4), 387–389.
Skidmore, M. and H. Toya (2002). Do natural disasters promote long-run growth?. *Economic Inquiry*, 40(4), 664–687.
United Nations Framework Convention on Climate Change (2015). Adoption of the Paris Agreement, Proposal by the President, Conference of the Parties. Twenty-First Session.

PART II

New core tasks: social security

5. The advantages and disadvantages of different pension system designs

Ian Koetsier

5.1 INTRODUCTION

Countries have developed very different set-ups of their pension systems. Even so, ultimately they share the same goal: to secure old-age income. For instance, the Austrian and German pension systems rely heavily on the public unfunded pillar, the so-called first pillar. In an unfunded pillar, the current generation of workers pays for the current retirees. In contrast, the Dutch pension system consists of multiple pillars. Besides the public unfunded pillar, a mandatory privately funded pillar exists in which current workers pay part of their income into a pension fund. These payments are used to generate returns. Returns and contributions accumulate over time, thus providing old-age income. Parallel to this so-called second pillar, voluntary funded private pension schemes form the third pillar of the Dutch pension system. Figure 5.1 illustrates the enormous differences between European countries regarding the importance of privately funded pillars. In the Netherlands, pension funds hold assets equalling almost 160 per cent of gross domestic product (GDP), whereas in France this is only 0.5 per cent of GDP.

It seems surprising that comparatively similar European countries choose such different paths to achieve a common goal, that is, old-age income security. Pension systems vary across countries, depending on their different attitudes toward risk-sharing, intergenerational and intragenerational redistribution, and other factors (Orszag and Stiglitz, 1999). The main reasons for these differences are rooted in history and path dependence of the pension system design. Therefore, this chapter does not try to find the one preferable pension system, because a one-size-fits-all approach does not seem appropriate. Instead the differences between the various types of pension systems are described, their advantages and disadvantages are discussed, and last but not least it attempts to assess the robustness of the different systems in an ever-changing environment.

The current situation is particularly difficult for the majority of

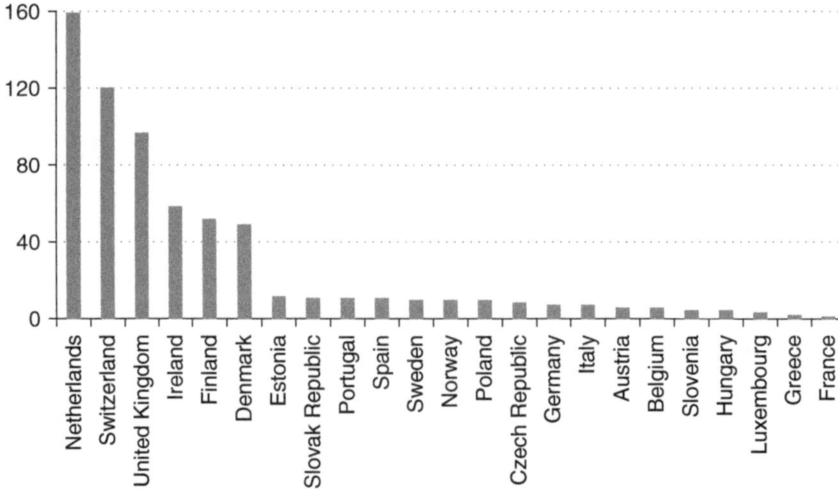

Source: OECD Global Pension Statistics (2015).

Figure 5.1 The size of pension funds relative to GDP

prevailing pension systems. The public unfunded systems face a deterioration of government finances, while the privately funded systems are confronted with low yields and high default risks. In difficult times such as these, it is crucial to understand the different pension systems and possible risks connected to them. Politicians increasingly experience pressure to reform pension systems, and policy failures could be very costly. This chapter helps to gain an understanding of the different systems and their advantages as well as their disadvantages. It provides ideas on how to deal with and how to mitigate some risks specific to them. Section 5.2 shows the different objectives of pension systems. Section 5.3 discusses the risks of the respective pillar designs. Section 5.4 concludes with the benefits of multi-pillar systems.

5.2 THE OBJECTIVES OF PENSION SYSTEMS

Different pension systems balance the primary objectives of pensions in different ways. These primary objectives include insurance (for example, protection against the risk of longevity), consumption smoothing (that is, enabling people to redistribute their means more evenly over their lifetime), poverty relief, and redistribution. However, pension systems are often judged on their secondary goals, such as higher savings and economic growth rates. These goals can interfere with the primary objectives or hinder the systems in achieving them.

One of the most important purposes of pensions is to smooth lifetime income and thus facilitate a more even consumption pattern throughout a person's life. This enables a person to transfer consumption from their productive middle years to their retired years, allowing them to choose their preferred time path of consumption over working and retired life (Barr and Diamond, 2006). The possibility to consume a part of the individual income at a later stage of life improves a person's welfare,[1] assuming that consumption preferences are time-consistent. A pension also provides some form of insurance, reducing some of the risks associated with retirement (for example, longevity risk). A pension scheme based on individual savings alone faces the risk that the beneficiary might outlive their savings, or would have stretch consumption in order to prevent that from happening (Barr and Diamond, 2006). In a pension system, assets and liabilities are pooled and in this way risks are shared, providing the individual with a higher probability to receive a sufficient income during retirement.

Pensions systems often possess a component of poverty relief. This component can take different forms, for example guarantees or uniform retirement benefits. They target those sections of the population who are unable to save enough for their retirement. Another important reason for government involvement is redistribution. This includes inter- and intra-generational redistribution. In the current context, redistribution is an intentional government action to ensure a more equal income composition. Pension systems can, for example, redistribute incomes on a lifetime basis, complementing the role of progressive taxes on annual income (Barr and Diamond, 2006).

Secondary goals of pension systems, often confused with main objectives, include economic and financial market development as well as contributing to economic growth. I regard the previously mentioned primary objectives as the most important aspects of pensions. It is clear that a private pension system cannot fulfil all of these goals. Private pension schemes do not allow for redistribution and poverty relief to the same extent as public schemes. However, it is also questionable whether a public pension scheme is able to yield the same returns as a private system.

5.3 THE RISKS CONNECTED TO THE DIFFERENT PILLARS

When comparing public and private pension systems we must be aware of the fact that there are no clear-cut differences between the two systems. A public system may involve some private firms: for example, a private firm may manage the assets for a public trust fund; and similarly, private systems make use of public services, at the very least to enforce their rules (Orszag and Stiglitz, 1999). Public systems are often unfunded, but this does not necessarily have to be the case. For instance, the public pension system in Norway is a fully funded system. There are also public systems which are partially funded. To avoid discussion of all exceptions, I use the three-pillar model to discuss the risks of the different pillars. The separate pillars serve different purposes in the pension system. The first pillar is an unfunded, state-run pillar focusing on redistribution and the alleviation of old-age poverty. The second pillar is generally a mandatory, privately managed component of the pension system. The contributions are invested in assets for return purposes, and its primary objective is consumption smoothening. The third pillar consists of voluntary savings in private pension funds, providing additional old-age income. The discussion focuses mainly on the differences between pillars one and two, because there is a considerable overlap regarding risks faced by pillars two and three.

Demographic Risks

Ageing

The demographic composition in almost all advanced economies is changing. We can distinguish two effects, a transition effect (the baby-boom generation) and a structural effect on the demographic composition (continuing changes in fertility and life expectancy). Figure 5.2 illustrates the development of the old-age dependency ratio. This ratio shows the relation between the working-age population and the retirees. In other words, an old-age dependency ratio of 0.5 means that two people of working age are supporting one retiree. In an unfunded system, the government makes promises to future retirees. This translates into future expenditures resulting in implicit public debts. These debts differ fundamentally from explicit government debts, insofar as they can be reduced by implementing successful pension reforms. In contrast to this, explicit government debts form part of the national accounts and cannot be changed significantly by fiscal reform (Eichhorst et al., 2011). It therefore makes good sense to keep these two occurrences of public debts apart. Even though it may be possible to change the basis upon which benefits can be claimed, the degree of

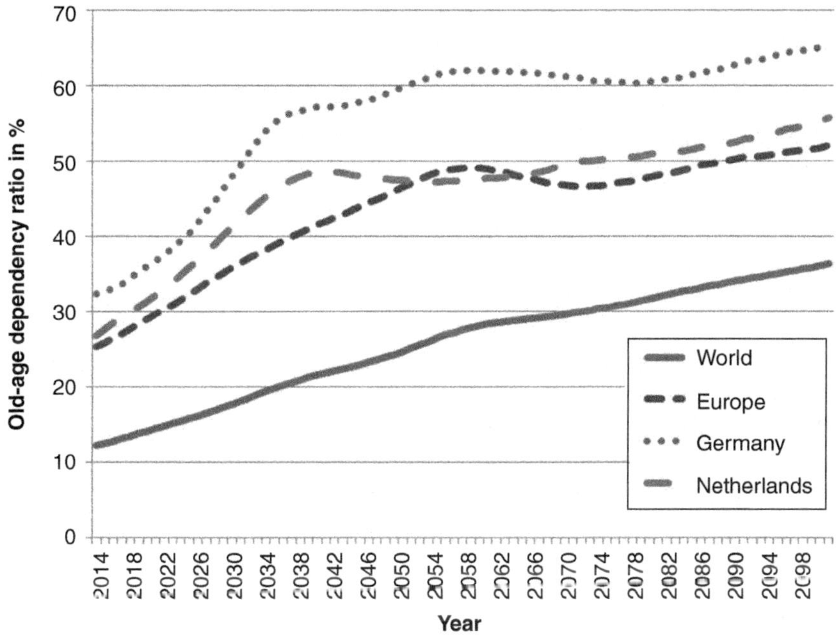

Source: Numbers from UN (2013).

Figure 5.2 Old-age dependency ratio, 2014–2100

change – that is, under the given circumstances in most cases, reduction – has social and political limits. After all, politicians are bound to keep their promises.

Fewer workers supporting more retirees living longer will put fiscal positions in Organisation for Economic Co-operation and Development (OECD)-countries increasingly under pressure, as public pension payments rise and absorb a growing share of total social expenditure (Eich, 2009). In countries where social security pensions are financed mainly through taxes, the link between pension expenditures and the government budget is closer than in systems where pensions are financed mainly by contributions of employees and employers (Eichhorst et al., 2011). Projections on the impact of an ageing population differ considerably, and the estimates of implicit public debts use different methodologies. Nevertheless all published estimates agree on the fact that there is a quite substantial level of implicit pension debts throughout the European Union (Eichhorst et al., 2011).[2]

It is often stressed that the effects of demographic change can be dampened by a funded pillar. Accordingly the international move towards funded pension systems can be explained to a great extent by the need to ensure adequate pensions against the background of increasing ratios in old-age dependency (Bebczuk and Musalem, 2009a). There are several reasons why the funded pillar is believed to perform better with an ageing population. First, pensioners pay for their retirement upfront and thereby avoid large payroll tax increases needed in a pay-as-you-go system with an ageing population (James, 1998). Second, these schemes are provided by private pension funds. Therefore, there is no direct link between a country's fiscal position and the ageing society. Third, it prevents large inadvertent intergenerational transfers from younger to older people (James, 1998). Even though a funded system seems better equipped to deal with an ageing society, an increased old-age dependency ratio will also affect the funded pillar. The inflow of contributions will decrease, whereas the payments of benefits increase. This makes pension funds more vulnerable as it becomes increasingly difficult to recover from adverse shocks or overcome initial funding deficits. However, I deem this risk less important than the risk to fiscal sustainability.

Longevity

A major risk facing both the unfunded and the funded pension pillar is the risk of unexpected longevity. From a welfare point of view, higher life expectancy can be seen as a positive effect. However, this effect is likely to undermine the sustainability of the pension system, especially when the retirement age is not adapted to the new situation. In that case, the working-age generation is faced with the task to support a growing number of retirees. This may prove problematic for pension funds as well, since the contribution rates are unlikely to be sufficient because they were based on 'faulty' life expectancy projections. At the moment, the evolution of life expectancy seems to be widely underestimated. As past projections of life expectancy have tended to underestimate the actual development in longevity, there is a real risk that populations could age even more rapidly than currently envisaged (OECD, 2005). Another problem concerning life expectancy estimates are unforeseen medical breakthroughs. Unexpected developments in longevity, and in particular sudden drops in mortality among the elderly (creating a 'fat tail' in the frequency distribution), can place a heavy burden on pension funds (OECD, 2005), and the public unfunded pillar as well.

Investment Risks

Interest rate risk

Protracted interest rates (low interest rates for a prolonged period of time, for example several years) have an adverse effect on the funding ratios of defined benefit pension funds. This is because the market value of pension liabilities increases while discount rates used to value them drop; and as pension liabilities typically last longer than the pension assets, the market value of liabilities rises faster than the value of the assets, leading to a funding shortfall (Ramaswamy, 2012).[3] The downward trend in long-term government bonds puts the funding ratio of defined-benefit plans increasingly under pressure.[4]

Low interest rates affect unfunded pension systems as well, mainly in two ways. Lower interest rates translate into lower interest rate payments on new issues of government debt. As a result, there is more room in government budgets for pension expenditures. Furthermore, Smid et al. (2014) state that 'an important effect of a low interest rate is an increase in the capital intensity of the economy'. This might also have positive effects on future government revenue due to higher labour productivity which translates into higher wages. Notice that with an increase of interest rates, the opposite is true.

Credit risk

Pension funds play an important role in the economy by channelling current retirement savings into investments in financial assets, and subsequently transforming these assets into a predictable post-employment income (Ramaswamy, 2012). Which side carries the main risk in these investments depends on whether the retirement income is based in defined benefits or defined contributions. In a defined benefit pension plan the investment risk regarding invested assets and potential funding shortfalls lies with the employer (Eichhorst et al., 2011). In a defined contribution scheme, the beneficiary carries the risk. Investments mistakes will lead to a lower nominal account resulting in a lower annuity during retirement.

Inflationary risk

Inflation risk is concentrated in the funded pillar of the pension system.[5] Previous experiences have shown that high inflation could potentially have a large effect on the adequacy of pensions. In the 1970s and early 1980s, many industrial countries experienced unexpectedly high inflation, which sharply reduced the purchasing power of fixed-income securities (Burtless, 2012). Furthermore, Perotti and Schwienbacher (2009) show that major inflation shocks erode on average 54 per cent of financial assets. Thus the entire asset side of a pension fund can potentially be eroded by a major inflation shock. Pension funds with large investments in fixed-income securities are unlikely to recover from these kinds of shocks. The 'real' value of their assets can decline dramatically, thereby reducing the future pensions of their beneficiaries.[6]

Market risk

Recent decades have proven that the risk of a financial or economic crisis is real (for example, the dot.com crisis, the financial crisis, the Great Recession and the European debt crisis). Following Impavido and Tower (2009), I identify the consequences as asset and liability shocks, lower investment income (rate of return) and contribution shocks. In a crisis, these impacts can materialize simultaneously. In the first stages of a financial crisis the stock markets fall, eroding the value of the assets of pension funds. During the dot.com crisis, the plunge of the equity markets during the years 2000 to 2002 sharply cut the funding ratios of pension funds which, in many cases, held equity allocations of 60 per cent or more (OECD, 2005). In 2008, European pension funds lost more than 20 per cent in real terms, although this varied considerably between countries (Casey, 2012). After the initial financial panic, the effects of the crisis began to impact upon the real economy. Central bankers reacted to this by applying expansionary monetary policies. These policies are problematic for pension funds, although lower interest rates generally benefit the economy. They had negative consequences for pension funds (Casey, 2012), because the lower discount rate increased the pension funds' liabilities at possibly the worst point in time. Falling asset prices and decreasing discount rates create what is called the 'perfect storm' for pension funds.

The rate of return on assets is likely to decrease during a recession (Impavido and Tower, 2009). This has an adverse effect on the funding ratio of pension funds, especially in the case of defined benefit pension funds, because they take on benefit promises based on projections concerning the rate of return on their investments. Furthermore, pension funds could be reluctant to increase contribution rates during a crisis. Another option is to compensate for the funding shortfalls by raising extraordinary pension contributions from their sponsors (Ramaswamy, 2012). This option is usually only open to defined-benefit pension funds. The likelihood of such measures depends on the rules and responsibilities provided for cases of funding shortfalls.

An unfunded pillar is confronted by very different consequences in a crisis. Furthermore, the consequences materialize at a different point in time compared to the funded pension pillar. An unfunded pension system cushions the immediate effects of a crisis for current retirees and as such could also act as a powerful automatic stabilizer within the welfare state during an economic downturn by maintaining pensioner incomes, which in turn would help to support domestic demand (Eich, 2009). This has a positive effect on the economic environment but the government finances are likely to deteriorate, at least in the short term. Lower payroll tax revenues in periods of high unemployment, and rising fiscal deficits in many advanced economies caused by reduced economic activity, are testing the sustainability of pay-as-you-go public pension schemes (Ramaswamy, 2012). The impact of an economic and financial crisis on a pay-as-you-go system will generally be of a more medium- to long-term nature, with contribution rates likely to increase and future retirement income generosity likely to decrease to ensure that the unfunded system remains financially sustainable in the long term (Eich, 2009). The first reforms clearly point in this direction as the statutory retirement age was increased in most advanced economies and the generosity of the unfunded pillar was reduced. The European debt crisis also affects the sustainability of the unfunded pillar. In the 'crisis' countries the sustainability of the first pillar is undermined. These countries face high interest rates, and increasing levels of government debt.

Political risks

Political risks are caused by government actions, that is, that the government could alter the conditions for retirement income. An obvious example is a change in the statutory retirement age or decreasing generosity of the public unfunded system. However, private pensions can also be affected by policy changes; for example, a favourable tax treatment in the present is by no means guaranteed for the future. Additionally, the statutory retirement age of the public unfunded system and the retirement age of the private system are often interlinked. Thus the private system is also subject to political risk. However, the degree of risk between these systems differs, and it is perceived to be more pronounced in the unfunded public system. Hence, a pension fund shields pensioners (at least to some degree) from sudden income shocks due to political action in order to restore short-term balance in the public pension system (Eichhorst et al., 2011).

Labour Market Risks

Labour market incentives

Large distortions in the labour market must be reckoned with, since the full amount of the contribution drives a wedge between the marginal product of labour and the required marginal compensation of the employees (Sinn, 2000). It is clear that this discrepancy will have a negative effect on labour supply. Whereas the wedge also exists in a private scheme, the link between contributions and benefits is clearer. Individual accounts are therefore often preferred from an incentive perspective. The transparency and simplicity of the relationship between contributions and benefits may reduce the labour supply distortions induced by a pension system (Burtless, 2010). In addition, private pensions (for example, individual accounts) are often organized at company or industry level. Therefore, the benefits resemble the previous contribution more closely. In a state pension system, the relation between contributions and benefits is relatively weak. This makes labour market distortions more severe in public pensions compared to private pensions.

Unemployment risk

Unemployment erodes the tax base for the unfunded pillar. Current employee contributions or tax payments are used to meet pension payments (Ramaswamy, 2012). Higher unemployment means fewer people pay for, *ceteris paribus*, the same number of retirees. Lower tax revenues and pension contributions received may require governments to temporarily fund pension payments by issuing public debt (Ramaswamy, 2012).[7] This has an adverse effect on the (future) sustainability of the unfunded pillar. Furthermore, the assumption that the number of retirees remains constant could prove overoptimistic. Empirical research shows a strong relationship between the number of early retirees and the business cycle (Eichhorst et al., 2011); the size of this effect of course depends on the possibilities for early retirement.

Funded systems are financed through worker and employer contributions, and if unemployment rises and wages decrease, the available revenue decreases as well (World Bank, 2009). This increases the vulnerability of the funded pillar because the inflow of new funds declines, undermining the ability of pension funds to recover from adverse shocks. This effect is exaggerated by the pension fund's expenditure side. The number of beneficiaries typically increases during a crisis, as people look to early retirement and disability as a means to cope with unemployment (World Bank, 2009). In sum, the dependence on labout market performance weakens the pension pillars simultaneously.[8]

The Rate of Return

Pensions should fulfil the consumption needs of retirees. The adequacy of retirement income depends to a great extent on the generated returns. The returns gained depend on the composition of the different pillars in the provisions for retirement income of a pensioner. It is important to stress that an unfunded pension pillar also generates returns for its participants. Aaron (1966) shows that these returns consist of two components: the growth of the labour force and the (real) wage growth. A similar measurement is used by Orszag and Stiglitz (1999): 'the real rate of return in a mature pay-as-you-go system is equal to the sum of the rate of growth in the labour force and the rate of growth in productivity'.[9]

The rate of return on financial assets – typically long-term bonds and equities – will play an important role in determining the level of benefits that can be guaranteed in a funded scheme (Ramaswamy, 2012). The pension fund's portfolio composition will explain a large part of the return performance. In general, the return of a funded system will be roughly equal to either the (real) interest rate, or some form of market index or a combination of the two. In a dynamically efficient economy, a funded system will always appear to offer a higher rate of return than an unfunded system (Orszag and Stiglitz, 1999). However, the range of observed historical returns is quite wide (Burtless, 2010). The finance literature notes that risk and return exhibit a clear positive correlation, so the large variation of returns is not unexpected. In the long run, the growth rate of aggregate public pensions, however, will certainly not be able to exceed the growth rate of GDP and the latter will be less than the rate of interest if the economy converges toward a steady state (Sinn, 2000). Following this rule the returns of a funded system will generally be higher compared to the returns of an unfunded system. Mitigating factors can be the choice of return rate, the extent of risk taking,[10] the poverty and redistribution component[11] and/or administrative and investment costs.[12]

I investigate the expected future return of the unfunded pillar. Current demographic predictions indicate that the labour force is set to decline in most advanced countries.[13] This will have a negative effect on the rate of return. A growth in labour productivity will play an increasing role in underpinning economic growth in many countries experiencing a rapidly ageing population (Ramaswamy, 2012). However, labour productivity is also affected by an ageing population. On the one hand, older workers will have more experience and on-the-job training which results in higher productivity. On the other hand, human capital and ability are likely to diminish over time, thereby reducing the productivity of older workers. Most empirical evidence points to the dominance of the latter factor. However, the changes in factor abundance will also have a price effect. The consequence is that labour becomes relatively more scarce compared to capital. This will drive up wages relative to the rate of return on capital (Börsch-Supan et al., 2002). Thus this will have a positive effect on the return of the unfunded system, and an adverse effect on the return on the funded system. Another argument related to labour supply points to the oversupply of capital for a shrinking labour force (for example, some capital might become obsolete). In addition, diminishing returns to scale will lead to lower returns if capital stock stays at the same level.

The future return of the private funded pillar largely depends on the materialization of the asset meltdown hypothesis. The number of people in the saving age (40–64 years) will decline and they start to dis-save their financial assets. Hence, they are putting downward pressure on prices. Siegel (2005) suggests that retirees will sell their financial assets to increase their retirement income to a sufficient level. He argues that the resulting imbalance between United States (US)-buyers and -sellers will drive asset prices down, leaving individuals in the future with far less resources than their account statements suggest today (Holzmann, 2009). The main counteracting factor could be foreign demand, especially from young developing economies. However, Siegel (2005) doubts whether this demand will be big enough to offset the sell-off of financial assets, concluding that the prices of financial assets will decline significantly. Other studies, most notable Poterba (2004), refute this claim. From a theoretical point of view, an asset meltdown should not occur as current prices are rational and forward-looking, and thus already internalize such a future scenario (Bebczuk and Musalem, 2009a). However, the main arguments against the hypothesis are put forward by Poterba (2004) using empirical data for the US. First, he shows that even though financial assets are accumulated quite rapidly, they decline only gradually after retirement. Second, he finds only a modest effect of the demographic mix on the return of different financial assets. Furthermore, increasing financial integration will dampen the effect as the ability to trade financial assets and the ease of trading improve over time.[14] In addition, policymakers are increasing the statutory retirement age in a number of advanced economies. This will also alleviate the downward pressure on financial asset prices.

5.4 DIVERSIFICATION OF RISKS

It is clear that with imminent demographic changes and the apparent volatility of financial markets no system can be developed that remains invulnerable and completely insulated from all outside challenges, whether they be demographic or economic in nature (Eichhorst et al., 2011). The recent financial and European debt crisis illustrates that a funded system suffers from turmoil in financial markets. However, the retirement of the baby-boom generation will also put increasing pressure on the unfunded pillar. Eichhorst et al. (2011) note that, therefore, risk sharing is essential.

A multi-pillar system facilitates maximal risk sharing, as adverse outcomes in one pillar could be balanced by another pillar. Whatever unpredictable disasters occur in the future – as they surely will – this diversified system is most likely to continue providing protection for the old, according to the old saying: 'do not put all your eggs in one basket' (James, 1998). As a consequence, an appropriate mix of the different pension pillars can help to create sustainable pension systems in a period of intense demographic change without endangering the objective of pension adequacy (Eichhorst et al., 2011). Partial funding gives a more stable contribution and benefit rate. Ramaswamy (2012) indicates that the main challenges for a funded pension system are poor financial market performance and low interest rates. For unfunded systems, the challenges lie predominantly in the demographic and the macroeconomic sphere. Therefore, it is possible to achieve better risk sharing and higher diversification benefits.

Some risks even affect the sustainability of the pillars in opposite directions (such as the inflation rate and the interest rate risk). For example, changes in interest and inflation rate influence the sustainability in different directions for the funded and unfunded pillar. These mutual exclusive effects strengthen the case for a multi-pillar system. This is fuelled by the notion that the long time horizon makes it impossible to foresee which of these risks will materialize in the future. Thus a preference for a specific pillar based on the likelihood of the materialization of specific risks is difficult, and surrounded by major uncertainties due to the long-term nature of pension provision. For instance, the Dutch multi-pillar system balances the consequences of an interest rate increase. The Dutch pension funds will benefit because they can discount their future liabilities at a higher rate, while the interest rate increase has an adverse effect on the sustainability of the public unfunded pillar. The government has to pay more for its pension obligations when it finances the contribution gap by issuing new debt.

Diversification in assets further contributes to the reduction of risks. Some contributions stress that the unfunded system is a funded system too, except that funding is based on human rather than financial capital. The understanding is that partial funding provides access to an asset – the human capital of the young – that is not normally tradable on the financial markets, thereby providing further diversification relative to the set of assets available on financial markets (Orszag and Stiglitz, 1999). Thus a multi-pillar system is also able to diversify between human capital and financial assets. In other words, multi-pillar systems allow for some degree of risk diversification between wage and interest income because the correlation between yields on securities and domestic wage growth is not perfect (Eichhorst et al., 2011). Portfolio theory suggests that a diversified investment portfolio offers the best way to balance risk and return (OECD, 2005). Numerous studies note that diversification reduces risk for the same rates of return, or increases the rates of returns at the same level of risk. Thus a multi-pillar system will have a positive effect on the mix between risk and return.

A private funded pillar allows for the opportunity to diversify internationally. A funded pillar opens possibilities to invest in financial and real assets. Private pension funds can enjoy the benefits of investment diversification, including international diversification that enables them to increase their yield and reduce their risk, by protecting them from inflation and other country-specific risks (James, 1998). Diversification in terms of geography is open only to funded pension pillars. This type of diversification can potentially lead to a more sustainable and a more stable pension system. First, international diversification will reduce the decrease in the rate of return since international capital mobility will diversify the demographic shock (Börsch-Supan et al., 2002), because the extent and the timing of the problems caused by an ageing society differ between counties. This makes it possible to engage in demographic arbitrage. Second, funded systems also allow smoothing out consumption internationally because the building up and running down of securities issued in foreign countries decouples domestic consumption from domestic production (Eichhorst et al., 2011). Third, international diversification is beneficial insofar as financial returns are not tightly correlated across countries (Bebczuk and Musalem, 2009b). Fourth, the rate of return is potentially higher because capital is transferred from a capital-abundant country to a capital-scarce country.[15] When a country makes only limited use of the funded private pillar, like for example Germany, it is almost entirely dependent on its own demographic developments and macroeconomic situation. It does not have the options for diversification in assets and for international diversification. For Germany, this is problematic because the old-age dependency ratio is projected to increase from just above 0.3 today to 0.6 in 2050. This means that instead of approximately three workers supporting one retiree today, three workers will have to support almost two retirees. Their current incomes have to provide for the current retirement income. Moreover, the German old-age dependency ratio is set to increase to the highest in Europe. This increases the urgency to diversify in terms of asset and country allocation.

The funded pillar is mostly designed to prevent massive intergenerational redistribution taking place. As a consequence, the absence of any intergenerational sharing of individual portfolio risk implies that workers face high uncertainty on their future pension wealth (Gollier, 2008). A public unfunded pillar allows for intergenerational redistribution. It is well established that intergenerational risk sharing can generate substantial welfare gains (Gollier, 2008). The ability to share risks between generations differs substantially between the public unfunded and private funded pillar. An unfunded pension pillar can spread the risk more broadly. Ultimately, the government can spread risk across this generation, but also over future generations. Furthermore, the budget deficit will lead to different consumption patterns between generations. In other words, the public budget can function as an effective intergenerational risk sharing device (Impavido and Tower, 2009). In addition, when a crisis occurs and the tax base declines, the budget can also keep the retirement income more stable (transferring the costs of this stabilization to the next generation). Although the public unfunded system allows for more intergenerational risk sharing than the private funded system, the ability to share risks across generations is not unlimited. When the gap between payment and returns widens, the new generation might opt out of the pension system.

In summary, it is clear that pensioners benefit from a multi-pillar system. It partly shields them from unexpected events that will materialize over time. It provides them with diversification opportunities far superior to the case of a single pillar. In addition, the combination of pillars makes sure that all the main objectives of a pension system are achieved to a sufficient degree now and in the foreseeable future.

NOTES

1. Please note that there are decreasing returns to consumption.
2. Funded systems are not considered here as these schemes do not have a direct claim on government finances.
3. Please note that the funds with the longest duration in terms of liabilities are also the

youngest pension funds. Therefore, these funds have a longer recovery period, and there is a higher possibility that interest rate developments will be in their favour.

4. Please note that this is exactly the opposite effect on a pension fund's balance sheet compared to the modest inflation.
5. The public pension pillar is maybe even more sustainable as inflation will lead to seigniorage. Therefore, the real value of public debts will decrease in real terms. In addition, the tax base might increase with inflation. However, whether these positive effects would materialize must be doubted because very high or hyperinflation has clear adverse effects on macroeconomic stability. High inflation is often seen as an indicator for a severe economic crisis.
6. Barr (2006) indicates that the workforce has to give up some consumption to facilitate pension provision in both unfunded and funded systems.
7. A pay-as-you-go system has a very broad base because it consists of the wage incomes of all subsequent generations (Sinn, 2000).
8. For the beneficiaries, unemployment will lead to non-contribution periods in their employment careers. These periods will lead to lower retirement income in a funded pillar because membership of employer and sector schemes ceases when employment contracts end (Casey, 2012). In the unfunded pillar, this depends on whether the provision of retirement income is related to work history or not.
9. Sinn (2000) concludes that 'the introductory gain of the first generation of retirees equals the present value of the implicit taxes that have to be paid by all future generations'. The low rate of return of the pay-as-you-go system is thus the result of these introduction gains.
10. Individuals could be risk-averse, and could prefer the safer low-return option.
11. Low-income households and women can benefit from the redistribution or poverty relief components to a greater extent than middle- and high-income households.
12. A simple rate of return comparison usually compares gross rates of return, even though administrative costs may differ even under idealized versions of the two systems and, *ceteris paribus*, higher administrative costs reduce the net rate of return an individual receives (Orszag and Stiglitz, 1999). Unfunded schemes have no investment costs, such as wages of portfolio managers and analysts, costs of trading facilities and transaction fees, or advertisement costs.
13. The extent of this decline depends on the effective retirement age of the population, migration, health situation and numerous other factors.
14. Increasing financial integration will also increase the correlation between financial markets, which will partly reduce the diversification benefits of international investment.
15. Even though considerable home bias remains. This can have to do with marginal productivity, human capital or better technologies. Foreign investments could result in higher costs if the home-country economic situation is not reflected in foreign returns. Furthermore, emerging markets have a different risk profile compared to more-developed economies. Another reason for foreign investment could be the relative size of the pension funds if domestic supply of financial assets is insufficient, or continuing investment will put massive upward pressure on the prices of financial assets.

REFERENCES

Aaron, H. (1966). The social insurance paradox. *Canadian Journal of Economics and Political Science*, 32(3), 371–374.

Barr, N. (2006). Pensions: overview of the issues. *Oxford Review of Economic Policy*, 22(1), 1–14.

Barr, N. and P. Diamond (2006). The economics of pensions. *Oxford Review of Economic Policy*, 22(1), 15–39.

Bebczuk, R. and A. Musalem (2009a). Can the financial markets provide sustained rates of return at large scale?. In R. Holzmann (ed.), *Aging Population, Pension Funds, and Financial Markets, Regional Perspectives and Global Challenges for Central, Eastern, and Southern Europe*, Washington, DC: World Bank, pp. 83–96.

Bebczuk, R. and A. Musalem (2009b). Does investing in emerging markets help?. In R. Holzmann (ed.), *Aging Population, Pension Funds, and Financial Markets, Regional Perspectives and Global Challenges for Central, Eastern, and Southern Europe*, Washington, DC: World Bank, pp. 97–118.

Börsch-Supan, A., F. Heiss, A. Ludwig and J. Winter (2002). Pension reform, capital markets, and the rate of return. MEA Discussion Papers, no. 23-02, May.

Burtless, G. (2010). Lessons of the financial crisis for the design of national pension systems. *CESifo Economic Studies*, 56(3), 323–349.

Burtless, G. (2012). Can improved options for private saving offer a plausible substitute for public pensions? *Politics and Society*, 40(1), 81–105.

Casey, B. (2012). The implications of the economic crisis for pensions and pension policy in Europe. *Global Social Policy*, 12(3), 246–265.

Eich, F. (2009). The financial and economic crisis and pension systems: international experiences, *Pension Corporation Research*. http://hdl.handle.net/10419/51557.

Eichhorst, W., M. Gerard, M. Kendzia, C. Mayrhuber, C. Nielsen, G. Rünstler, et al. (2011). Pension systems in the EU – contingent liabilities and assets in the public and private sector. IZA Research Report, No. 42.

Gollier, C. (2008). Intergenerational risk-sharing and risk-taking of a pension fund. *Journal of Public Economics*, 92, 1463–1485.

Holzmann, R. (2009). Will population aging affect rates of return?. In R. Holzmann, *Aging Population, Pension Funds, and Financial Markets, Regional Perspectives and Global Challenges for Central, Eastern, and Southern Europe*, Washington, DC: World Bank, pp. 119–138.

Impavido, G. and I. Tower (2009). How the financial crisis affects pensions and insurance and why the impacts matter. IMF Working Paper, WP/09/151.

James, E. (1998). New systems for old age security: experiments, evidence and unanswered questions. *World Bank Research Observer*, 13(2), 271–301.

OECD (2005). Ageing and pension system reform, implications for financial markets and economics policies. *Financial Market Trends*, 2005(Supplement 1). http://www.oecd.org/daf/fin/private-pensions/35810991.pdf.

Orszag, P. and J. Stiglitz (1999). Rethinking pension reform: ten myths about social security systems. Presented at the conference on ‘New Ideas About Old Age Security’, 14–15 September, World Bank.

Perotti, E. and A. Schwienbacher (2009). The political origin of pension funding. *Journal of Financial Intermediation*, 18, 384–404.

Poterba, J. (2004). Impact of population ageing on financial markets in developed countries. *Federal Reserve Bank of Kansas City Economic Review*, 89(4), 43–53.

Ramaswamy, S. (2012). The sustainability of pension schemes. BIS Working Papers, No. 368.

Siegel, J. (2005). *The Future for Investors*, New York: Crown Publishing Group.

Sinn, H. (2000). Why a funded pension system is useful and why it is not useful. *International Tax and Public Finance*, 7, 389–410.

Smid, B., H. ter Rele, S. Boeters, N. Draper and A.W. Nibbelink (2014). *Minder zorg om vergrijzing*, Den Haag: Centraal Planbureau.

World Bank (2009). Pensions in crisis: Europe and Central Asia. Regional Policy Note, 12 November.

6. Pension provision: (still) a public task?

Florian Blank

6.1 INTRODUCTION

Comparative studies point out that many pension systems show distinct combinations of public and private provision of pension benefits (Döring, 2010; Ebbinghaus, 2011a). These combinations come together with different interpretations and regulations of what is public and what is private as well as with different institutions and actors involved in welfare provision and regulation: public pension provision includes both tax-financed basic pension systems run by state institutions and social insurance systems administered by the social partners (that is, representatives of both sides of industry) with a strong contribution–benefit link; private pension provision may refer to both voluntary pension insurance and mandatory occupational pension schemes. Differences between countries and, possibly even more so, policy changes within countries cannot only be traced to changes in the constellations of political actors but are also linked to changing perceptions of what ought to be a public task and what is to be left to the private sector.

This chapter uses the German case as an example to discuss the changing role of the public sector in pension provision, but also the legitimacy of public involvement in this policy area. For a long time, private elements – however they are defined – were not a prominent feature of the German pension system and of social policy-making; without much exaggeration one can say that there was no public–private mix according to the official understanding of the system. This system has been subject to major reforms in recent years. In particular, the 2001 reform not only adjusted the statutory pension insurance, but shifted the whole pension system from a single-pillar model of pension provision towards a multi-pillar model, thus redefining the public–private mix in pension provision. While prior to the 2001 pension reform employees could rely on statutory pension insurance alone, it is now up to them (and their spouses) to use the new system of statutory pension insurance and additional occupational and private pension schemes according to their own needs and calculations, and to build their pension portfolio. However, occupational and private schemes are subject to specific legal regulations. In addition, occupational pensions are regulated by the social partners, which leads to new questions about the definition of the public and private sectors of welfare provision.

This chapter will argue that the privatization of pension policies leads to problems with respect to adequate and encompassing pension provision. While according to Heath (2011) public provision of pensions may be justified because it is more efficient than private provision, it will be argued in this chapter that the main reason why there is public responsibility for the provision of old-age benefits rests on communitarian reasoning as understood by Heath, that is, a decision of what should (not) be traded in markets. Following the decision that the provision of old-age benefits is indeed a public responsibility, efficiency and distributive concerns play a role in the actual design of the pension system.

The chapter is structured as follows: section 6.2 describes recent pension reforms in Germany, sketches the design of the new system and presents data on the development of the reformed system. Section 6.3 provides an analysis of these changes, referring to categories and concepts of comparative welfare state research and sometimes more specific studies of the German case. It is argued that the concept of privatization may help to understand general developments in German pension policies. In comparative welfare state analyses, privatization has been conceived as a rather complex phenomenon that may not only consist of a shift from public to private provision, but may also include a new definition of the role of the state. A second strand of analysis that is discussed focuses on the reform of occupational pensions in the wake of the reform of the statutory pension insurance system. These analyses lead to a more complex picture of welfare provision and add to the debate by pointing to the role of employers, employers' associations and trade unions in the regulation and provision of pension schemes. Section 6.4 focuses on justifications for public involvement in pension provision, referring to the work of Heath (2011). It is shown that Heath's analysis and his considerations of a public goods model of the welfare state may be applied to pension policies and the German case. His arguments, however, need to be amended, because they seem to fail to grasp what constitutes the core of public involvement in the pension system. It is argued that while the correction of market failures is surely important, the provision of benefits that contribute to the de-commodification of labour can best be justified by communitarian arguments as defined by Heath. Section 6.5 concludes.

6.2 THE PRIVATIZATION OF GERMANY'S PENSION SYSTEM

The 2001 pension reform has often been called a paradigm shift by observers (see Schmähl, 2007). The reform altered the overall structure of the German system of old-age pension provision. What was a single-pillar system before 2001 was turned into a multi-pillar system. As a consequence, citizens today face more personal responsibility for organizing their individual pension mix, and they have to deal with various providers of pension insurance.

The statutory pension insurance (*gesetzliche Rentenversicherung*) continues to be the core of the pension system. Membership in statutory pension insurance is mandatory for most employees (and some groups of self-employed persons; civil servants, farmers and some other occupations are covered by specific pension schemes). In 2014, 53 million people were insured in the statutory pension insurance; in 2015, 21 million pensioners received benefits (Deutsche Rentenversicherung, 2016, p. 9).

The statutory pension insurance is financed by earnings-related contributions of employees and employers (in 2016, 18.7 per cent of the individual gross wage, shared by employer and employee) as well as subsidies from the federal budget. There is an upper limit for contributions and – because of a strong link between contributions and benefits – for benefits. Total revenues from employee and employer contributions and additional federal subsidies amounted to an estimated €276 billion in 2015. That year, the additional governmental subsidy paid out of general tax revenue was €62 billion (Deutsche Rentenversicherung, 2016, p. 9). In 2014, the benefits under the statutory pension insurance made up 30.7 per cent of the German social budget, which totalled €849 billion (estimate; BMAS, 2015b, Table 2, Table 3).

The statutory pension insurance scheme works on a pay-as-you-go basis with a strong link between benefits and contribution records, so that the benefits reflect individual life courses (especially the employment career). The scheme is organized as what is called a *Parafiskus* in German, a somewhat independent public organization for whose day-to-day administration the contributors' representatives (employers and members of the social pension insurance, often trade unions) are responsible (self-administration; see Ebbinghaus, 2011b).

The 2001 Pension Reform

Prior to the reform of 2001, the statutory pension insurance had the main task to protect the standard of living of (future) beneficiaries after retirement. Pensions were adjusted annually following a formula that made sure that pensions increased in parallel to wages. In addition to the statutory pension insurance, there were other ways to save for old age (such as occupational pension schemes or products offered by private insurance companies) but they were not seen as an integral feature of the pension system and social policy-making.

While many features of the statutory pension insurance scheme are still intact today, its overall task was newly defined by the 2001 reform: in order to contain future increases of contribution rates – which were projected to rise massively as a consequence of demographic change, a development that was seen as damaging to the German economy (see Schmähl, 2007, pp. 322–323) – future benefits were reduced. To this end, the formula according to which benefits are adjusted annually was altered in a way that loosened the connection between benefits and the development of wages. Now, as a rule, benefits grow at a slower rate than wages. As a consequence, the benefit level of the statutory pension insurance has decreased as a percentage of average wage. Still, the statutory pension insurance scheme is considered to be the main pillar of old-age security now and in the foreseeable future. The adjustment formula was changed again in 2004, again with the intention of slowing the increase in contribution rates and benefits.

The 2001 reform did more than just alter the statutory pension insurance scheme. Citizens are now expected to individually fill the pension gap – the difference between pre-2001 benefit levels and projected public benefit levels – by voluntarily taking out funded private pension insurance or using occupational pension schemes.[1] To encourage and support employees and their spouses in actively creating or, rather, buying their pension portfolio, the government introduced tax breaks and subsidies for old-age saving plans. They can be used for certified pension plans provided by insurance companies or savings banks (so-called 'Riester' plans, named after former minister Walter Riester who was responsible for the reform). Also, employees were granted a right to transfer part of their wages into occupational pension schemes and to enjoy breaks in taxes and social insurance contributions (earnings conversion). However, if wages are paid on the basis of collective agreements, these collective agreements must allow this kind of transfer. This way, employers' organizations and trade unions play a special role in the new system of old-age security. The new system introduced a considerable amount of choice into the pension system (Blank, 2009). It is noteworthy that when an employee decides to use an occupational pension scheme through earnings conversion, both the employee's and the employer's contributions to social insurance are reduced (see Blank, 2014). But whether the employer gives the money saved to the employee as a subsidy to the latter's saving efforts or keeps it is a matter of collective agreements or pure goodwill.

The 2001 reform changed the overall architecture of the German pension system. As shown above, this included a shift from a single-pillar model to a three-pillar model of pension provision, consisting of the statutory pension insurance as the main pillar and/or occupational pensions and private pensions as additional pillars. The second and third pillars thus turned from supplements into substitutes. On the individual level, however, the new pension system is supposed to work as a two-pillar system. According to the then-governing coalition's plan, employees can reach past benefit levels by using either private or occupational pension schemes in addition to mandatory pension insurance. Empirical data show, however, that the multi-pillar model was never fully accepted by the people (see below).

While the declining benefit level of the statutory pension insurance has already been mentioned above, a second development affects the performance of the first pillar: analyses show that younger generations acquire fewer entitlements to benefits from the statutory pension insurance than members of older generations (see Blank and Schulze Buschoff, 2013). This is a consequence of changed life courses and employment careers that, among other aspects, now include longer spells of unemployment but also longer phases in education. This development is even more problematic because reckoning of such periods as pensionable has been reduced due to reforms of the pension system. Thus one can say that the statutory pension insurance scheme is under pressure from two sides: its general level of benefits has been politically reduced, and at the same time individuals are less able to build up sufficient entitlements.

Development of the Three-Pillar Model

The number of people covered by occupational pension plans increased after 2001. A survey by TNS Infratest (2014, p. 12) shows that in 2013, 59.5 per cent of public and private sector employees subject to social insurance were covered by occupational pension schemes. For the private sector alone, the most recent numbers refer to 2011, when 50 per cent of employees in the private sector were covered by occupational pension plans, and 50 per cent of companies offered an occupational pension scheme (TNS Infratest, 2012a, pp. 19–23). With respect to both the share of employees covered and to companies offering such schemes, the increase in the spread of occupational pensions has slowed down considerably in recent years. Focusing on employee-financed occupational pension schemes alone (earnings conversion), less than one-quarter of employees in the private sector use this kind of old-age provision (see Blank, 2014, p. 136). There are significant differences between economic sectors and individual companies with respect to coverage of employees with occupational pension schemes and the use of earnings conversion. Not surprisingly, the 2001 reform has also caused a shift in the financing of occupational pensions. Schemes financed by employers and employees together or by employees alone are relatively more common today than they were prior to the reform. Thus, traditional occupational pensions – with the employer granting employees a pension because of paternalistic concern or as a consequence of their human resource management objectives – have been supplemented by occupational pensions that are also a vehicle for individual saving activities.

In the wake of the 2001 reform, employers' associations and trade unions agreed on various collective agreements that specify rules relating to earnings conversion. The regulations for the economic sectors or single companies differ quite widely, including on the amount of employer subsidies (Huke, 2011; Blank, 2014). The rules laid down in collective agreements usually apply to all employees of companies covered by a particular collective agreement, not only to trade union members. The social partners also founded or reoriented existing institutions (*Versorgungswerke*) to administer occupational pensions, sometimes in cooperation with insurance companies.

As of early 2016, about 16.5 million Riester plans have been taken out (net, that is, without plans cancelled by savers; BMAS, 2015c). This contrasts with the estimated 39 million people eligible for subsidies (Fasshauer and Toutaoui, 2009). Also, one person can own more than one Riester plan. After years of increasing numbers of plans, it seems that the market for this kind of fostered plan is now saturated. In 2011 (the last year for which numbers are available) about 11 million people received subsidies (Kruse and Scherbarth, 2016, p. 91). People often do not receive the full subsidies because they fail to meet the savings target (that is, 4 per cent of the last year's gross income minus the subsidies). Still, costs to the federal budget are not to be neglected; the subsidies alone (without tax breaks) amounted to €2.7 billion in 2012. Total public costs (subsidies and tax breaks) were estimated at €3.6 billion in 2012 (Kruse and Scherbarth, 2015, p. 91).

Neither private pension plans nor occupational pension schemes can be said to cover all employees (and their spouses). Do they complement each other and cater to different segments of those eligible for subsidies? A survey among employees aged 25–65 who are subject to social insurance shows that a significant share of them are not covered by any supplementary pension scheme: 20 per cent of them had an occupational pension scheme and used a Riester scheme; 36 per cent were members of

Table 6.1 Share of people with 'Riester' schemes by level of available household income (1)

	Western Germany		Eastern Germany		Germany	
	2004	2010	2004	2010	2004	2010
1st quintile	5.7	22.9	12.8	20.0	7.5	22.1
2nd quintile	7.1	25.1	9.1	36.2	7.5	27.2
3rd quintile	8.4	30.2	13.4	30.3	9.3	30.2
4th quintile	10.2	30.7	12.4	32.5	10.7	31.0
5th quintile	10.4	34.3	14.3	32.2	11.3	33.9

Note: Equivalence-weighted with the modified Organisation for Economic Co-operation and Development (OECD) scale; quintiles are based on the whole population, not only on people eligible for Riester subsidies.

Source: Geyer (2011, p. 19); the data were provided by the German Socio-economic Panel – SOEP v27; the calculations were made by DIW Berlin.

an occupational pension scheme; 15 per cent used a Riester scheme; and 29 per cent used neither (TNS Infratest, 2012b, p. 37). Available data also show that both Riester plans and occupational plans are unevenly distributed across employees. As a general rule, it is safe to say that the higher the income of employees is, the more likely they are to use both kinds of pension schemes (see Table 6.1).

The empirical data on the spread of private and occupational pension plans lead to the conclusion that what is formally a three-pillar system is in fact a one-, two- or three-pillar system at the individual level. The regulation of mandatory public pension insurance and voluntary additional pension schemes has led to a situation where the design of pension policies is not matched by individual citizens' abilities and behaviour.

As a consequence of this malfunctioning of the German three-pillar model, growing inequality is to be expected with respect to future old-age incomes. This is due to: (1) rather different conditions under which employees and their spouses can use the different pension schemes; (2) a growing heterogeneity of life courses; and (3) individual decisions about the use of private and/or occupational pension schemes. However, with respect to the three-pillar model it has to be noted that this model works better for people with a higher income than for the others. Also, comparisons by the Organisation for Economic Co-operation and Development (OECD) demonstrate that the benefit level of the German pension system is low, even if private pensions are taken into account (OECD, 2015, p. 141).

6.3 ANALYSING PENSION REFORMS

The reforms of Western welfare states over the last decades have received much attention. The debate about how to analyse and interpret these changes has led to the insight that many reforms cannot be understood as a simple more or less of welfare provision (see Blank, 2011b, pp. 17–22). Instead, various distinct developments can be found even in individual welfare states. One of the tendencies identified in the current welfare state reforms is the privatization of hitherto public systems of welfare provision. Gilbert, who identified a shift from public to private provision as one of four tendencies of welfare state change, defines privatization as follows:

> The meaning of *privatization* is thus defined as a change in the initial organization of state and market responsibilities for social welfare toward more market and less state. This course of change is guided by policies that aim to limit the direct role of the state and to increase private activity in the financing and provision of social benefits. (Gilbert, 2004, p. 101)

Privatization policies should not solely be understood as a simple 'less state, more private sector' trade-off, as the understanding of the state and its tasks may also change in the process. This observation of a changing role of the state is reflected in concepts such as the 'enabling state' (Gilbert, 2004) or the 'regulatory state' (Leisering and Mabbett, 2011). According to this line of argument, the state reduces its involvement in directly running the social security system or providing benefits. Instead it provides a legal framework or fiscal incentives to organize the provision of welfare goods and services by markets or civil society (not-for-profit) actors.

In the application of the concept of privatization, Seeleib-Kaiser (2008, p. 11) proposes to distinguish three different modes of social policy intervention that can be affected by privatization: financing, provision and regulation. Pointing to problems in the definition of public and private – especially when simply equating 'state' with 'public' – he sketches an understanding of a wider welfare system that is not restricted to the state in a narrow sense but recognizes the variety of actors and organizations that act on behalf of the state or fully independent of the latter in the provision of welfare:

> [A] welfare system could be imagined as a social arrangement, which insures against social risks in a collective, highly regulated and/or redistributive manner with a relatively high degree of certainty to future claims [*Erwartungssicherheit*] . . . Governance within this domain primarily relies on democratic, legal, and professional peer accountability. Within a welfare system thus defined, *social* policy can ideally be provided by 'public' and/or 'private' actors without necessarily violating the boundaries of the 'public domain', because of a subordination of profit motives. (Seeleib-Kaiser, 2008, pp. 10–11)

The central point of this approach is that the classification of systems of welfare provision as belonging to the public or private domain depends on their actual characteristics and not so much on the (legal) definition of actors or institutions. As a consequence, one can argue that a move from the 'provider state' to the 'regulatory state' may not necessarily weaken the public domain.

Comparative analyses of pension systems show rather wide differences in the public–private division of labour without always specifying the underlying understanding of what is public and what is private. Even so, it is important to note that these arrangements are not to be found on a simple continuum (with one end being pure private and the other pure public provision). Rather, different national pension systems show different qualitative interpretations of the role of public and private actors, reflecting different national trajectories and different values on what different institutions should do (Döring, 2010; Ebbinghaus, 2011a). Consequently, even though some pension policy reforms may actually contain elements of a less public, more private logic (and in some cases even the contrary logic), other reforms may transform the qualitative features of both public and private institutions as well as their quantitative relation. This transformation may even – if one follows Seeleib-Kaiser (see above) – lead to a strengthening of the public domain even though the actual providers are private enterprises.

How should one view the German case following these general considerations? Using Seeleib-Kaiser's (2008) modes of policy intervention as a guide to an analysis of privatization, the pension reform of 2001 can be described as follows. First, there was an open attempt to contain contributions to statutory pension insurance and to encourage spending on private or occupational pension plans. This was accompanied by the creation of public subsidies for individual saving efforts but most of all by a shift from employer and employee contributions to private investments of employees and their spouses.

Second, pension provision was shifted from the statutory pension insurance – whose future benefits were cut – to private providers. The latter include market actors in the strict sense (such as insurance companies) but also publicly owned savings banks or institutions run by employers alone or jointly by employers and trade unions.

Third, public regulation of the pension system was amended to include new rules on funded pension plans in order to organize the subsidies; a new class of certified pension insurance plan was created this way. Most importantly, the decision about old-age security was partly shifted from the public domain (mandatory pension insurance) to the private domain (individual choice).

Taken together, these points hint at both a new understanding of the welfare state that fits the concept of the regulatory state and an individualization of responsibility. Following the definition of the public domain given above, it may be argued that in particular the latter aspect – individual responsibility – justifies talking of privatization since the collective protection against social risks was weakened despite new public regulations and subsidies.

While the general path of reform can thus be understood as privatization, the reform of occupational pensions raises some interesting questions about the notions of public, private and privatization. These questions relate to social policy analyses that acknowledge that several actors or sectors are engaged in the provision of welfare goods and services and together constitute a 'welfare mix' (Rose, 1986), 'welfare pluralism' (Evers and Olk, 1996) or, as already noted above, a 'welfare system' (Seeleib-Kaiser, 2008; Schubert et al., 2008; see Kaufmann, 2003). These approaches allow for a differentiation of actors and institutions that belong to the private sector and recognize the difference between households, for-profit enterprises and not-for-profit organizations such as charitable organizations or communities. The above analysis of pension privatization may be seen as compatible with this differentiation, as it includes a shift towards both households (responsibility, costs) and commercial providers of pension products.

Table 6.2 illustrates the new system of pension provision. It should be noted that the classification of social partners (that is, trade unions and employers' associations) as belonging to the community sector is debatable since they are voluntary associations of market actors whose agreements are in some cases similar to the law (see below).

The new regulation of occupational pensions and the redefined role of the social partners, however, is not easy to grasp, and the reforms have attracted some attention by social policy researchers. Berner (2008, p. 411) singled out distinctive aspects of the post-2001 system of occupational pensions; the system changed towards being:

- a social policy issue (instead of a matter for human resource management and the regulation of financial services alone);
- a matter of corporatist regulation (that is, a matter of regulation through collective bargaining);[2]
- market-based (that is, many occupational pension schemes are provided by competing providers such as insurance companies); and
- individualized (earnings conversion means that individual employees decide about their membership in a scheme as opposed to the employer protecting their employees collectively).

Table 6.2 The German pension system after the 2001 reform

	State	Community	Market
Provision	Public pension insurance as the main pillar	Institutions founded/run by social partners (occupational pensions)	Insurance companies and other private organizations (occupational and private pensions), individual employers
Funding	Mandatory insurance contributions (employers and employees); public subsidies for occupational and private schemes	Collective agreements including employers' subsidies to earnings conversion	Private savings
Regulation	Social law, public regulation and supervision of the second and third pillars	Collective agreements on earnings conversion	Private responsibility to invest (level, product)

Berner (2008, p. 383) argues that, as a consequence of the features of the new system of occupational pensions, the border between occupational pensions and private pension schemes is blurred. While this is certainly true, the involvement of social partners has led to the development of various concepts to understand the new system of occupational pensions. Berner's notion of corporatization signifies an element within the set of rather heterogeneous developments in welfare reform that can hardly be reduced to a public–private shift.[3]

These strands of analysis and observations point to a distinct category or space between the public and the private that makes it difficult to use concepts such as 'privatization'. It raises questions about the status of welfare provision by employers and/or social partners and/or trade unions (sometimes called occupational welfare). While employers' associations and trade unions are voluntary associations of individuals or institutions in the economic sphere (they are regulated by private law), collective agreements have similar effects as the law, they are compulsory and directly binding to members. This 'in-between' was already described in the post-war period, when British sociologist T.H. Marshall used the term 'industrial citizenship' to denote a status or rather a set of social rights that derived from the collective use of civil rights (rights to form associations and to bargain in the market sphere): 'Trade unionism has . . . created a secondary system of industrial citizenship parallel with and supplementary to the system of political citizenship' (Marshall, 1963, pp. 97–98, 116).

So while old-style occupational pension schemes provided by the employer to their employees can be qualified as a private matter, the inclusion of occupational pensions in the design of social policy and their treatment in collective agreements may even be understood as a move towards more public elements within the field. Compared to the Riester schemes, the involvement of collective actors may be seen as some kind of step towards public responsibility, which frames the individual decision to use an occupational pension scheme.[4]

While the above-mentioned concepts illuminate the question of who plays a role in the new system of pension provision and how this can be grasped conceptually, from a social policy point of view, however, it has to be asked whether the German system of regulating occupational pensions really qualifies as a system of industrial citizenship, and whether this kind of collective framing of individual decisions by social partners can be equated with the public domain as understood above. Since the coverage of occupational pensions is 50 per cent of private sector employees and usage of earnings conversion is much lower than that, it has to be concluded that, despite the social partners' efforts and despite the corporatization of pension provision, occupational pensions have not become a public matter. This does not contradict the assumption that collective agreements and collective bargaining are in between the public and the private sphere (or neither public nor private); it simply acknowledges that the specific agreements and regulations to date do not serve as an *ersatz* public responsibility, especially if the coverage of collective agreements is taken into account.[5]

There are two examples to the contrary, however, which illustrate how the system of occupational pensions could be changed towards more public responsibility: first, in the German confectionery industry, employers' subsidies to occupational pensions are given to employees not only as a matter of right (which employees have to claim), but it is the duty of employers to transfer these subsidies to specific pension savings accounts. Here, one could talk of industrial citizenship, but the limits are still clear: these rules apply to one sector of the German economy, and the employers and their employees in this sector who are bound by a collective agreement.

Second, in the construction industry, collective agreements dealing with occupational pensions have been extended by the state to all companies in Germany (*Allgemeinverbindlicherklärung*). Thus, these contracts are now applicable to other companies, not only those that are members of the employers' associations. While the first example shows a way to include into an occupational pension scheme all employees to which a collective agreement applies, the second shows that there are ways to make all employees of a sector profit from the results of collective bargaining.

6.4 PENSION POLICIES AS PART OF THE *RES PUBLICA*: JUSTIFICATIONS

The discussion of German pension policies and the consequences of reforms in terms of coverage of private and occupational pension schemes points to problems in pension provision that follow from privatization. But why is this a (public) problem at all? In his discussion of justifications of the welfare state, Heath (2011) distinguishes three lines of arguments that have been brought forward to justify political interventions in, or substitutions of, the market. First, there is the redistributive argument: 'There are more or less egalitarian versions of this view, but what they all share in common is the idea that the central defect of the market economy is that it produces distributive outcomes that are in some way unacceptable' (Heath, 2011, p. 16). The second, communitarian argument focuses on moral reasons why specific goods are not to be traded on markets, that is, why they should not be commodified. The third, the public goods model, which Heath finds the most convincing, argues that state intervention is necessary to correct for market failures: 'The economic model of the welfare state should therefore be interpreted as the view that the state should strive to resolve collective action problems in cases where it can do so more efficiently than other institutional forms' (Heath, 2011, p. 26). While Heath sticks to a simple public–private (or rather state–market) dichotomy, leaving aside welfare production by households, communities, social partners or not-for-profit enterprises, his distinction is nevertheless useful to clarify what role the state or the public should play in pension provision.

In his discussion, Heath refers to old-age provision a few times. Old-age policies as part of the social safety net can be described as universal, state-run insurance programmes:

> It is also sometimes forgotten that both life annuities and defined benefit pension schemes are both essentially insurance products, and that most state-run pension schemes amount to the provision of this type of insurance on a national scale. The social safety net is, from this perspective, just a special instance of state provision in the face of missing or inefficient private markets. It merits its own heading, however, because it is often misclassified as a redistributive transfer scheme, rather than a risk-pooling arrangement. (Heath, 2011, pp. 26–27)

According to Heath, labelling social insurance programmes such as pension systems as redistributive is a misclassification. Nevertheless, he points out that pension insurance redistributes money from those who die early to those who live longer (that is, it is a protection or insurance against the risk of longevity). With respect to pension provision in the social security programme, Heath states that this programme works as 'a collectively purchased life annuity. And a life annuity is an insurance product, designed to protect individuals from the risk of outliving their savings' (2011, pp. 36–37). In addition, 'many welfare-state programs engage in . . . "horizontal redistribution," viz. reallocation of income over the individual's own life-cycle' (2011, p. 39). Still, an argument for public pension provision follows from market problems:

> So again, there is a strong case to be made for pooling retirement savings, which is precisely what a life annuity does. The market for private life annuities, however, is subject to adverse selection problems, which means that there are efficiency gains to be achieved through public administration of such a program. (Heath, 2011, pp. 36–37)

Heath is certainly right in arguing that social insurance systems solve problems that can be classified as market failures. The German example serves as an example of how privatization may create new problems.[6]

Compared to a mandatory public scheme, transaction costs may be higher in a privatized system with competition among providers. This includes the costs of information gathering and processing by users as well as the marketing costs of providers. From the point of view of (future) pensioners, the transaction costs of a public mandatory system without elements of choice are close to zero. In the privatized setting, a decision needs to be taken by individuals about the need to save (versus consumption), the correct way of saving (occupational versus private pensions versus other ways of saving) and the pension product (in early 2011, 5100 Riester pension schemes were certified, that is, allowed to be sold in the market, but much fewer were actually offered; see Blank, 2011a, p. 113). Even though a direct comparison of the efficiency of public pay-as-you-go systems and private funded schemes is difficult to undertake (the German system of private pensions has also been criticized for lacking transparency with respect to the costs of pension schemes; see Blank, 2011a, p. 110), two numbers may serve as an indication: the federal government calculates 10 per cent costs on contributions for Riester plans (BMAS, 2015a, p. 40); by contrast, the public pension insurance's expenditures for administration and proceedings (*Verwaltungs- und Verfahrenskosten*) accounted for 1.5 per cent of total expenditures in 2015 (Deutsche Rentenversicherung, 2016, p. 20, author's calculation).

Even if a pension scheme market works, its users may show irrational behaviour. Research in the field of behavioural economics has shown that the assumption of a rational consumer is often inadequate (see Ratner et al., 2008). However, problems of low use of private pension schemes cannot only be traced to cognitive failure, since studies show that the level of income, of course, plays an important role in determining whether someone saves for old age (see Table 6.1; see Corneo et al., 2015; Blank, 2011a). This not only has consequences for protection in old age, but also has additional distributional effects. The authors of a recent study of Riester subsidies summarize their findings: 'First, we find that about 38% of the subsidies accrue to the top quintile of the income distribution, while only about 7% accrues to the lowest quintile. Second, we find that the effect from the progressive schedule of the subsidy is almost exactly offset by the regressive effect from self-selection into the program' (Corneo et al., 2015, p. 3).

The German example also shows that users may not save more but differently as a consequence of public subsidies (windfall gains; see Blank et al., 2016, p. 6; Corneo et al., 2015, p. 2). Finally, insurance markets may be subject to specific problems such as cream skimming and adverse selection as noted by Heath (see above).

These are problems that may be overcome through state intervention, which may be regulatory in nature, that is, not necessarily a return to direct state provision of benefits. State intervention may take the form of making private or occupational pension insurance mandatory, even if the actual provider is a for-profit or not-for-profit enterprise, and setting standards for providers and products.

With respect to pension provision, reference to the public goods model to justify public involvement as argued by Heath seems only partly correct, however. While it rightly stresses that the state should intervene if pension benefits are to be provided, the argument does not seem to justify why the state should be in the pension business at all. In other words: why should the public regulate or even organize the provision of old-age income, that is, deal with the problems that people may outlive their savings? In order to answer this question it seems worthwhile to consider what pensions are: they are incomes provided to a group of people who are permanently unable to earn a living wage from selling their labour power or who have limited or declining abilities to do so. More specifically, in modern welfare states, old-age pensions are provided to a specific age group for which it is assumed that many or most of its members have limited abilities to sell their labour power due to their declining capabilities, or who should be rewarded for their past contributions to the welfare of a community. Invalidity pensions, by contrast, are provided following an individual medical assessment rather than following a political consensus on benefit provision for a certain age group. In other words, pensions are a means of de-commodifying labour permanently.[7] They follow from the decision that a specific group should not need to rely on market income, which seems to point to the relevancy of the communitarian argument in social policy – as Heath calls it – that focuses on the discussion of what should be left to the market (and what should not).[8]

The actual design of pension systems may finally be influenced by distributive motives such as the wish to eradicate old-age poverty, to provide a flat-rate pension as a citizens' right, or to protect employees' living standards by providing benefits that mirror contributions. The decision of how to design such a system follows after the decision that public intervention is necessary at all. From a comparative point of view, the general aim of de-commodifying labour in old age can be realized through social insurance systems as well as basic pensions systems in combination with occupational or private pension schemes that reflect the employment career or individual income position. While flat-rate benefits financed by general tax revenues may be much more (re)distributive than contribution-based social insurance systems, private and occupational schemes are even less so. Three examples from European countries may illustrate the different interpretations of de-commodification.

As noted above, the German system is geared towards status protection: public, occupational and private schemes are to contribute jointly to this aim. While occupational and private schemes are regulated by legal rules and collective agreements (in the case of occupational pensions) and publicly subsidized, their use is not mandatory. Poverty prevention is a task of a specific, means-tested social benefit scheme that is organized outside the pension system. According to OECD calculations (2015, p. 141), the overall benefit level (replacement rate) is low even if private pensions are taken into account. Gross replacement rates are the same for different income groups in this simulation.

The Dutch case provides an example of a division of labour between pillars: a flat-rate basic pension provides benefits that serve as a protection against old-age poverty. Benefits from occupational pension schemes have the task to protect living standards in old age. More than 90 per cent of employees are covered by occupational pension schemes regulated by the social partners. This is due to state intervention: companies have to join sector-level funds, and collective agreements on occupational pensions are declared binding. This is accompanied by specific tax regulations (Trampusch, 2014, pp. 101–102). OECD calculations (2015, p. 141) show that overall gross replacement rates are very high. With respect to the distributive aspect, the gross replacement rates of basic pensions decline with increasing income, while replacement rates of occupational pensions increase with income. In total, the pension system's replacement rates decline mildly with increasing income.

Austria, finally, builds its pension provision on a statutory pension insurance system that covers most employees and self-employed persons (see Blank et al., 2016). While there is a strong link between benefits and contributions, there is also a means-tested minimum pension for people with at least 15 insurance years within the pension system. This way, the same system deals with the maintenance of living standards and poverty reduction. Occupational and private pensions play only a minor role. The Austrian system's gross replacement rates are roughly the same for different wage earners according to OECD simulations (2015, p. 141), thus reflecting the contribution–benefit link. This is not least due to the fact that the minimum pension is not considered in this calculation. Overall gross replacement rates are high.

In all three countries, the provision of old-age pensions relies heavily on public benefit provision and regulation: pensions are seen as a public task. There are differences with respect to overall benefit levels and the character of public intervention. A comparison of Austria and the Netherlands shows that both countries seek to protect the living standards of employees but use different instruments to achieve this goal. Both countries have mechanisms in place that provide protection against old-age poverty (public provision of benefits). Thus they combine different distributive objectives in their pension systems, and public benefit provision guarantees a basic income.

If the argument is correct that the general approach to public pension provision is a communitarian one and that the specific public involvement in pension provision and regulation is justified because of economic and distributive reasons, the different lines of argument distinguished by Heath may have a more complex relationship than being alternative approaches to justify the welfare state. Rather, they should be thought of as interlinked, as being able to provide justification at different stages of the debate on what is public and what is not. While communitarian arguments point more to the general question of whether welfare provision should be a task of the public or not, economic and distributive arguments tend to point out why and how the state should intervene, given the decision that access to certain goods and services should be open to the whole population or specific parts of it. Table 6.3 summarizes this line of argument.

Reflecting on the German case, one has to conclude that if there is political consensus that older people should be relieved from the need to sell their labour power, public intervention is justified (communitarian argument). This public intervention can have different shapes and may

Table 6.3 Justification of public intervention in pension provision

	Equality	Community/ Morality	Efficiency
Provision	State provision may be required if benefit levels of private providers differ too much		Depends on cost–benefit ratio of a (single) public provider versus (competing) private actors
Funding	If distributive goals (poverty reduction, equal benefits) are to be reached, state funding from general tax revenue is necessary		
Regulation	Specific decision about design being more or less redistributive or egalitarian (flat-rate benefits versus maintenance of living standards)	General decision of whether or not pension provision is a public issue	Regulation is needed to correct market failures

include regulatory policies as well as a direct benefit provision by the welfare state. The debate on market failures and the outcome of current welfare markets in Germany points to the need of more public intervention (economic argument). Some non-public forms of collective provision of pensions, such as sector-wide occupational pension schemes, can be treated as a specific hybrid of public and market-based forms of pension provision, especially if they are made mandatory (which is a public decision). These hybrid forms, however, lead to differences between (future) retirees regarding the level and conditions of their protection.

6.5 CONCLUSION

The chapter discussed pension policies and the public role in pension provision. Using the German case as an example, it described past pension reforms and their consequences. Referring to concepts from comparative welfare state research, the reforms were analysed using a concept of privatization that distinguishes between the privatization of financing, provision and regulation. Also, the new role of social partners in pension provision was highlighted. An understanding of welfare state change that is restricted to a simple public–private or state–market dichotomy does not seem to capture this role. Finally, the chapter discussed reasons for a public role in pension provision and regulation. Referring to a distinction made by Heath (2011), it was argued (contrary to Heath's assessment) that the communitarian argument seems to provide the best foundation for public pension provision (or adequate public regulation of welfare production), since pension schemes need to be understood as provisions that serve to permanently de-commodify labour and hence limit markets. Heath's public-economy arguments for public pension provision, however, provide strong arguments for the direct public provision of benefits or strong public regulation – if there is a consensus that labour should be de-commodified.

Further discussion of the analysis of 'normative models of the welfare state' and the public role in providing social benefits in particular, and in limiting or regulating markets in general, should go beyond a simple dichotomy of the public and private sector and acknowledge the role that communities, not-for-profit organizations and households play in addition to state and market actors. Even so, the analysis provided by Heath clarifies the role of the public.

NOTES

1. For a summary of the criticism of the government's expectations and calculations, see Blank et al. (2016, pp. 5–6).
2. According to Berner (2008, p. 411) there has been no liberalization in the field of occupational pensions, as regulation through laws and collective agreements means that occupational pensions are now subject to more regulation than before.
3. Jeanrond (2014, p. 474) even talks of trade unions as 'semi sovereign' who assume a *hoheitliche* (sovereign) function in the field of occupational pensions. In a similar manner, Fehmel (2013) talks of social policy by collective agreements (*Tarifsozialpolitik* or *Vertariflichung*) in pensions and early retirement policies, which exists as a tendency alongside privatization.
4. 'Whether occupational pensions are collectively negotiated, employer-provided or individual schemes has major consequences for the overall scope of private pensions and the benefits in retirement. The more state or collective regulation intervenes, the larger the coverage of supplementary pensions and the larger is the scope to pool risks and guarantee rights. Encompassing coverage and collective regulation depends on bargaining institutions, the willingness of employers to negotiate, and the overall bargaining coverage as well as state support (erga omnes extension of collective agreements). In addition, coverage varies strongly by sector and size of firms due to the different strength of unions' (Ebbinghaus and Wiß, 2011, p. 380).
5. In 2014, 50 per cent of employees were covered by sector-level collective agreements, and 8 per cent by company-level agreements. Of the remaining 42 per cent, roughly half of the employees worked under conditions oriented towards the regulations defined by collective agreements (WSI-Tarifarchiv, 2016, Table 1.7).

6. This has been discussed more broadly in the debate on welfare markets. See Blank (2011c).
7. The concept of de-commodification was popularized in welfare state research by Esping-Andersen (1990, pp. 21–22): 'Stripping society of the institutional layers that guaranteed social reproduction outside the labour contract [in pre-capitalist societies] meant that people were commodified. In turn, the introduction of modern social rights implies a loosening of the pure commodity status. De-commodification occurs when a service is rendered as a matter of right, and when a person can maintain a livelihood without reliance on the market.'
8. Why some political actors (including voters) are convinced that certain groups should be de-commodified in old age is another question. Motives may include paternalistic concern, the feeling that older people should be rewarded for a lifetime of work and/or the wish to decrease labour market supply.

REFERENCES

Berner, F. (2008). Steuerungsprobleme im regulierenden Wohlfahrtsstaat, Die Vermarktlichung und Individualisierung der betrieblichen Altersversorgung, *Zeitschrift für Sozialreform*, 54(4), 391–417.

Blank, F. (2009). When 'choice' and 'choice' are not the same, institutional frameworks of choice in the German welfare system. *Social Policy and Administration*, 43(6), 585–600.

Blank, F. (2011a). Die Riester-Rente – Überblick zum Stand der Forschung und sozialpolitische Bewertung nach zehn Jahren. *Sozialer Fortschritt*, 60(6), 109–115.

Blank, F. (2011b). *Soziale Rechte 1998–2005, Die Wohlfahrtsstaatsreformen der rot-grünen Bundesregierung*, Wiesbaden: VS.

Blank, F. (2011c). Wohlfahrtsmärkte in Deutschland – Eine voraussetzungsvolle Form der Sozialpolitik. *WSI-Mitteilungen*, 64(1), 11–18.

Blank, F. (2014). Die betriebliche Altersversorgung durch Entgeltumwandlung – Regulierung, Verbreitung und verteilungspolitische Aspekte. *Vierteljahreshefte zur Wirtschaftsforschung*, 83(3), 129–142.

Blank, F., C. Logeay, E. Türk, J. Wöss and R. Zwiener (2016). Alterssicherung in Deutschland und Österreich: Vom Nachbarn lernen? WSI-Report 27, 1/2016.

Blank, F. and K. Schulze Buschoff (2013). Arbeit, Leistungsgerechtigkeit und Alterssicherung im deutschen Wohlfahrtsstaat. In F. Blank and K. Schulze Buschoff (eds), Altern in der Arbeitsgesellschaft, Special Issue of *WSI-Mitteilungen*, 66(5), 313–320.

Corneo, G., C. Schröder and J. König (2015). Distributional effects of subsidizing retirement savings acounts: evidence from Germany. FU Berlin School of Business and Economics Discussion Paper 2015/18, Berlin.

Deutsche Rentenversicherung (2016). *Rentenversicherung in Zahlen 2016*, Berlin: Deutsche Rentenversicherung Bund.

Döring, D. (2010). Betriebliche Altersversorgung/Pensionsfonds und Staat-Privat-Arbeitsteilung in ausgewählten europäischen Ländern. Arbeitspapier der Hans-Böckler-Stiftung 187, Düsseldorf.

Ebbinghaus, B. (ed.) (2011a). *The Varieties of Pension Governance, Pension Privatization in Europe*, Oxford: Oxford University Press.

Ebbinghaus, B. (2011b). The role of trade unions in European pension reforms:

from 'old' to 'new' politics?. *European Journal of Industrial Relations*, 17(4), 315–331.

Ebbinghaus, B. and T. Wiß (2011). The governance and regulation of private pensions in Europe. In B. Ebbinghaus (ed.), *The Varieties of Pension Governance, Pension Privatization in Europe*, Oxford: Oxford University Press, pp. 351–383.

Esping-Andersen, G. (1990). *The Three Worlds of Welfare Capitalism*, Cambridge: Polity Press.

Evers, A. and T. Olk (1996). Wohlfahrtspluralismus – Analytische und normativ-politische Dimensionen eines Leitbegriffs. In A. Evers and T. Olk (eds), *Wohlfahrtspluralismus – Vom Wohlfahrtstaat zur Wohlfahrtsgesellschaft*, Wiesbaden: Westdeutscher Verlag, pp. 9–60.

Fasshauer, S. and N. Toutaoui (2009). Die Anzahl des förderberechtigten Personenkreises der Riester-Rente – eine Annäherung, *Deutsche Rentenversicherung*, 2009(6), 478–486.

Federal Ministry of Labour and Social Affairs (BMAS) (2015a). Bericht der Bundesregierung, Rentenversicherungsbericht 2015. Available at https://www.bmas.de/SharedDocs/Downloads/DE/PDF-Pressemitteilungen/2015/rentenversicherungsbericht-2015.pdf?__blob=publicationFile&v=3 (accessed 6 June 2016).

Federal Ministry of Labour and Social Affairs (BMAS) (2015b). Sozialbudget 2015. Available at http://www.bmas.de/SharedDocs/Downloads/DE/PDF-Publikationen/a230-14-sozialbudget-2014.pdf?__blob=publicationFile&v=2 (accessed 6 June 2016).

Federal Ministry of Labour and Social Affairs (BMAS) (2015c). Statistik zur privaten Altersvorsorge. Available at http://www.bmas.de/DE/Themen/Rente/Zusaetzliche-Altersvorsorge/statistik-zusaetzliche-altersvorsorge.html?cms_searchArchive=0&cms_submit=Senden&cms_dateafter=tt.mm.jjjj&cms_sortString=-dateOfIssue&cms_searchIssued=0&cms_datebefore=tt.mm.jjjj&cms_templateQueryString=%22riester-rente%22 (accessed 6 June 2016).

Fehmel, T. (2013). Tarifsozialpolitik und Insider-Solidarität, *WSI-Mitteilungen*, 66(6), 405–411.

Geyer, J. (2011). Riester-Rente: Rezept gegen Altersarmut?. *DIW Wochenbericht*, 78(47), 16–21.

Gilbert, N. (2004). *Transformation of the Welfare State: The Silent Surrender of Public Responsibility*, Oxford: Oxford University Press.

Heath, J. (2011). Three normative models of the welfare state. *Public Reason*, 3(2), 13–43.

Huke, R. (2011). Tarifliche Vereinbarungen zur betrieblichen Altersversorgung – Stand und Perspektiven. *Betriebliche Altersversorgung*, 66(1), 21–41.

Jeanrond, H. (2014). Gewerkschaften und soziale Sicherung. In W. Schroeder (ed.), *Handbuch Gewerkschaften in Deutschland*, Wiesbaden: Springer VS, pp. 465–484.

Kaufmann, F. (2003). *Varianten des Wohlfahrtsstaats, Der deutsche Sozialstaat im internationalen Vergleich*, Frankfurt a.M: Suhrkamp.

Kruse, E. and A. Scherbarth (2015). Förderung der Riester-Rente durch Zulagen und Sonderausgabenabzug: Mehr als 10,8 Millionen geförderte Personen im Beitragsjahr 2012 – fast 50 % der Zulageförderung als Kinderzulage. *RVaktuell*, 2016(5), 91––103.

Leisering, L. and D. Mabbett (2011). Introduction: towards a new regulatory state in old-age security? Exploring the issues. In L. Leisering (ed.), *The New*

Regulatory State, Regulating Pensions in Germany and the UK, Basingstoke: Palgrave Macmillan, pp. 1–28.
Marshall, T.H. (1963). Citizenship and social class. In T.H. Marshall (ed.), *Sociology at the Crossroads and Other Essays*, London, UK; Melbourne, Australia; Toronto, Canada: Heinemann, pp. 67–127.
OECD (2015). Pensions at a Glance 2015. OECD and G20 indicators. Paris.
Ratner, R.K., D. Soman, G. Zauberman, D. Ariely, Z. Carmon, et al. (2008). How behavioral decision research can enhance consumer welfare: from freedom of choice to paternalistic intervention. *Marketing Letters*, 19(3), 383–397.
Rose, R. (1986). Common goals but different roles: the state's contribution to the welfare mix. In R. Rose and R. Shiratori (eds), *The Welfare State East and West*, Oxford: Oxford University Press, pp. 13–39.
Schmähl, W. (2007). Dismantling an earnings-related social pension scheme: Germany's new pension policy. *Journal of Social Policy*, 36(2), 319–340.
Schubert, K., S. Hegelich and U. Bazant (2008). Europäische Wohlfahrtssysteme: Stand der Forschung – theoretisch-methodische Überlegungen. In K. Schubert, S. Hegelich and U. Bazant (eds), *Europäische Wohlfahrtssysteme, Ein Handbuch*, Wiesbaden: VS, pp. 13–43.
Seeleib-Kaiser, M. (2008). Welfare state transformations in comparative perspective: shifting boundaries of 'public' and 'private' social policy?. In M. Seeleib-Kaiser (ed.), *Welfare State Transformations: Comparative Perspectives*, Basingstoke: Palgrave Macmillan, pp. 1–13.
TNS Infratest (2012a). Situation und Entwicklung der betrieblichen Altersversorgung in Privatwirtschaft und öffentlichem Dienst (BAV 2011). Endbericht, München. Bundesministerium für Arbeit und Soziales Forschungsbericht 429.
TNS Infratest (2012b). Verbreitung der Altersvorsorge 2011. Endbericht, München. Bundesministerium für Arbeit und Soziales Forschungsbericht 430.
TNS Infratest (2014). Trägerbefragung zur betrieblichen Altersversorgung 2013 (BAV 2013). Endbericht, München. Bundesministerium für Arbeit und Soziales Forschungsbericht 449/1.
Trampusch, C. (2014). Strukturen der tariflichen Altersvorsorge im internationalen Vergleich. *Soziales Recht*, 4(3), 100–107.
WSI-Tarifarchiv (2016). Statistisches Taschenbuch Tarifpolitik, Düsseldorf.

7. Protection against unemployment: a *res publica*?

Brigitte Unger*

7.1 INTRODUCTION

Workers can be protected from unemployment and loss of income in several ways. First, unemployment could be prevented by following a full-employment macroeconomic policy, with deficit spending, in order to fill in the demand gaps of the market economy. This suggestion of John Maynard Keynes dates back to the 1930s and was a reaction to the major economic crisis and mass unemployment of that time. With this policy, the phenomenon of unemployment would simply not occur. Another way is to establish the right to work in the constitution. Here the state would have to provide public jobs in case the private economy did not offer them, or to give subsidies to the private sector in order to employ people. A third possibility is to pursue an active labour market policy and help people find an adequate job. A fourth way is unemployment insurance, which is a passive form of labour market policy. When unemployment occurs, the jobless receive a compensation for their income through the insurance. The following chapter will focus mainly on this passive instrument of unemployment protection. Did and should the state intervene in unemployment insurance? Is it a *res publica*?

Protecting people from unemployment is – from a historical perspective – a relatively late development in the system of social security. But beginning in the late eighteenth century, with the development of factories and labour markets, all social laws were very much centred on work (Deakin, 2000; Garside, 1990). They aimed to keep the industrial worker in sound condition by providing food, shelter and income, thus ensuring sufficient manpower for manufacturing and industry. And they usually became a national public task, a *res publica* seen by the state as a response to large economic and political crises such as famine, political unrest and revolutions. In the same way, unemployment insurance became a *res publica* as a reaction to the mass unemployment of the 1920s.

In the following an overview of the development of unemployment insurance will be given for European countries, in particular for the United Kingdom (UK), Germany and the Netherlands. These countries took a different path towards creating a welfare state. Studying unemployment insurance in different countries aims at finding out whether there is a core of *res publica*; whether there are some tasks and responsibilities that have to be public and cannot be left to the market or the individual.

7.2 THE EMERGENCE OF UNEMPLOYMENT INSURANCE

Unemployment insurance was a response to increasing unemployment in many capitalist countries in the early twentieth century, which grew into mass unemployment during the Great Depression in the 1920s and 1930s. In many European countries trade unions had started to offer mutual private unemployment insurance benefits under voluntary plans. In Sweden, 'Help Funds' were created in the 1870s, which were closely linked to the unions (Lundgren, 2006, p. 3). Famous early examples were also small local unions in Belgium, established in Liege in 1897 and Ghent in 1901, which set up voluntary mutual unemployment insurance plans (Wynnyk, 2014, p. 1). Today the term 'Ghent system of unemployment insurance' still refers to a system in which unions are in charge of paying out unemployment insurance benefits.

The next step was the establishment of municipal, provincial and national government subsidies to voluntary benefit plans organized for non-union workers. Berne, Switzerland, was the first city to inaugurate this plan, which started in 1893. St Gallen (only from 1985 to 1987) and Basle (1910) followed (BSV, 2013), and similar municipal funds were created in Cologne, Germany, in 1896, in Leipzig in 1903, and in Bologna, Italy, in 1896 (Committee on Economic Security, n.d.).

Beginning in 1917 the Swiss federal government subsidized unemployment insurance provided by cities and municipalities (cantons). When parliament enacted the first federal unemployment insurance law in 1924, only 10 per cent of the working population was insured, 94 per cent of this through trade union insurance funds. The 1924 law made the Ghent system a federal law (BSV, 2013) but did not include compulsory unemployment insurance. Rather, the state claimed the right of supervision with it (BSV SECO, 2013).

In 1911,[1] 13 years prior to the Swiss federal law, the first Compulsory Unemployment Insurance was introduced in the UK (Table 7.1). It covered only 2.5 million workers in a few sectors, such as mechanical engineering, building and shipbuilding (IRC, 1934). It was funded by

Table 7.1 State involvement in unemployment insurance in Europe

Laws subsidizing voluntary insurance systems		'Compulsory' unemployment insurance laws	
France	1902	Great Britain	1911
Denmark	1907	Italy	1919
Norway	1915	Austria	1920
Netherlands	1917	Irish Free State	1920
Switzerland	1917	Poland	1924
Finland	1917	Switzerland	1924
Belgium	1920	Bulgaria	1924
Czechoslovakia	1921	Germany	1927
Spain	1931	Netherlands	1949
Sweden	1934		

Sources: Wynnyk (2014, p. 2), InfoNU (2011), BSV (2013).

flat-rate contributions from employers, employees and the national government and – in a later amendment – covered almost all non-agricultural workers between the ages of 16 and 64. In 1919 Italy became the second European country to introduce compulsory unemployment insurance laws.

In the Netherlands, the Unemployment Act (*Werkloosheidsbesluit*) of 1917 regulated the involvement of the government in social security. The government gave subsidies for the voluntary unemployment insurance schemes of the trade unions and for unemployment benefit arrangements made by employers. In exchange for subsidizing the unemployment insurance system, the government insisted on defining the eligibility criteria for unemployment benefit payments (InfoNU, 2011).

An important driver for insuring the unemployed and defining who was eligible was to distinguish the group of workers from the poor and those receiving social aid (Engbersen et al., 1993). Attaining this goal was aided through the Support of Unemployment Regulation of 1932 (*Steunregeling aan werklozen*). In 1949 the first compulsory Unemployment Insurance Act (*Werklosheidswet, Wet van 9 September 1949 tot verplichte verzekering van werknemers tegen geldelijke gevolgen van onvrijwillige werkloosheid*) was enacted after long and arduous debates (https://search.socialhistory.org/Record/548891) and was followed by the Unemployment Insurance Act of 1963 (*Wet Werkloosheidsvoorziening*; http://zakelijk.infonu.nl/juridisch/72671-geschiedenis-van-het-sociale-zekerheidsrecht.html).

Austria introduced compulsory unemployment insurance in 1920 and Germany only in 1927 (*Gesetz über Arbeitsvermittlung und*

Arbeitslosenversicherung), in order to combat the social unrest and mass unemployment of the Great Depression (see Talos and Wörister, 1994; Frohman, 2008).

7.3 TYPES OF UNEMPLOYMENT INSURANCE SCHEMES IN EUROPE TODAY

One can distinguish unemployment insurance schemes in Europe along several criteria. In the following, three criteria will be used:

1. Benefits. Who is covered by the programme? All unemployed? And how much is paid to an unemployed person?
2. Duration of benefits. How long are benefits paid?
3. Financing. Who pays for the unemployment insurance? Which actors bear the costs, and in what proportions?

Benefits

Unemployment insurance is generally given only to those registered as unemployed, and often on the conditions that they seek work and do not currently have a job. Today, basic elements of voluntary state-subsidized programmes can still be found in Denmark, Finland and Sweden, where entitlement is based on voluntary membership, often combined with contributions to an unemployment insurance fund (Esser et al., 2013). Historically, benefits were paid in daily flat-rate amounts. Nowadays, earnings-related benefits are also paid, albeit often affected by relatively low earnings ceilings for benefit purposes. The state exercises a regulatory and supervising role, but has also often contributed to the financing of benefits through state subsidies, particularly in times of economic downturns and high unemployment (Esser et al., 2013).

Whereas the Nordic countries still rely on voluntary unemployment schemes (but often also combined with some basic insurance, such as in Sweden; see Lundgren, 2006), many European Union (EU) countries today have compulsory unemployment insurance programmes. One can distinguish between comprehensive schemes and state corporatist schemes. In a comprehensive scheme everybody who is unemployed is eligible, while in a corporatist scheme only specific occupations qualify. Comprehensive unemployment insurance can be found in regimes with flat-rate unemployment benefits, such as Ireland, Malta and the United Kingdom, and they can be graduated by earnings. Comprehensive income security is provided in Bulgaria, the Czech Republic, Estonia, Hungary,

Latvia, Lithuania, Portugal, Romania, Slovenia and the Slovak Republic (Esser et al., 2013):

> It should be noted that in all these ten countries, except for Slovenia, there are maximum ceilings for benefits purposes that modify the degree of income security in the downward direction for many groups of workers, in some cases even to the extent that benefits are so weakly graduated by earnings that they in practice may appear to be flat-rate. (Esser et al., 2013)

Many continental European countries, including Germany, Austria, Belgium and the Netherlands, have state corporatist unemployment insurance programmes, which belong to the group of compulsory insurance. State corporatist systems are characterized by statutory income protection that is separated along occupational lines. Yet there has been a tradition in state corporatist systems to exclude not only groups with weak labour market attachment, such as seasonal workers and domestic employees, but sometimes also high-income earners. Although many of these exclusions have disappeared, some still remain and influence coverage negatively. State corporatist unemployment insurance programmes are administered jointly by employer and employee representatives. Over the years, occupational segregation in these programmes has often been reduced, either through harmonization of eligibility conditions and entitlements levels, or by abolition of segmented structures altogether. Contribution rates are the same for all groups of employees in most state corporatist unemployment insurance programmes, although some countries differ from this general pattern (Esser et al., 2013).

How much of his former income does a worker get when he becomes unemployed and is eligible for benefits? Replacement rates are expressed as a percentage of an average production worker's wage for a single-person model family. Gross replacement rates (before taxes) vary greatly, ranging from 80 per cent in Luxembourg to 13 per cent in the United Kingdom (Figure 7.1). Gross replacement rates are on average somewhat higher in eurozone countries, around 50 per cent, as compared to slightly below 40 per cent in countries outside the common currency (Esser et al., 2013). Note that net replacement rates, which is what is left to the worker after paying taxes, can be substantially different, depending on the tax system. They do, however, become more stable over time (see Seils, 2014). Luxembourg, the Netherlands and Slovenia have the highest gross replacement rates, while the UK, Malta, Lithuania and Poland are at the lowest end with replacement rates of 15–25 per cent of gross income.

An index of unemployment insurance generosity from Scruggs (2014), which includes benefit replacement rates, benefit duration, benefit

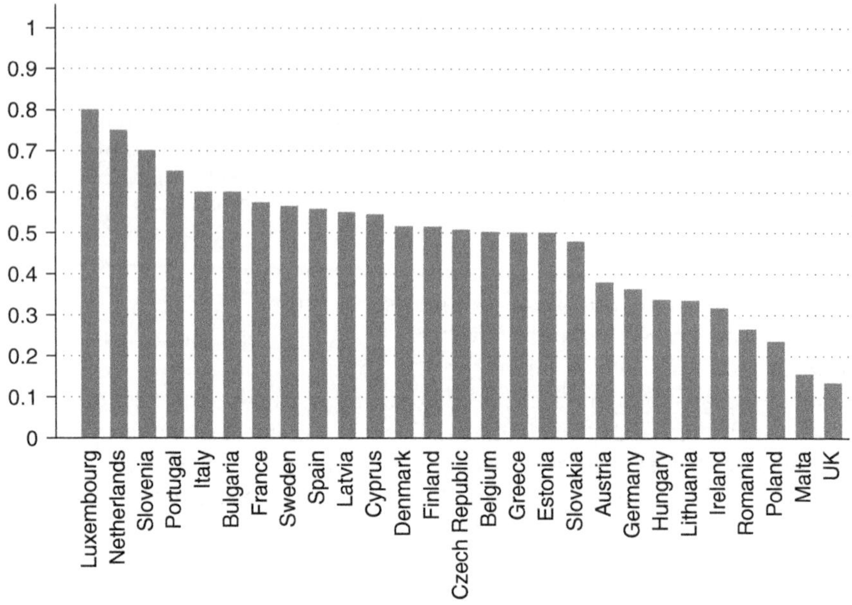

Source: Social Policy Indicator Database (SPIN), quoted in Esser et al. (2013, p. 11) and Scruggs et al. (2014).

Figure 7.1 Unemployment insurance gross replacement rates in the EU-27, 2010

eligibility and waiting days, as well as insurance coverage, shows that unemployment generosity has declined since the 1980s in some, and since 2010 in almost all European countries. Figure 7.2 displays unemployment insurance generosity of Germany, the UK and the Netherlands. It is the highest in the Netherlands, followed by Germany and the UK. The decline in unemployment insurance generosity was the most drastic in Germany (and in Sweden, which is not shown in this graph).

Duration of Unemployment Benefits

The duration of unemployment benefits (Figure 7.3) ranges from an almost unlimited length in Belgium, and 200 weeks in Denmark until 2010, to a minimum of 26 weeks in Lithuania, Slovenia, Slovakia, Malta and Cyprus. As the Institute of Economics and Social Sciences WSI found, the duration of unemployment benefits has been substantially reduced in many European countries since the 1990s (Seils, 2014).

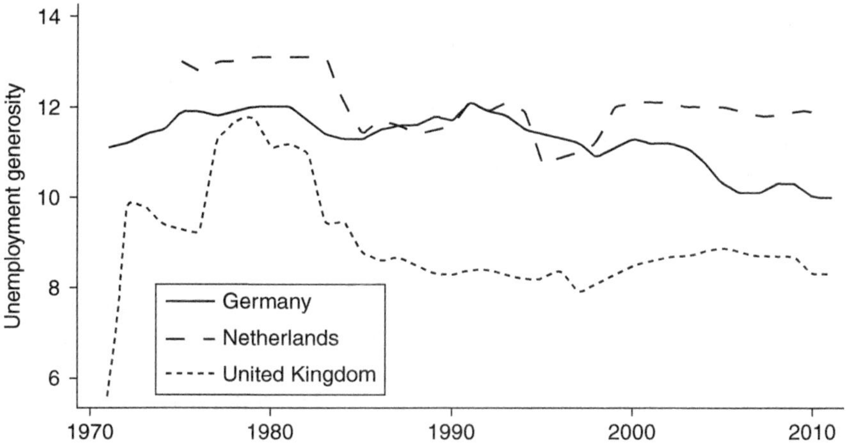

Source: CWED2 (2014), courtesy of Swantje Falcke.

Figure 7.2 Unemployment insurance generosity in Germany, UK and the Netherlands

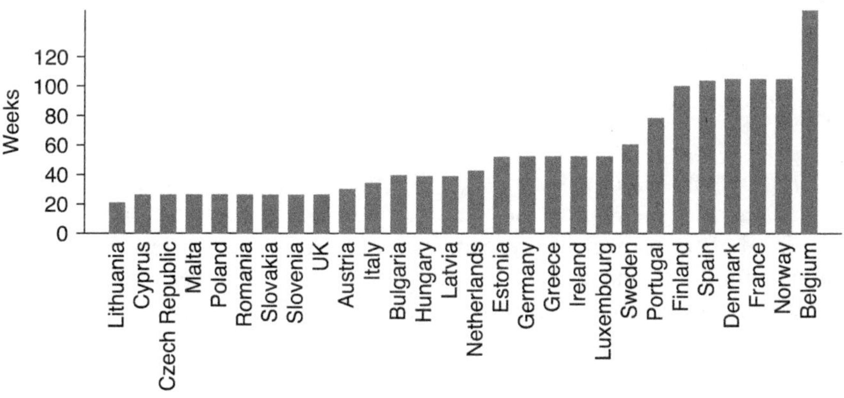

Source: Social Policy Indicator Database (SPIN), quoted in Esser et al. (2013, p. 12) and Scruggs et al. (2014).

Figure 7.3 Duration of unemployment insurance benefits in 27 EU member states, 2010 (weeks)

When unemployment benefits end, the long-term unemployed have access to unemployment assistance. This is organized very differently in 27 EU countries. In 2010, 15 countries provided specific unemployment assistance. In ten of these it is income-tested – Austria, Czech Republic, Finland, France, Germany, Ireland, Malta, Portugal, Spain and the United Kingdom – whereas benefits are flat-rate in Estonia, Greece, Hungary, the Netherlands and Sweden. Some EU countries make no distinction between social assistance and unemployment assistance (Esser et al., 2013, p. 13).

The Hartz IV reforms in Germany in 2010 introduced *Arbeitslosengeld II*, which changed the unemployment system substantially. If a worker is not eligible for full unemployment benefits, or after receiving the full unemployment benefits for the maximum of 12 months, he is able to apply for benefits from the so-called *Arbeitslosengeld II* (Hartz IV) programme, an open-ended welfare programme which, unlike the US system, ensures that people do not fall into penury. A person receiving Hartz IV benefits is paid €399 (2015) a month for living expenses plus the cost of adequate housing (including heating) and health care. Couples can receive benefits for each partner plus their children. A worker who gets this fixed (very low) amount of Hartz IV receives the same amount as a person getting social aid (*Sozialhilfe*). With this, once the worker drops out of the first phase of unemployment insurance, he becomes a beneficiary of social aid. This measure functions like a poverty trap; it is very contested in Germany and needs urgent reforms in light of the high and increasing number of low-income receivers in Germany.

Financing

Unemployment benefits were originally financed by the potentially unemployed themselves. Mutual insurance organized by trade unions was the first form of insurance. Today insurance still can be financed by the potentially unemployed themselves (the employees), but employers and the state can contribute to the financing as well. In some countries, a significant proportion of unemployment benefits are distributed by trade unions, an arrangement known as the Ghent system, dating back to the first voluntary arrangements in Ghent, Belgium, in 1901 (see above under The Emergence of Unemployment Insurance).

The role of the state in financing unemployment insurance varies (Table 7.2). In some countries, such as Luxembourg, Cyprus and Malta, the state pays a fixed contribution. In others, the state covers the insurance deficit. These include corporatist states such as Austria, Belgium and the Czech Republic, but also other types of welfare states such as Ireland

Table 7.2 Forms of state participation in financing unemployment insurance schemes in the EU-27, 2010

Form of participation	Eurozone countries	Non-Eurozone countries
Fixed contribution	Luxembourg, Cyprus, Malta	
State covers deficit	Austria, Belgium, Finland, Ireland, Slovakia	Czech Republic, Lithuania, Poland, Romania
State provides subsidy	Germany, Greece, Italy, Slovenia, Spain	Denmark, Latvia, Sweden, the United Kingdom,
State does not contribute	Estonia, France, the Netherlands, Portugal	Bulgaria, Hungary

Source: Social Security Programs Throughout the World (SSPTW, 2010), quoted in Esser et al. (2013, p. 18).

and Finland. In some countries the state provides subsidies, such as in Germany and the UK. And in others the state does not contribute, such as in the Netherlands.

7.4 THE LEGITIMATION OF PUBLIC UNEMPLOYMENT INSURANCE

As mentioned above, the historic reason for the establishment of unemployment insurance was very closely related to mass unemployment and the failure of private mutual insurance companies under such circumstances.

Normative Arguments: Efficiency

Unemployment can be seen as a waste of resources. The allocation of labour that could produce goods and services which increase overall welfare is not optimal if labour is left idle. From a purely economic mainstream reasoning, unemployment should not occur. Supply creates its own demand, and prices and wages are flexible, so market clearing and full employment does exist unless workers are not willing to work at the (low) market wage. Following the Great Depression and the theory of John Maynard Keynes, unemployment was considered to be a phenomenon which the state had to take care of. Musgrave (1959) called it the stabilization function of the state, to create stable and predictable income to all its citizens.

Unemployment insurance can be seen as an automatic stabilizer of the economy (see Musgrave, 1959). Benefits automatically increase when unemployment is high and fall when unemployment is low, smoothing the business cycle. Unemployment benefits increase the income of the unemployed, their consumption and thus the aggregate demand in the economy, in turn increasing employment.

Full employment can be seen as a public good. There is no rivalry in consumption: everybody profits from it, from the safe political climate, the safety in the streets, the stable income of workers and the profits of entrepreneurs. Exclusion from consumption of this good is also not possible. In an economy of full employment nobody can be excluded from experiencing a full employment situation, whether they like it or not. The market cannot provide full employment, as the falling prices and wages during the Great Depression showed. Though wages fell tremendously, unemployment grew. Therefore, when there is a market failure, the government must step in to provide this public good. One way of stepping in is to provide unemployment insurance in order to maintain the income of the unemployed, consequently increasing aggregate demand as well as national income and employment.

The economic argument for (and against) unemployment insurance, however, comes more from a microeconomic efficiency approach. Unemployment insurance itself is seen as a market failure because it suffers from adverse selection and moral hazard, so that private insurance companies cannot supply a sufficient amount of unemployment insurance without going bankrupt.

Adverse Selection

Incomplete information of the insurance company about the likelihood of a worker becoming unemployed makes it impossible for insurance companies to charge different workers different premiums. Asymmetric information implies that the insurance company does not know the probability of an individual worker becoming unemployed, while the worker themself does. Insurance companies therefore set an average insurance premium. This attracts workers who have a high probability of becoming unemployed, while workers with a low risk of unemployment will stay out of the insurance market. Adverse selection causes profit-maximizing private insurance agencies to set excessively high insurance premiums because there is a high likelihood that they will have to make payments to the insured, since the low-risk workers will not insure themselves. High premiums work to exclude many individuals who otherwise might purchase the insurance. The government has to step in and enact a compulsory state programme in order to avoid the adverse selection problem.

Moral Hazard

The fact of being insured might change the behaviour of the worker. They might become less hard-working and try to make an income without work, paid from the unemployment insurance, or they might not accept a job easily; that is, moral hazard problems might occur. The moral hazard issue of whether unemployment insurance encourages unemployment by discouraging workers from seeking a job or accepting a job has recently been strongly supported by Robert Barro, who talks about 'the folly of subsidizing unemployment'. In 2010 Barro found that the unemployment rate in the United States (US) could have been as low as 6.8 per cent, instead of 9.5 per cent, if unemployment benefits had not been extended from 26 weeks to 99 weeks by President Obama (see Barro, 2010). University of California, Berkeley Professor Jesse Rothstein contradicts this and sees demand shocks and not workers' laziness as the main reason for high unemployment in the US. He finds that moral hazard from the extension from 26 to 99 weeks amounted to only 0.3 per cent of extra unemployment rather than Barro's figure of 2.7 per cent (https://newrepublic.com/article/97971/would-extending-unemployment-benefits-increase-unemployment).

Howell and Azizoglu (2011) try to put the pros and cons of the debate on moral hazard together. They assess moral hazard problems of unemployment insurance from different angles. They find that the theoretical predictions of large work disincentive effects follow from a model that focuses attention on the 'value of unemployment' (when benefits replace earned income and workers prefer 'leisure' to work). But disincentive effects are much smaller when one also includes the 'value of employment' (there are large non-pecuniary benefits to holding a job, and substantial social, psychological and future employment costs to idleness) as well as the institutional realities of the unemployment insurance system, which require acceptance of reasonable job offers. Unemployed persons who collected benefits did not find themselves out of work longer than those who did not have unemployment benefits; and unemployed workers did not search for work more or reduce their wage expectations once their benefits ran out (Howell and Azizoglu, 2011).

Redistribution

Unemployment insurance can also be seen as a redistributive task of the state between the employed and the non-employed, between the income earners and the non-income earners. Engström (2009) models unemployment insurance as a redistributive task showing that optimal unemployment insurance benefits of the low-skilled workers are higher than efficiency purposes would predict. He claims that unemployment insurance can be used for redistribution purposes. But unemployment insurance was and is discussed mainly under the aspect of efficiency.

Stabilization

The moral hazard debate shows that unemployment insurance is a highly politicized issue. One finding which is neglected in the above debate is stability. As Sinn (2003), for example, shows, state-administered social insurance, which redistributes income only when the insurance claim occurs, may not increase the expected national income but will definitely reduce the variance of income. For the welfare of citizens, the stability of income is a value per se. Being able to plan household expenditures ahead without being immediately shaken by a layoff is an added value of public insurance. In addition, unemployment insurance functions as an automatic stabilizer in macroeconomic terms as well (see above).

7.5 MUTUAL DEPENDENCE OF RISKS, SPILLOVER EFFECTS

Furthermore, public unemployment insurance was introduced during times of mass unemployment. These are times when employment risks are not independent of each other. A precondition for private insurance is that risks are independent. Mutual dependence on risks – such as a hurricane or mass unemployment – makes private insurance impossible. Even mutual insurance of insurance companies among themselves does not help when they are affected by the same risk. Unemployment is a risk that the private sector cannot insure, not (only) because of moral hazard but because of its spillover effects through the whole economy.

7.6 IS THE PROTECTION AGAINST UNEMPLOYMENT A *RES PUBLICA*?

The history of unemployment insurance development shows that – as with almost all public tasks – it was first a voluntary insurance organized by trade unions. In many countries, this was then taken over by the state as a public task. Features of the original principal architecture of unemployment insurance were:

Table 7.3 Actors and justifications for the res publica of unemployment insurance

Dimensions \ Who: the actors	State	Community/ corporatist institutions	Market
What: provision	In some countries	Trade unions, funds	–
Funding	Sometimes co-funding	Major funding	
Regulation	Eligibility, duration,. . .	Involved in regulation	

	Dimensions \ Justification	Equality	Community/ morality	Efficiency
'Supply' side of activities	Production (direct/ indirect provision)			Adverse selection and moral hazard
	Funding			Mutual risks, spillovers
	Regulation/standard setting			Prevent idle workers and laziness, create income and demand

1. Contribution-based insurance (employees paid a flat rate into the insurance pot and were mutually insured).
2. The equivalence principle (insured over the entire period, the total of the premiums must match the total of the benefits paid out including administration costs and so on).
3. No means testing.

Different European countries took different paths. Table 7.3 gives an overview over the role of the state, the community and the market with regard to the provision, funding and regulation of unemployment insurance. Elements of basic comprehensive insurance were introduced in many countries. Often the state assumed the role of the regulator and supervisor, sometimes of co-financier. In some countries employers and employees share the contributions; in some countries trade unions are in charge of distributing unemployment benefits. Interest associations – organizations between the market and the state – have historically initiated the organization of unemployment insurance. Purely private unemployment insurance on a voluntary and individual basis has not existed, but instead there has been mutual insurance, organized by trade unions in times of increasing unemployment. Today, unemployment insurance is still left (partly) in the hands of trade unions and the social partners. It is of public concern but not necessarily an element of the state's agenda. Interest associations can also take over this task. The state usually regulates eligibility and duration and often acts as a co-financier. It is efficiency arguments (to prevent market failures like adverse selection and moral hazard explained in the previous section) that prevail as a legitimation for unemployment insurance to be a *res publica* or a semi *res publica* in the hands of trade unions and the social partners.

NOTES

* With thanks to Eric Seils and Dorothee Spannagel from the Wirtschafts- und Sozialwissenschaftliches Institut (WSI) in Düsseldorf, Germany, for their presentation at the second Res Publica Workshop in Utrecht and for helpful comments. Also many thanks to WSI EUCOS PhD Swantje Falcke at Utrecht University for providing some of the tables.

1. Unemployment insurance in the US followed the British example, but came much later. From 1916 on several bills failed in Congress. And it was only when the total number of unemployed workers in the United States was estimated to number between 11 million and 15 million that unemployment insurance benefits were first considered as part of the (national) Social Security Act in 1934 and 1935 (Wynnyk, 2014, pp. I–1).

REFERENCES

Barro, Robert (2010). The folly of subsidizing unemployment. *Wall Street Journal*, 30 August.

BSV (2013). Bundesamt für Sozialversicherungen, Geschichte der Sozialen Sicherheit in der Schweiz. http://www.geschichtedersozialensicherheit.ch/risikogeschichte/arbeitslosigkeit.

BSV SECO (2013). Staatssekretariat für Wirtschaft (SECO) homepage. http://www.geschichtedersozialensicherheit.ch/institutionen/staatssekretariat-fuer-wirtschaft-seco/.

CWED2 (2014). Comparative Welfare Entitlement Dataset. In Lyle Scruggs, Detlef Jahn and Kati Kuitto, *Comparative Welfare Entitlements Dataset 2. Version 2014-03*, University of Connecticut and University of Greifswald. www.cwed2.org.

Deakin, Simon (2000). The historical process of wage formation. In Linda Clarke, Peter de Gijsel and Jörn Janssen (eds), *The Dynamics of Wage Relations in the New Europe*, Dordrecht: Springer Science and Business Media, pp. 38–39.

Engbersen, Godfried, Kees Schuyt, Jaap Timmer and Frans van Waarden (1993). Cultures of the welfare state. In Godfried Engbersen, Kees Schuyt, Jaap Timmer and Frans van Waarden, *Cultures of Unemployment: A Comparative Look at Long-Term Unemployment and Urban Poverty*, Political Cultures Series, Boulder, CO and San Francisco, CA, USA; Oxford, UK: Westview Press, pp. 7–41.

Engström, P. (2009). Unemployment benefits as a means for optimal redistribution. *FinanzArchiv / Public Finance Analysis*, 65(1), 21–36.

Esping-Andersen, Gospa (1990). *The Three Worlds of Welfare Capitalism*, Princeton, NJ: Princeton University Press.
Esser, Ingrid, Tommy Ferrarini, Kenneth Nelson, Joakim Palme and Ola Sjöberg (2013). EU Directorate Employment, Social Affairs and Inclusion: unemployment benefits in EU member states. European Commission.
Frohman, Larry (2008). *Poor Relief and Welfare in Germany from the Reformation to World War I*, New York: Cambridge University Press.
Garside, W.R. (1990). *British Unemployment 1919–1939, A Study in Public Policy*, Cambridge: Cambridge University Press
Howell, David R. and Bert M. Azizoglu (2011). Unemployment benefits and work incentives: the US labor market in the Great Recession. *Oxford Review of Economic Policy*, 27(2). http://www.economicpolicyresearch.org/images/docs/research/employment/Howell%20WP%202011_7.pdf.
Industrial Relations Counselors (IRC) (1934). Analysis of the provisions of certain European Laws, An Historical Basis for Unemployment Insurance. NED-New edition Vol. 21, 79–164.
InfoNU (2011), http://zakelijk.infonu.nl/juridisch/72671-geschiedenis-van-het-sociale-zekerheidsrecht.html, 11 May.
Lundgren, Bo (2006). Recent development in unemployment insurance in Sweden, International Experts Workshop of the ISSA Technical Commission on Unemployment Insurance and Employment Maintenance, Brussels, 10–11 April. https://www.issa.int/html/pdf/workshop/bruxelles06/2lundgren.pdf
Musgrave, Richard (1959). *The Theory of Public Finance, A Study in Public Economy*, Cambridge: McGraw Hill.
Scruggs, Lyle (2014). Social welfare generosity scores in CWED 2: a methodological genealogy. CWED Working Paper 01, February.
Seils, Eric (2014). Die Vermessung des Wohlfahrtsstaates. In E. Seils, C. Bogedan and S. Leiber (eds), *Sozialversicherung: Wandel, Wirkung, Weiterentwicklung*, Wiesbaden: Springer.
SSPTW (2010). Social security programs throughout the world: Europe 2010. https://www.ssa.gov/policy/docs/progdesc/ssptw/2010-2011/. . ./ssptw10europe.pdf.
Sinn, Hans Werner (2003). *The New Systems Competition*, Hoboken, NJ: Wiley-Blackwell.
Talos, Emmerich and Karl Wörister (1994). *Soziale Sicherung im Sozialstaat Österreich. Entwicklung – Herausforderungen – Strukturen*. Baden-Baden: Nomos.
Wynnyk, Bohdan M. (2014). The history of unemployment insurance legislation in the United States and New York State 1935–2014. New York State Department of Labor, July. http://www.dol.gov/ocia/pdf/75th-anniversary-summary-final.pdf.

8. More health care or more beer? A curious paradox of making some economic tasks a *res publica*

Frans van Waarden*

8.1 INTRODUCTION: A CURIOUS PARADOX

Some time ago, I opened my daily Dutch newspaper (*Volkskrant*, 24 April 2014) and found a 'good news' message on the front page: 'Heineken's sales went up', a few days later followed by headings like 'More growth and profit beer industry' and 'Stocks Heineken up' (see also Figures 8.1 and 8.2). More

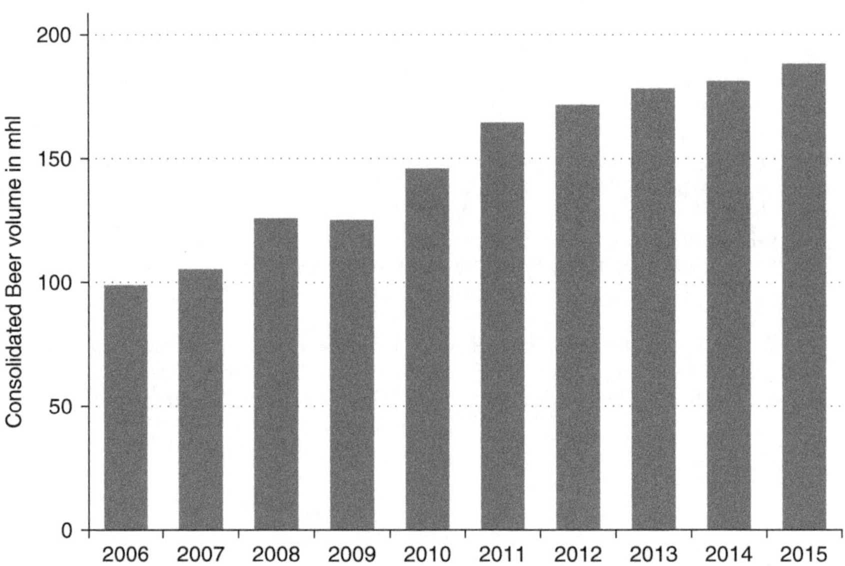

Source: Heineken Annual Reports 2010 and 2015.

Figure 8.1 The good news: Heineken beer sales, 2009–2014, by world region (in hectolitres)

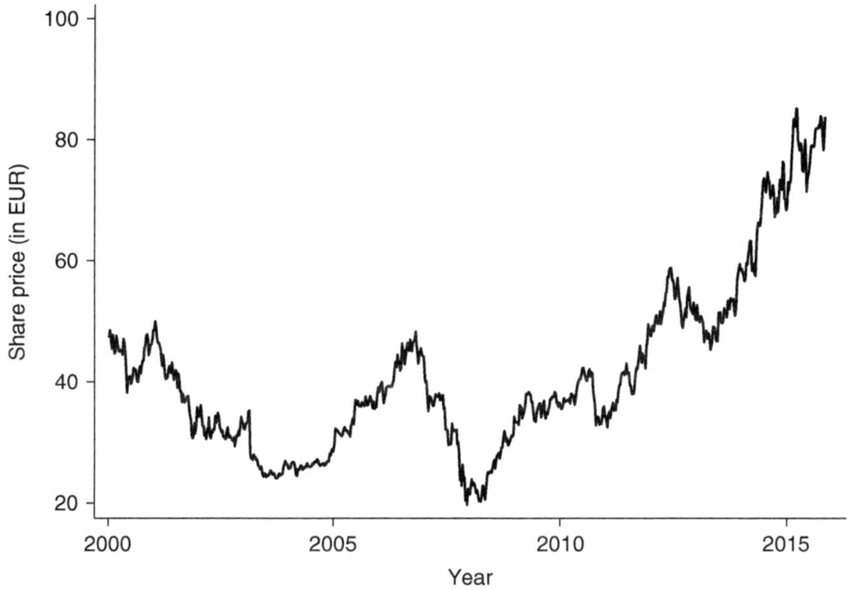

Source: Reuters, Amsterdam Stock Market.

Figure 8.2 The good news: Heineken stock prices at the Amsterdam Stock Exchange

recently, a newspaper (*NRC Next*, 1 June 2016) reported that Heineken is the most popular future employer among Dutch economics students, ahead even of KLM (place 2), Google (3), Nike (4), Apple (5) and Unilever (6).

The attentive newspaper reader will have come across many similar examples in other countries as well. Thus, for example, the *Wall Street Journal* (11 February 2015) also praised the beer industry with the headline: 'Heineken raises dividend after reporting 11% rise in profit'. Increasing beer production, consumption, prices and sales as well as a rise in profits from this seem to be something positive, something we value highly. Worldwide, 'beer is the third important drink after water and tea', and newspapers seem to support Benjamin Franklin's quote that 'beer is living proof that God loves us and wants us to be happy' (http://www.slideshare.net/cadeler/beer-industry).

The emphasis in such reports, curiously enough, is not on the value of the services, but on the costs. Since 2006, public health expenditures have risen in Europe and in the United States (US). In 2013 they were 7.8 per cent of gross domestic product (GDP) in the European Union (EU), 8 per cent of

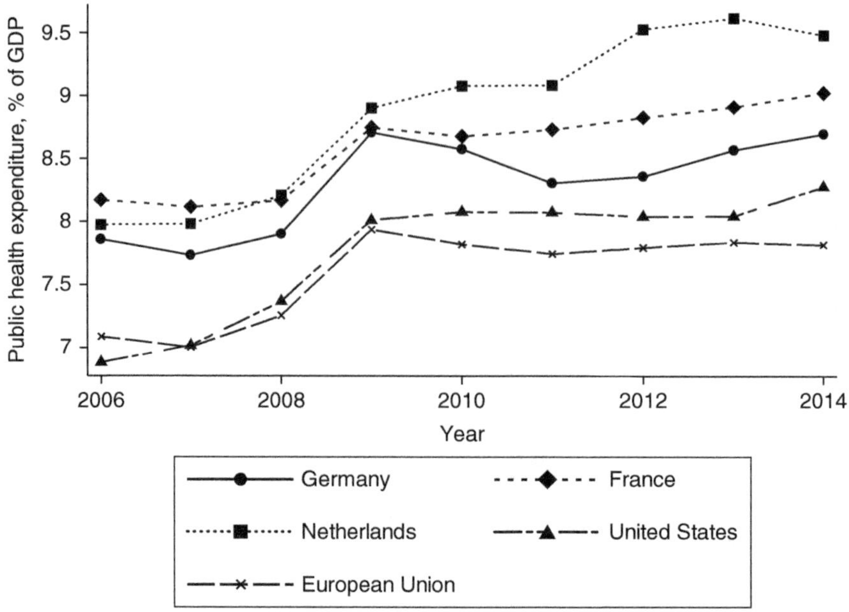

Note: Public health expenditure consists of recurrent and capital spending from government (central and local) budgets, external borrowings and grants (including donations from international agencies and nongovernmental organizations), and social (or by the state compulsory) health insurance funds.

Source: World Bank.

Figure 8.3 The bad news: public health expenditure as % of GDP, 2006–2013

GDP in the US and 12 per cent of GDP in the Netherlands. Thus when reporting about the health care sector, typical newspaper headings have stressed the costs of health care, using such terms as 'debacle' and 'shock': 'Costs of health care beyond all bounds!' (*Volkskrant*, 24 April 2014), a topic somewhat later more thoroughly elaborated by the also leftist weekly the *Green Amsterdammer* in its 6 June 2014 dossier, 'The care-cost debacle' by the 'Research Editorial Staff'; 'The catastrophic care debacle' (*New York Times*, 9 October 1989); 'The coming shock in health-care cost increases' (*Wall Street Journal*, 7 July 2015). The growth of the health care sector, the increase in health care provision, expenditures and consumption, increasing health care prices, and a rise of profits in the health care sector seem to be something negative, something we place a low value on.

Rarely is there any appreciation – at least in the economic sections of the newspapers – of any growth of health care services, of their innovation in new products, services or technologies to keep us all alive longer and in an ever healthier condition; perhaps mindful of Benjamin Franklin's opinion that 'Health care seems to be living proof that God does not love us and does not want us to be happy'? God made us human creatures prone to disease (and other creatures even to serve as food for others). Do we have the right to interfere with His creation? Is the medical sector perhaps blasphemous? Some religious sects do indeed nurture such ideas.

In the Netherlands, long waiting lists for health treatment are now suddenly seen as something that is perhaps not so bad, since this would be a way to reduce health care costs. Letting people wait for treatment and operations in order to reduce health care costs is quite a cynical proposal. Health care seems to burden the budget and to be provided at the cost of other potential expenditure – as if this is more valuable than our health.

The paradox was even explicitly present in the 2014 Throne Speech (*Troonrede*) of the Dutch government at the opening of the new parliamentary year, an annual tradition in which the government outlines its policy priorities for the upcoming year. On the one hand, the national government proclaimed that it 'needed to work on a structural recovery and growth of the economy and employment', but only a few lines further it complained that 'the costs of health care grow faster than the economy . . . Hence there is a need to increase cost-consciousness, counteracting waste and tackling fraud'; as if the healthcare sector is not part of the economy at all. Among the measures that the government took was a strategy of shifting the responsibility for home care for the elderly and health care for youngsters to local government, without providing them with sufficient funds to pay for it. This has resulted in more than 30000 lay-offs of care workers (www.ontslagenindezorg.nl), and elderly people left without sufficient home care. So much for the professed goal of 'stimulating the recovery and growth of the economy and employment': clearly not by stimulating the growth and employment of such a useful sector as that of health care. The Minister of Health countered with the remark that 'his business was not to care for employment and income'. But apparently neither is it to care for care services, given the lay-offs. The newspapers commented: '*De zorg is een zorg*' (care is a concern).

This is a curious paradox. Both beer production and health care services are economic sectors that do basically the same, at least at a somewhat higher level of abstraction. They provide goods and services that are high in demand, employ people – that is, provide employment – and they contribute to the GDP, that is, to the much-desired holy grail of economic growth. All these are typical indicators of prosperity. So, why is beer expansion good news and health care expansion bad news? In both cases there is consumption – that is, they satisfy societal needs – and production, and both sectors have their costs and benefits, and both provide jobs and income for others.

Why, then, do we emphasize the benefit side in the beer case? It may be that beer is often a source of human happiness. But too often it has also been a source of miserableness. This then often has to be 'repaired' by the health care sector. Yet here we seem to emphasize the cost side more than the benefit side. And we seem to value the growth of the beer industry more than the growth of the health care sector. This is puzzling. Why do newspapers not write that 'costs of beer consumption are exploding', while 'the health care sector is dynamically growing, providing more jobs and more care'? Why do we stress the benefit side when it comes to beer and the cost side when it comes to health care? Would it not make more sense to do exactly the opposite, with newspaper headlines such as 'Costs of beer consumption exploding' and 'Healthy booming growth of the health care sector'?

8.2 SOME EXPLANATIONS OF THIS CURIOUS PARADOX

There may be quite a few possible explanations for this curious paradox. Is it perhaps because beer consumption starts happily but ends miserably? Whereas with health care it is the opposite: starting with miserableness (sickness and sometimes pain of treatment) but ending with happiness?

More seriously: beer consumption is – perhaps with the exception of alcoholics – a free and voluntary choice. We buy it when we feel like it. And only some of us do. By contrast, health care consumption is usually involuntary, not a free choice. The need arrives not because we like it, but because we feel the necessity once we are struck by a disease. Yet we ought to be happy that there are skilled doctors and nurses and effective treatments and medicine available once we need them, especially when we need them urgently.

Health care payment is even less voluntary. In many countries we are forced to pay for the service by the government; that is, it forces us to pay for health insurance. This is akin to taxes that we are also forced to pay by the state, and which we dislike having to pay. The difference is that with health care insurance the payments go under public government pressure to private health insurance companies, while tax money is not only required by, but is also largely meant as and spent as a resource for the government and its agencies. Both taxes and health insurance contributions share the principle of compulsory payment, and often long before the service is being 'consumed', and in both cases 'consumption' may not really or always imply personal 'enjoyment'. Thus compulsory health insurance comes down to an earmarked tax. This is why it was resisted by a great many Americans when President Obama tried to introduce it in the USA, a policy which became known as 'Obamacare'.

Why is health care payment compulsory in many countries, and beer consumption compulsory nowhere? Perhaps this is a ridiculous question, but it helps in identifying the differences between beer consumption and health care consumption. Beer consumption is in a way a 'luxury', something special and not necessary for most people, except for those who have become alcoholics (and perhaps also in cases of social pressure among friends, where it can be considered 'not done' if one does not join in the drinking or share in the costs, for example by taking turns in buying a round of drinks). By contrast, health care is no luxury, but sooner or later it is a basic necessity for almost all human beings, when it is their turn to be struck by a more or less serious disease. That means that beer consumption as a non-necessity can wait, whereas health care consumption often cannot wait, although that depends on the seriousness and urgency of the disease that has struck.

However, this health care need arises on average more often later than sooner. For most of us the need for (more) health care increases with age. As our body grows older the need for 'servicing' it with health care increases, as is even more the case with ageing cars, houses, computers, and so on. But unlike these, the human body has during a very long evolutionary process developed the capacity to defend itself against threats to its health from a great variety of attackers, varying from viruses, bacteria and predators to members of our own species in warfare, and even the weather. These defences – many of which have become routines for, in and by the human body – have been quite successful over the ages and more recently have been aided by modern medical knowledge and technology, thus extending the average life expectancy of human beings in the Netherlands from 37 years in 1860 to 79 years for men and 83 for women in 2012 (CBS 'Historische overlevingstafels voor Nederland'). As a result, most of the remaining serious threats to our survival come as our bodies wear out and become more vulnerable with ageing. Therefore, it has even been estimated that on average half of our health care costs arise in our senior years. For survivors to age 85, more than one-third of their lifetime expenditures will accrue in their remaining years (Alemayehu and Warner, 2004). (So if one wants to save money kill the elderly, or don't treat them any more).

Yet we are expected to start paying for health insurance early on, to pay now for services needed much later. When we are younger we pay for but do not need so much health care, at least in relative terms. Since our time perspective tends to be short, we tend to overemphasize costs to be made now rather than benefits to be received eventually, mostly in a more distant future. Hence we may dislike this forced 'consumption' of a 'security' which we often may not need for some time. And for health care insurance, we are often forced to pay for a long, if not very long, time before we may really start enjoying the service. Paradoxically, due to the health care successes themselves, allowing us to live longer and grow older, this time distance between payment for and enjoyment of the services grows ever longer.

Related to this is the absence of the 'profit principle' in the case of transactions over health care. With compulsory health insurance we usually do not immediately 'profit' from our payment after we have made it. This profit principle for the individual consumer – here, the patient – that is, goods and/or services in immediate exchange for money, is common in most other market transactions that we engage in. The reverse occurs on the labour market: in exchange for labour, you get your money. But with health care insurance one pays up front without immediately profiting from the goods or services that one has paid for. The exchange of money gives you 'security', the peace of mind that you have in being sure of getting health care goods and services when you may need them in the near or distant future. This certainty and reduction of risk is actually what you buy with this and most other insurances.

In between beer and health care, there is food. It shares with beer the attribute that it is consumed by the body. However, food shares the attribute with health care that it is a basic necessity for survival (while for beer one cannot say that). In order to stay alive, we need liquid and food as well as health care. We spend quite a bit on both food and health care. Americans spend more on food than on health, Dutchmen about equal amounts for both. Over their lifetime Americans spend around $300 000 on health and about $520 000 on food. Dutchmen spend €277 000 on health and almost the same amount (€278 000) on food. With their thrifty food expenditure, Dutchmen lie below the EU average of €320 000 (calculated in 2014). As the saying goes: the Dutch eat to live, while the Italians, for example, live to eat. For beer, Americans spend US$29 000 and Dutchmen €25 000 over their lifetime (in 2014). Lifetime beer expenditure therefore amounts to about 5–11 per cent of food expenditure in the US and the Netherlands, respectively, and 10 per cent of lifetime health expenditure in both countries.[1]

Though we pay more or equal amounts for food as for health, we find it perfectly normal that we pay for our food directly ourselves, following the 'profit principle'. We exchange money in a single transaction for the finally consumed good or service. We usually pay in immediate exchange for the food that we buy. And that too we find also perfectly normal: we do not expect the government or an insurance institution to pay for it (except perhaps beggars and the homeless). That is so because the probability of being hungry at the day's end is close to 100 per cent and the frequency of needed payments is way too high. There is no uncertain risk involved here, and hence no commercial organization could insure it. The only collective satisfaction of this need could be by a generous charity or a concerned government caring for food provision for the poor.

Food has on the whole become cheaper over time through its mass production and modern technologies of production, conservation and transport; this notwithstanding the increasingly longer distances between farm and fork. By contrast health care costs – thanks to our advanced modern medical science and technologies – on the whole have become more expensive. Food for survival is still more or less affordable for most people. Such is often not, or less, the case with the need for health care. When the need is there, modern advanced medical technology may offer solutions, but often at a price which is unaffordable for many.

Yet the difference between food and health care is that the need for food (and drinks such as beer for some) is usually frequent, regular, and hence more or less predictable, but in small amounts; whereas the need for health care is for most of us infrequent, irregular, and unpredictable as regards when and how much care will be needed and at what price. The costs of care can turn out suddenly to be quite high. And we seem to be less inclined individually to put money or other resources aside to help us out in times when we could get sick: as long as we are healthy, we do not consider that possibility very much. So that when we do get seriously ill, many of us have not saved sufficient resources to pay for the sudden possibly high costs of health care.

Given that the need for food is regular and hence predictable, people can put aside the money required for it. That is less the case with the need for health care. Disease is often an unpredictable event, and when it strikes people may not have saved enough to pay for necessary treatment. However, for the unpredictable event of a disease a probability can still be calculated, and hence insurance is possible. Insurance companies have developed such health insurance and people can and do voluntarily buy such health insurance. Such insurance becomes relatively cheaper the more people participate, especially the young and healthy together with older and more often sick people; that is, the more the risk of the need for health-care is spread. In all cases we are forced to pay, first and foremost by our needs: in the case of food and drink, by our hunger, thirstiness and taste; in the case of health insurance, by our own need to insure the risk of sickness.

More in general, we are forced by our needs and our usual dependence upon other people for food and health care. We could of course 'do it ourselves' to some extent in both cases: grow our own vegetables and keep chickens in the garden or on the rooftop to satisfy our need for food, and herbal medicines for self-medication if we believe in it. Such 'do it yourself' in the care sector has recently become more popular for health care in the Netherlands, where the government with its austerity measures is cutting back on professional home care for the sick and elderly, with the message that just like care for young children, care for the elderly should also be a task of the family and not of home-care professionals paid by the government. This is all under the deceptive ideological slogan of 'the Caring Society' ('*Zorgsame Samenleving*'), to disguise the cutbacks of the no longer 'Caring Government'. If they are lucky, a family could get some government funding for this family home care, to compensate family members who have to reduce their paid work outside of the home to care for the family member.

Whom do we pay? Rarely the eventual goods and services provider. A major difference is that payments for food and drinks are usually made in direct exchange for those goods; that is, the buyer immediately gets real value for money. In the case of health insurance such a 'profit principle' does not really exist. Someone who pays for insurance does not immediately see what value for money they will eventually get in the form of health care service. The financial transaction of buying insurance can be, and is usually, substantially separated from the consumption of the insured health care service or good; that is, payment is not in direct exchange for the care service as is common with many other economic transactions. Hence the buyer cannot sanction the service provider for poor service by being unwilling to pay the full price, as is not uncommon in other market transactions.

To ensure maximum spreading of the costs and risks of the need for medical care it is important that as many people as possible participate in this insurance to spread the funding base, including especially those who might be the least inclined to insure themselves because they consider themselves healthy and for the time being not in need of health care. However, on a voluntary basis those people who consider themselves to be low-risk might rather spend their money on other goods – including fancy food – in the here and now rather than on 'saving' or 'investing' it for the (possibly distant) future. They might not participate in voluntary insurance. Hence, in order to correct for this problem, the state became involved.

8.3 WHY HAS HEALTH CARE (INSURANCE) BECOME A 'PUBLIC CONCERN' (*RES PUBLICA*)?

How to make sure that everyone participates in health care insurance? This is certainly not the first kind of insurance which can be more secure, stable and more affordable, the more people participate in it. The standard repertoire of incentives consists of the sermon, the carrot and the stick. Which one is best used here?

The sermon could be an appeal to a sense of solidarity. This has certainly been used in the early days and still is, here and there. And it has been shown to work best in relatively closed and not too large sub-communities with a strong shared identity ('us versus them') and also strong mutual social control, that is, organization, producing a strong sense of social cohesion, as found formerly in guilds and now in their successors, some trade unions.

But as such organizations increased in size with the growth of cities and countries in terms of population, instruments of mutual social control needed to be complemented with the carrot and the stick, initiated and provided by someone or some group in a position of power. And as indicated, the larger the group, the easier it is to spread risks and costs. Hence eventually they were extended to whole cities or even countries, led by the rulers and their government. First political leaders took responsibility for food as the basic condition for human survival; and once prosperity and medical knowledge grew, they eventually also took responsibility for some health care, although that took a while.

The importance of providing such basic resources for the people has been brought home to political leaders through social unrest. History has taught that insufficient supply of food, or overly expensive food, has not infrequently been a motive for revolts and revolutions. It was one of the concerns that set off the French Revolution. In emergency situations, direct or indirect public concern for sufficient food supply of a reliable quality has been a factor in the survival of the regime. It has not infrequently been the foundation of a new state authority. That was even the case with the European Union authorities. One of their first major policies was the Common Agricultural Policy (CAP), motivated by a concern for a sufficient and affordable domestic healthy food supply, also in times of war and conflict, a need people were well aware of so shortly after World War II. Eventually this basis of human survival has become complemented with a broader public concern for the health of the people. Thus the availability, safety and quality of food, and later also of health care, have over time become partly a public responsibility; in addition to some older private and semi-public initiatives, concerns and responsibilities, as for example of the guilds and the churches.

Early health care used alcoholic drinks such as wine and beer as medicine, not yet knowing the mechanism by which they worked, namely that alcohol killed disease-spreading germs. Given the importance of these drinks, their quality and quantity were regulated early on. The Romans had laws against the adulteration of wines; adding water was a criminal offence. In the late Middle Ages the Germans had their well-known *Reinheitsgebot für Bier*, the German Beer Purity Law. Ever since, food and its production have been heavily regulated with regard to origin, purity, quality and composition of ingredients, production processes, hygiene, workers' qualifications and the organization of food inspection. Enforcement of all such regulations has been paid out of general taxes, which we do not see specifically, as with earmarked taxes.

But the food sector is not regulated with regard to the amounts the consumer should or is allowed to consume (except in the case of extreme shortage, as in wartime when food may be scarce) and we are not forced to consume food. There is no need for that: people's hunger takes care of that. And if people do not eat, this usually has no contagious consequences for others.

In some countries, such as currently the United Kingdom, health care has become a fully public concern, with public funding, public provision, public quality standards and other public regulation. Other countries have compulsory health funding, but not as taxes to a government, rather as legally imposed insurance premiums to be paid to private health insurance companies. In both cases citizens are compelled to pay for health care in advance.

Why this compulsory insurance? Is that not paternalism of and by the state? Does the citizen not know what is good for them? The advantages have been outlined already: spreading the risk is the asset of insurance in general; social solidarity; as more people participate, it can be cheaper and hence more or less affordable for those on lower incomes; reducing the risk of the spreading of infectious diseases. That is why quite a few communities (such as nation states) have decided to protect citizens from their own possible short-sightedness by imposing collective and compulsory measures in the form of compulsory insurance for all citizens against the risk of sickness (or similar measures funded by compulsory taxation); a kind of forced collective saving for bad times. It is relatively new that the state thinks it is a government task to ensure health care savings or insurance: the idea is relatively new in the Netherlands, but even more so in the US with 'Obamacare', which unleashed fierce resistance from people who did not want to be forced to pay for such insurance, which came down to an earmarked form of taxation.

However, historically, the system of health insurance started as a more or less private initiative. It can be traced back to the medieval guilds. These formed mutual funds of assistance associations for a small number of workers under the auspices of their craft guild. It developed from wage replacement and a death benefit into payment for and/or the provision of outpatient physician services, inpatient hospital care and pharmaceuticals:

> Once the guilds disappeared (were banned), there was an extended period in which various collective not-for-profit as well as private for-profit attempts were made to organize the provision of health insurance. These civil society efforts produced mixed results, varying by country and by historical and/or cultural situation. In the Netherlands, for example, private commercial insurers tried to establish a market for health insurance, with unsatisfactory results. (Saltman and Dubois, 2004, p. 23)

Eventually, what had begun as voluntary worker co-operatives turned into a state-mandated compulsory health insurance system. Germany under Bismarck is often considered to be the first to introduce health insurance, as it was the first Western European country to codify existing voluntary structures into mandatory state-supervised legislation in 1883. Subsequently, throughout the twentieth century other countries followed: from the Netherlands in 1941 to Switzerland in 1996.

8.4 TYPES OF HEALTH CARE INSURANCE

In the Netherlands the government obliges all citizens to join one of the publicly recognized private health insurance companies. Though companies can compete on price, the basic coverage that has to be offered as well as the franchise is regulated by a publicly appointed council of healthcare experts and politicians. For special care costs such as for the elderly (home care, and so on) there is a separate universal fund called AWBZ (General Law for Special Health Care Costs).

Health care insurance can be funded through social security funds and earmarked contributions or through taxes:

> The concept of social health insurance (funding through social security funds and provision of doctors) is deeply ingrained in the fabric of health care systems in western Europe. It provides the organizing principle and a preponderance of the funding in seven countries – Austria, Belgium, France, Germany, Luxembourg, the Netherlands and Switzerland. Some countries subsequently changed to predominantly tax-funded arrangements in the second half of the twentieth century – Denmark (1973), Italy (1978), Portugal (1979), Greece (1983) and Spain (1986). Moreover, there are segments of social health

> insurance based health care funding arrangements still operating in predominantly tax-funded countries like Finland, Sweden and the United Kingdom, as well as in Greece and Portugal. In addition, a substantial number of central and eastern European (CEE) countries have introduced adapted SHI models since they regained control over national policy-making – among them Hungary (1989), Lithuania (1991), Czech Republic (1992), Estonia (1992), Latvia (1994), Slovakia (1994) and Poland (1999). (Saltman and Dubois, 2004, p. 22f)

'Often, the state is not seen to be the owner of these social security structures, but rather their guardian and administrator – their steward' (Saltman, in Saltman et al., 2004, Chapter 1, p. 5).

8.5 LEGITIMATION OF STATE INTERVENTION

Economists give several reasons why the state intervenes in health care (see Barr, 2004), which mainly legitimize state intervention by efficiency arguments:

1. Health can be considered a 'merit good' (Musgrave, 1957, 1987; Lee Mendoza, 2011) which the government in a paternalistic way wants to provide for us in both our individual and collective interest (like we are also forced to pay for pension insurance). The government does so for various reasons, among them that a healthy population has various positive externalities. For example:
    a. Infectious diseases, that could harm others, have less chance to spread around. People might not take into account the negative spillover effects that a disease like the measles could have on others. So there is a market failure of negative external effects of diseases on others that the government should correct.
    b. A healthy population means content citizens and voters and good workers for the economy, which in turn is in our collective interest.
    c. A healthy population would also mean healthy families and hence good family care for the children and elderly.
2. There is also the idea that the individual would be too short-sighted to save sufficiently for the bad days and hence there would be too low a consumption of health care. A disease is not predictable, ill-health strikes unexpectedly (like a car accident) and the damage is distributed unequally between the healthy and the sick, or the sick and very sick. Though we know that one needs more health care with age and that the 'costs' of health care can go also up with age, so with age one's health gets more expensive. People might underinsure themselves,

therefore the government should intervene, in both setting insurance standards and making insurance obligatory.

3. Asymmetric information about the need for medical care and treatment can lead to inefficient care provision. Asymmetric information about the risks of the insured (which they themselves are more likely to know, but the insurance company will not) can lead to mainly 'bad risks' (people who are more likely to need expensive medical care) insuring themselves, to too-high insurance fees that deter 'good risks', and so to bankruptcy of private insurance companies (Barr, 2004, p. 260).
4. To fill gaps in coverage of private insurances for chronic and congenital illness, the medical needs of the elderly and primary health care (Barr, 2004, p. 262).
5. Moral hazard might occur because patients may be able to influence the provision of treatment. Insured skiers might take fewer precautions and incur higher risks of breaking a leg. Insured people might decide to go more often to the doctor, which involves higher costs. Moral hazard occurs also through the third payment problem. The insurance company is largely divorced from the decisions of doctors and patients, and the doctor is paid a fee for service. If medical insurance covers all the costs, health care is free to the patient, and the doctor is not constrained by the patient's ability to pay. The result is overconsumption of health care and there are social costs though zero private costs to doctors and patients. So, a private insurance company would not cover this.
6. There are also principal–agent problems involved in health care provision. The doctor is an agent to two principals: the patients and the insurance company. Public insurance has lower accounting costs and therefore is cheaper.
7. There is also the argument of solidarity, which was at the origin of mutual health insurance funds: the argument of equality and solidarity of the healthy with the sick. So there is also an equity concern for the government to intervene.

8.6 SOLVING THE DILEMMA BY MAKING HEALTH CARE MORE PRIVATE?

Sufficient health care provision and funding is seen as a public responsibility. This is why health news is always focused on the cost side. The public sector produces costs, while the private sector produces goods like beer, and hence produces benefits. But this view on health care is biased.

Do doctors and nurses deserve to be seen as a burden or cost, instead of looking at the provision of their services? Doctors are a cost when they make mistakes, but in principle their services should be stressed positively. Why do we not focus on beer brewers causing us to get drunk and die earlier through alcohol-related liver diseases or car accidents, and on doctors helping us to stay alive?

For a long time one had to pay for health care. But could a publicly provided good under public responsibility today be turned into a private health insurance? Could parts be put into private hands? Could we pay cash for medicine? Once medicine is expensive, public insurance often refuses to pay for it. Several health care systems in different countries have introduced a certain amount of self-payment before the insurance pays. Would it be a solution to:

1. Turn public into private goods, that is, privatize health care (again)?
2. Make it a regular transaction, with consumer 'paying when profiting' (profit principle)?
3. Appreciate a growing health sector? We should be happy that the health care sector is growing, that doctors and nurses provide good service and that medicines can be prescribed and consumed.

With regard to the development of health care, provision and funding has been privatized. First a basic compulsory insurance was introduced with a standard service package. Then provision became more and more variable and privatized. Doctors had to become more commercial, looking at their watches in order to save costs, saving on medicine and treatment, and so on. Steven Vogel (1998) showed in his book on market liberalization in Japan, the US and Europe that as markets became more privatized and liberalized, more regulations were needed. 'Freer markets, more rules' were the consequences of the privatization of the supply of the service provision. In health care this was a privatization of the demand for medical services, where there are two parties: the patient and their insurance company. Following privatization their relationship became more regulated, except for the segment of the market where the consuming patient pays themself. This is or should be the case for a small amount spent by people privately, for cheap medicine, just as we have no insurance for food. For minimum food needs there could also be food funds, collected by taxes, and food rations as supplied to the poor or the homeless. Small medical expenses could be paid out privately. The insurance should be for larger expenses and treatments.

In a newspaper article the Dutch Minister of Finance once suggested that consumers should spend no matter on what. The same minister, however, said that one should save on health care expenditures. I hope however that I have shown the paradox contained in such a statement. One solution proposed here would be a more or less partial privatizing of minor health care expenditures, leaving only the more expensive segment as a *res publica*. In the beer sector the opposite would hold, with at most a publicly paid gift of cheap beer to citizens on certain special occasions, but whoever wants a fancier beer or more of it has to foot the bill themself.

8.7 CONCLUSION

It should be clear now that there are pros and cons, costs and benefits, to organizing health care as a public or a private responsibility, a *res publica* or a *res privata*, or a shared *res pub-priv* (or *PuPri* or *PP*?) responsibility. The benefits are usually known, as they form the legitimation for the public involvement, whether public regulation, funding or even direct provision of the service. As to the cost side, hardcore economists claim that public provision can be less efficient in the absence of market competition. Here I have stressed an additional disadvantage, namely a negative public perception of health care services, overemphasizing the cost side of the services in comparison to the benefit side; something our health care providers do not deserve. There are costs involved in making health care a public responsibility, but not only and not so much the material economic costs themselves: on top of that there is also the negative imagery of this 'service', in which its cost side tends to be overemphasized to the detriment of its benefits, which deserve better.

The balance between costs and benefits may vary depending on the degree of public involvement with health care. This could range from, at one extreme, a fully publicly funded and provided service (the British model), as for example with the army, the police and the jails in many countries (public safety being among the historical core business of the state); to at the other extreme, a complete public absence from this economic sector – for which it is difficult to come up with an example. Perhaps the illegal drug market comes close to it (if one overlooks the passive role of the state here: its criminalization of drugs has actually created that underground market). In between these extremes there are in principle a wide variety of financial, regulatory, organizational and managerial involvements of the public sector with health care services. And such a variety has also become an empirical reality, dispersed over different countries and their governments. There are good arguments imaginable for the diversity of public choices.

The need for public health care can be legitimized mainly on the grounds of efficiency, but also on equity and moral grounds. However, it is not up to wisecracking, arrogant, soothsaying economists, social scientists, historians or legal scholars to decide this or even to recommend what should be done. The best science can do is to identify, analyse and compare the pros and cons, the costs and benefits of the various options, give empirically founded arguments and make these 'public'. But in a democratic society it should be up to the demos to take that decision democratically. The very choice whether something should be a public responsibility – that is, a *res publica* – ought also to be itself a *res publica*, a matter for 'public choice'; here not understood as that curious American conservative-liberal social and political movement, but more simply and broadly as the whole democratic public discussing the options in public and deciding along the rules of democratic decision making. And so it has often been. This chapter has added to the pros and cons of public involvement, if not public provision or finance, of these health care services. But the choice should be left to the demos, and preferably a well-informed demos.

NOTES

* I thank the participants of the WSI Res Publica Workshop for helpful comments. In particular I want to thank Swantje Falcke and Leydi Breuls for providing and calculating data on lifetime health, beer and food expenditures.

1. Lifetime expenditure calculations need a lot of heroic assumptions. A direct comparison of food, beer and health could not be found, so different sources were used: US Bureau of Labor Statistics, LISS Data (Longitudinal Internet Studies for the Social Sciences, https://www.lissdata.nl/lissdata/about-panel), Alemaheyu and Warner (2004), Brunello et al. (2009, Table 5, p. 575), Beer Statistics (2014), World Bank (various years); and it was assumed that half of beer was consumed in bars and half at home at a beer price in bars of €5 and $5. The results were also tested for robustness using survey data (LISS for the Netherlands) and national statistical data.

REFERENCES

Alemayehu, Berhanu and Kenneth E. Warner (2004). The lifetime distribution of health care costs. *Health Services Research*, 39(3), 627–642. http://www.ncbi.nlm.nih.gov/pmc/articles/PMC1361028/.

Barr, Nicholas (2004). *Economics of the Welfare State*, 4th edition, Oxford: Oxford University Press.

Beer Statistics (2014). The brewers of Europe. http://www.brewersofeurope.org.

Brunello, Giorgio, Pierre-Carl Michaud and Anna Sanz de Galdeano (2009). The rise of obesity in Europe, an economic perspective. *Economic Policy*, 59(July), 551–597.

Lee Mendoza, Roger (2011). Merit goods at fifty: reexamining Musgrave's theory

in the context of health policy. *Review of Economic and Business Studies*, 4(2), 275–284.
Musgrave, Richard (1957). A multiple theory of budget determination. *FinanzArchiv*, New Series 25(1), 33–43.
Musgrave, Richard (1987). Merit goods. In *The New Palgrave: A Dictionary of Economics*, Vol. 3, pp. 452–453.
Saltman, Richard and Hans Dubois (2004). The historical and social base of social health insurance systems. In Richard Saltman, Reinhard Busse and Jossep Figueiras (eds), *Social Health Insurance Systems in Western Europe*, Open University Press. http://www.who.int/health_financing/documents/shi_w_europe.pdf.
Vogel, Steven K. (1998). *Freer Markets, More Rules. Regulatory Reform in Advanced Industrial Countries*, Ithaca, NY: Cornell University Press
WHO (2015). Global Health Observatory Data Repository: Life expectancy – Data by country (CSV). World Health Statistics 2015. Geneva: World Health Organization.
World Bank (various years). *World Bank Databank*. http://data.worldbank.org/indicator/SH.XPD.OOPC.ZS/countries/EU-NL-DE-FR-US?display=graph.

9. ECEC: childcare markets in the Netherlands and England[1]

Trudie Knijn and Jane Lewis

9.1 INTRODUCTION

Early childhood education and care (ECEC) for children below school age is still a contested issue. In most European countries, childcare (unlike education, healthcare, social housing and social benefits) was for a long time not framed as a matter of public interest, despite women's campaigns. Those days are gone. For various reasons, the European Union (EU) has proved to be an advocate of gender equality. At the Barcelona Summit in 2002, the European Council (EC) set targets for the provision of childcare and pre-primary education in the EU member states. These targets require that at least 90 per cent of children between three years old and the mandatory school age (varying from five to seven years) and at least 33 per cent of children under three years of age should have access to formal childcare. In many European countries, these targets were met by 2015, but the number of hours available vary. However, the EC did not provide guidelines on how childcare should be provided or on how it should be purchased; these issues are left to the discretion of the member states in accordance with the principle of subsidiarity.

Regarding the central question in this book of what legitimizes state intervention, ECEC is an interesting case due to the various path-dependent routes member states have followed in developing the provision and funding of ECEC. The ways in which responsibilities are divided among the institutional settings and actors differ. In some European welfare regimes (the Scandinavian countries, Belgium, France and parts of Germany), both the provision and funding of childcare are mainly seen as a public issue. In other countries (the United Kingdom and Ireland, and most continental European countries), childcare is seen primarily as a familial responsibility or a mix of private (family and market) and public responsibilities (Knijn and Saraceno, 2010; Saraceno and Keck, 2010). That division reflects other differences in the aims and objectives of childcare. First, public and political opinions differ on whether childcare is needed, above all, to stimulate women's labour market participation and overcome child poverty (Leseman and Slot, 2014; Lewis, 2009; Esping-Andersen, 2009), or whether the main goal is to stimulate children's development, which according to many researchers is better served outside the family by professional and group provision for children, in particular for children from disadvantaged backgrounds (Heckman, 2006; Leseman and Slot, 2014; Esping-Andersen, 2009). Second, a divide exists between those who assume that childcare is better served by publicly provided services and those who accept the idea that the service should be provided by a market in which providers compete and clients have a free choice. However, even if childcare is provided by the market, state intervention is still needed, as will be shown in this chapter.

We explore current developments in childcare in two countries that have quasi-markets in childcare: ECEC provision is mainly private in England, and wholly private in the Netherlands. In both countries, the childcare market receives substantial public funding, enough to put both countries in the middle of the Organisation for Economic Co-operation and Development (OECD) range, and the two have different degrees of regulation. While there is a broad consensus in the EC and the OECD that ECEC should be available, affordable and of high quality, there are problems with all of these aspects, albeit to different degrees. In both countries, there are signs of failure in a fragmented and fragile market that offers mainly private providers, ranging from large chains to small businesses and childminders (all of which may provide early years education and care in England) alongside not-for-profit providers and, again in England, some public providers. Employers' childcare services are minimal in both countries. While early years education is funded by the state in both countries, early years care is funded by parents with the help of tax allowances (Netherlands) and childcare tax credits together with childcare vouchers administered by employers (England). The two systems are regulated to different degrees by the state. In both countries, no attempt has been made to increase public childcare provision. England is virtually alone in Western Europe in providing both early education and care via the market (Penn, 2007; Lewis, 2009; Knijn and Saraceno, 2010; Stewart, 2013). In the Netherlands, the 2005 Childcare Act (*Wet Kinderopvang*) abolished all public childcare centres, leaving only playgroups (for a maximum of ten hours per week) and early education to the responsibility of local authorities, while the British 2006 Childcare Act made local authorities the providers of last resort.

Nevertheless, in both countries public expenditure on childcare has expanded enormously since 2000, resulting in a flourishing childcare market. In 2007, spending on childcare and pre-primary education made up about 0.7 per cent of GPD in the Netherlands and about 1.3 per cent of gross domestic product (GDP) in the United Kingdom (UK) (OECD, 2009), although these data also include non-compulsory early education delivered by schools (very large numbers of four-year-olds go to school in both countries; OECD, 2015). Balancing private (employers' and families') costs against public expenditure in this new market, while guaranteeing value for money as well as access to a quality service for those who need it most, has been a major policy challenge.

Since the 1980s, two parallel trends have formed the background to these developments in childcare provision in the Netherlands and the UK: increasing rates of female employment and the neoliberal impetus to outsource social services to the market. Under these conditions, policy decisions in the Netherlands and policy path dependence in the UK have resulted in private providers entering the childcare business, even though they have been subject to different amounts of regulation (for example, regarding inspections, monitoring for health and safety, staff-to-child ratios). The assumption underlying the commitment to a childcare market rather than public provision is that the market would be better able to create services in line with parents' wishes and would be more efficient than public services, as competition would achieve cost savings. Another characteristic of both countries is the increase in public funding and thus the assumption that childcare is not a wholly private familial nor a wholly private market responsibility. In this respect, the analysis of the situation in England and the Netherlands corresponds to the results obtained for most similar cases (Skocpol and Somers, 1980).

In this chapter we argue that childcare needs state intervention in respect of financing and regulation and cannot be left to the private market alone. First, we consider the theoretical arguments for defining childcare as a 'public good' in line with the arguments put forward in the introduction of this volume. We then demonstrate the extent to which the childcare market is fragile and fragmented, and as such to a considerable degree dependent on public funding. We also argue that because of the fragmented market, parents' free choice is limited in less well-off parts of the country and poorer neighbourhoods. In addition, as Plantenga (2012) has indicated, parental choice is limited due to difficulties in assessing quality, poor information, lack of transparency, switching costs related to policy decisions on tax allowances and tax credits, and because children need continuity of care. Market provision tends to be fragile and therefore unsustainable and sometimes inaccessible, especially in poor areas. Finally, the childcare market has exclusionary effects, which are linked to policy decisions on eligibility. In this context, issues of affordability, entitlement and service quality come to the fore. However, high-quality ECEC is what children need and what the childcare market cannot be relied on to provide, which implies the need for good regulation.

9.2 STATE INTERVENTION IN CHILDCARE: THEORETICAL ARGUMENTS

One of the intriguing questions in the 'Introduction' to this book is why state intervention is considered legitimate for some public interest goods and services but not others. It suggests the following reasons for state intervention.

First, redistribution. Market forces may result in (democratically) unacceptable levels of income or wealth inequality, in which case government may intervene to make either service availability or quality (or both) more equal (cf. Musgrave and Musgrave, 1989). Although redistribution is more often associated with cash rather than services, this argument has force in respect of childcare if equal access as well as high-quality care are to be guaranteed. The costs of good-quality care offered by skilled childcare workers are far beyond the price that low- and middle-income families can afford (Folbre, 2008). Redistribution of childcare costs becomes an argument for policy intervention to make ECEC provision non-exclusionary.

Second, producing goods which on moral grounds should not be treated as commodities on the market. The argument put forward in the 'Introduction' to this book is that the state should engage in activities that purposely limit the scope of markets if moral goods are involved: 'examples of goods that should be provided publicly on moral grounds include water utilities, education, health care, military defence, police and court services . . . For certain goods one may argue everyone should have equal access (for example, primary education, basic health care, national statistics bureaux, cultural institutions, nature reserves)'. The communitarian argument used here is that private corporations are driven by profit, whereas the state is driven by the public interest and a desire to avoid the corruption of moral and civic goods by market provision. If commodification is deemed not morally permissible, then, the authors argue, it is appropriate for the free market exchange of that good to be blocked.

This communitarian argument seems debatable with regard to childcare. On the one hand, the moral grounds for providing childcare are varied, politically contested and unclear: is childcare designed to promote mothers' employment, to overcome child poverty or to promote child development? On the other hand, though, state intervention and regulation by the state might be legitimized for two moral reasons. First, childcare concerns a vulnerable group of the population: young children, whose care and protection should be in good hands and whose future will be crucial for the prosperity of society. Second, childcare can help poor families to overcome poverty if mothers are employed. This female employment argument has been the main reason for the European Council to implement childcare place targets. Interestingly, economists define services that should not be treated as commodities as 'goods'. Social policy scholars (as we are) prefer to keep more distance from the idea of services as 'goods' at all, whether these be publicly or privately delivered services. For that reason we define childcare just as a matter for state intervention.

Third, state intervention is legitimate and necessary for the production of those goods where the public sector generally outperforms markets. When this criterion is applied to what is already a developed childcare market, research has shown that public provision provides better-quality ECEC (e.g. Sylva et al., 2004) but is expensive to run. However, whether public services outperform private services depends to a large degree on public investment, especially in the training and guidance of practitioners, and on the character and quality of regulation. There is certainly a need for state intervention in the childcare market to guarantee access to quality care. The publicly supported market is rather fragile, fragmented and vulnerable to public policy decisions; it cannot achieve sustainability on its own, and tends to control costs at the expense of quality. Our overall conclusion will be that: (1) in the end, it is public policy that determines whether a high-quality, affordable market for public services is able to flourish; and (2) private markets for public goods need adequate and stable state regulation.

Before we elaborate on these conclusions, we will first outline the nature of the childcare markets in England and the Netherlands. Two aspects of state intervention will be highlighted: regulation of the fragile and fragmented market, and public funding by way of tax reliefs and vouchers.

9.3 THE CHILDCARE MARKET IN ENGLAND AND THE NETHERLANDS

ECEC is a complicated market with some similarities in England and the Netherlands. Both countries have a variety of providers for children aged 0–4: private for-profit and non-profit providers of formal childcare, some public providers (playgroups in the Netherlands and nursery schools in England) as well as private childminders. Also, in the Netherlands, 98 per cent of children aged four go to school, while in England a majority of four-year-olds go to school for part of the year before they turn five years old, and there is almost universal take-up of the 15 free hours of early years education among three- and four-year-olds, which is provided by both for-profit and not-for-profit providers.[2]

Both countries have also developed initiatives that focus on securing children's development, such as Sure Start Children's Centres in England (which were set up to provide some early education as well as other services for pre-school children, but which have suffered major cuts since 2010) and *Voorschoolse Educatie* (pre-school education) in the Netherlands. Finally, both countries have invested on a large scale in ECEC. Public expenditure in the Netherlands rose from €1.3 billion to €3.4 billion between 2005 and 2010, and declined again to €2.3 billion in 2013 (CPB, 2011; Rekenkamer, 2014; Brancheorganisatie Kinderopvang, 2015). In England, expenditure on early years education rose rapidly under successive Labour governments from £1040 million in 1997/98 to £4395 million in 2009/10. Expenditure continued to rise under the coalition government of 2010–2015, reaching £4784 million in 2013/14 (HM Treasury, 2015). However, expenditure via tax credits in respect of early years care fell after Labour left office, from £2508 million in 2009/10 to £882 million in 2012/13, which is close to the figure recorded for the early 2000s. Childcare vouchers administered by employers account for around £500 million, an amount which has held steady since 2010 (Stewart and Obolenskaya, 2015).

Turning to the differences between the two ECEC systems, first, a variety of groups and individuals can provide subsidized childcare in the Netherlands: playgroups (for children aged 2–3 and for a maximum of ten hours per week[3]), so-called guest parents (often linked to childcare centres) and also grandparents, and other informal caregivers, provided that they are registered. In England early years education is provided by a relatively small number of public nursery schools (around 28 000) as well as in nursery classes and reception classes of primary schools. Subsidies also go to private and voluntary providers of formal ECEC and to childminders (who are similar to Dutch guest parents) to fund the part-time entitlement to early years education, as well as to parents for early years care. Second, more children in England than in the Netherlands are cared for outside the home: 53 per cent of English children versus only 43 per cent of Dutch children under four.

The Childcare Market: Fragile and Fragmented

In the childcare market with its multiple service providers – from national for-profit childcare chains, to small local private and not-for-profit providers, to childminders – services and facilities differ in scale, quality, focus, intention and financial health. A recent Dutch study (CPB, 2011) shows that while the childcare sector has expanded rapidly, its structure has become more complicated. Commercial providers have succeeded in taking a larger share of the market (rising from 40 per cent in 2003 to 70 per cent in 2010). The providers themselves have also increased in size and have taken over, merged with or replaced non-profit providers (CPB, 2011). Moreover, the market is characterized by some very large commercial organizations and many very small-scale providers, which have tempered the oligopsonistic threat from the large providers, and consumer choice has increased a little. The largest group providers in the Netherlands are the for-profit companies (HIG/Smallsteps and Partou/Kinderopvang Nederland BV) and the non-profit foundation *Stichting Kinderopvang Humanitas* (Berkhout et al., 2009). In England, the main for-profit providers are the Busy Bees Group, Bright Horizons and Asquith Day Nurseries and Pre-schools (Gaunt, 2014). Taken together, the largest childcare provider chains in the Netherlands hold about 10–12 per cent of the market (Berkhout et al., 2009), while they occupy 25 per cent of the market in England (DfE, 2015). These figures do not tell the whole story because in the larger Dutch towns (more than 50 000 inhabitants) the market share of large chains is about 55 per cent. Further analysis by Berkhout et al. (2009) shows that the large chains have a 40 per cent market share in 75 per cent of the towns with 50 000+ inhabitants. These data are relevant for understanding the extent of parental choice, which is one, though not the only, policy argument for the marketization of childcare. An incomplete local market dominated by one or only a few providers limits consumer choice.[4]

The 2011 Centraal Planbureau (CPB) analysis of the childcare market drew the conclusion that, from an economic perspective, the childcare market functions well with a return of 5 per cent. However, in a market failures happen, and sustainability is difficult to achieve for private providers of childcare. Another concern in the political and public debate in both countries has been whether the big chains are making a substantial profit at a cost to parents and taxpayers (CPB, 2011; House of Lords Select Committee on Affordable Childcare, 2015). However, it has been concluded that there is no evidence of profiteering. In contrast, and in spite of the CPB's optimistic predictions, in the Netherlands about 80 childcare centres went bankrupt in 2014, and another 25 in the first half of 2015 (Brancheorganisatie Kinderopvang, 2015). Such a dramatic decline in the supply of childcare has not been observed in England, although the number of childminders has declined steadily, and entry into and exit from the market is common. In addition, for-profit providers of early years education feel that the public money they receive to fund the 15 free hours is insufficient. It has been shown that they attempt to offset this shortfall by charging parents more for the additional hours of early years care that they need (House of Lords, 2015). The government has announced that it will increase the number of free hours to 30. But if these are not funded more generously, for-profit providers might either refuse to provide the extra hours or might find that the business is not sufficiently profitable for them to continue.

An explanation for the bankruptcy of so many for-profit childcare centres in the Netherlands is the partial withdrawal of financial subsidies by the Dutch government at a time of economic crisis. Indeed, European comparative scholars had predicted that the rising social expenditure on childcare and other forms of 'social investment' (Hemerijck, 2013; Bonoli and Natali, 2012) since 2000 would come to an end and most likely reverse in the face of austerity measures (Schäfer and Streeck, 2013). However, comparative data for the years 2000–2011 does not show an overall impact of austerity on early years education; in the UK, public expenditure on early education clearly continued to rise (Kvist, 2013). In the Netherlands in contrast, the prediction proved to become reality. Since 2011, the percentage of Dutch children in childcare has declined by a substantial 30 per cent (about 100000 children) due to the combined effects of the economic crisis (unemployment) and policy measures (cutbacks in subsidies) (Brancheorganisatie Kinderopvang, 2015; Rekenkamer, 2014). As a consequence, for-profit providers have merged, reorganized and aimed for greater efficiency; more than 30000 childcare workers lost their jobs between 2011 and 2014 (Brancheorganisatie Kinderopvang, 2015). While it appears that ECEC policy has been embedded in the policy agendas of both countries, early years provision is still a sector vulnerable to austerity measures.

One of the big companies to go bankrupt in 2014 was Estro. This case exemplifies the risks of private equity funds entering the sector. The company owned 370 childcare centres that employed 3600 childcare workers. A few years before the bankruptcy, the company had been taken over by private equity funds (for example, Bencis and Providence), which forced private childcare providers to meet the whole of their loan repayments. Estro was unable to continue, and other investors (HIG/Smallsteps) 'rescued' the company. During the two huge reorganizations that followed, about 1200 childcare workers lost their jobs, permanent jobs were replaced by flexible jobs and the quality of childcare was under pressure for a long period. A review by Brancheorganisatie Kinderopvang (2015) shows that Estro was not the only childcare company facing financial difficulties. Even after the bankruptcy of 80 childcare centres in 2014 and another 25 in 2015, 40 per cent of childcare providers report financial problems, in terms of either solvency or profitability. Probably in reaction to this financial fragility, the Dutch government intends to abolish the income-related tax allowances implemented in 2004 and to replace them with direct subsidies for childcare centres (*Kinderopvangtoeslag*). However, Brancheorganisatie Kinderopvang fears that this policy change will lead to a rise in administrative costs.

A second major type of privately provided childcare is that offered by registered childminders taking care of children either at the parents' home (in the Netherlands) or in their own homes. *Gastouders* (guest parents), as they are called in the Netherlands, may also include grandparents. Their work is subsidized via the tax allowance for parents, and they have to pay income tax on this (additional) income. In England, private childminders are required to register with the national Office for Standards in Education, Children's Services and Skills (Ofsted), and in the Netherlands they have to register with a guest parent agency at the *Landelijk Register Kinderopvang en Peuterspeelzalen* (National Register of Childcare Providers and Playgroups). In both countries, childminders are subject to health and safety regulations and to requirements regarding the number of children of different ages they can take. They provide the cheapest form of childcare for parents in both countries because they incur lower housing and administrative costs. In the Netherlands, the qualifications required of guest parents and informal caregivers, such as grandparents, are similar to those of workers in formal centres, whereas in England they are the least-qualified childcare workers and also the least well paid (Boogaard and Bollen, 2014; Brind et al., 2014). In the Netherlands, the number of guest parents operating through 722 registered guest parent offices is relatively stable at 40 000, while in England there are about 56 000 childminders on the register (Brancheorganisatie Kinderopvang, 2015; Brind et al., 2014). In the Dutch model, all guest parents and informal caregivers, such as grandparents, are required to register with a guest parent agency. The agencies are responsible for verifying qualifications (at least a three-year qualification in the domain of care and welfare), checking health and safety aspects of their homes (a clean, safe and smoke-free home), the maximum number of children they care for at any one time (no more than four children under the age of 12), and also their financial accountability and insurance. In 2013, the British coalition government announced that it would follow the example of the Netherlands by setting up childminder agencies to take care of the paperwork for childminders and, they hoped, to encourage new entrants (DfE, 2014). However, at the time of writing in February 2016, the process has been very slow and childminder numbers have continued to decline.

Insofar as conclusions can be drawn from the composition of the childcare market, these are:

- The market is fragmented in terms of provider size, which varies from very large to very small operators, with a trend toward large for-profit organizations.
- It is a market in which large (for-profit) providers, whose financial basis is sometimes fraught with risk (in the Netherlands), operate alongside many small-scale providers, who are also facing financial challenges (in England). Although the large companies do not completely dominate the market, they do so in many towns in the Netherlands. It has to be concluded that the supply side of the local markets is anything but transparent.
- The market is financially fragile. Profits are low in the Netherlands and difficult to ascertain in England; state subsidies are indispensable but do not guarantee sustainability. As a result, the quality and continuity of childcare are in jeopardy, as is the job security of the workforce. The for-profit companies operating in the market are subject to movements in the wider economy and fluctuations in government subsidies.

In the following, we will look at the exclusionary effects observed in the childcare markets of the two countries and at the quality and regulation of childcare.

Exclusionary Effects of the Childcare Market

The structure of the ECEC system in the UK, which until the late 1990s evolved in the absence of any large-scale government intervention, has exhibited strong continuity, with a profoundly mixed market and a large role for the private sector in both care and education for children under school age. In the Netherlands, the childcare system evolved with the help of some government financial support in the 1990s to assist employed mothers but without substantial educational aims for children. However, there has been change in policy goals and the ideas driving them since 2000. In both countries, childcare policy is struggling to balance several goals: the desire to promote child development and/or mothers' employment while at the same time controlling budgets. In the UK, these goals have been complicated further by the desire under the Labour governments prior to 2010 to address the problem of child poverty (Lewis, 2009), and the desire under governments since 2010 to address the cost-of-living crisis (Morgan, 2014). In consequence, changes in the component parts of childcare policy and in policy instruments tend to lack coherence (a problem noted as early as 2006 by Wincott).

Childcare is a matter of social and cultural preferences, as well as of weighing costs and quality. With regard to preferences, less-well-educated parents and ethnic minority families in England and the Netherlands prefer informal care by mothers, grandparents or other kin (DfE, 2012; Portegijs et al., 2014; Knijn and Saraceno, 2010), even if children are less well prepared for primary school. Simon et al. (2015) highlighted the high reliance on informal care (kin and neighbours) by young and unemployed mothers, who are also likely to be disadvantaged (see also Speight et al., 2015).

In both countries, many parents are not yet using ECEC on a full-time basis for children under school age. There are many reasons for this, which may include the quality of provision available and its costs, in addition to normative ideas about childrearing. But governments in both countries have invested heavily in ECEC.

In the Netherlands, full-time childcare is available for babies from ten weeks at a low cost for low-income families, but costs are reimbursed only if the parent(s) is/are employed, and only in relation to the working hours of the parent with the fewest working hours. Therefore, while full-time childcare is available, data show that the 43 per cent of children under age four who are in childcare use only 600 hours per year on average, a decline of 200 hours since 2013 (Brancheorganisatie Kinderopvang, 2015). Dutch data also show that childcare is mainly used by middle- and higher-income families (CBS, 2016). Akgündüz and Plantenga (2014a) have found that there are no differences in attendance at formal care settings when both playgroups and childcare centres are taken into account, but that higher-income parents are more likely to use childcare centres while lower-income parents tend to use playgroups. Noailly and Visser (2009) conclude that parents in low-income neighbourhoods may have no access to formal childcare at all and may be isolated from the larger market. This is because markets react to the demand and purchasing power in neighbourhoods, which implies that policies are needed to make childcare accessible for low-income families. However, such policies also have to be sensitive to what parents want for their children.

The English system of financing ECEC is complex, with different exclusionary effects. All providers are eligible to receive public funding for the free hours of early years education (so long as they offer the early years foundation stage curriculum). In addition, private for-profit, not-for-profit and independent providers (which include childminders) also offer early years care, which is state subsidized via tax credits and employers' vouchers, both of which go to employed parents. Part-time early years education is funded out of taxation and is available to all three- and four-year-olds and to disadvantaged two-year-olds. The government relies on demand-side funding: the amount of money spent on the free early education entitlement depends on the number of children participating, while the tax credits for early years care go to parents who are employed 16 or more hours a week and who then buy care. Vouchers, which are administered by employers and are less generous than tax credits, are available to parents who do not draw tax credits. In addition, the entitlement to part-time free hours of early education is universal for three- and four-year-olds, while the free hours for two-year-olds are restricted to the 40 per cent most disadvantaged. The take-up of part-time free early education is very high in England, but there are substantial differences between the poor and better-off: while 94 per cent of parents earning more than £45000 a year take advantage of the free hours, only 80 per cent of parents earning less than £10000 a year do the same. Only 58 per cent of parents take up the free hours offered to disadvantaged two-year-olds (NAO, 2016). A report commissioned by the Department of Education (NAO, 2016) found that awareness of the entitlement was particularly low among Bangladeshi, Somali and Polish parents. Also, many parents need to buy extra hours of early years care, but in 2011, the proportion of childcare costs covered by tax credits was cut from 80 to 70 per cent. While tax credits benefit the less-well-off, it has remained difficult for parents to afford the extra childcare that would allow them to increase their hours of work.

With regard to the exclusionary effects of the childcare market, the costs of childcare are shared by three parties under the 2005 Dutch Childcare Act: employers, the state and parents. After a policy based on voluntary contributions failed (Yerkes, 2014), employers have paid a fixed tax in the amount of about 0.50 per cent of the gross wage of all employees (not just those with children) since 2007. In effect, employers contribute one-sixth of the cost of childcare per child, and if both parents are employed, this contribution covers about one-third of the costs per child. Since 2012, (household) income-related tax allowances in the Netherlands have been based on the working hours of the parent who works the fewest hours per week (childcare costs are compensated for 140 per cent of these working hours) alongside the parent's income (the higher the income, the smaller the tax reduction) and the costs per hour of the selected childcare provider (up to a maximum of about €6). The introduction of this new working-hours-related calculation means that the costs of childcare have increased for many parents, which in large measure accounts for the withdrawal of children from formal childcare.

It is therefore not straightforward to work out the winners and losers in the childcare market. These rather diverse and fragmented market-based systems have an effect on the fees that parents must pay. In the Netherlands in 2011 (most recent data available), parents had to pay a higher rate per hour than the legally set maximum in 50 per cent of the childcare centres, and they had to pay the difference out of their own pockets (CPB, 2011). In addition, until 2012, many childcare centres offered only full-day childcare. In consequence, parents with a part-time job had the choice between paying for the full 12 hours of care per day or doing without childcare completely. Due to this combination of strict funding policies and for-profit provision in a period of economic downturn (from 2012), low-income parents in particular withdrew their children; their use of childcare decreased by 15 per cent from 2014 to 2015, while the figure was about 7 per cent for middle-income parents and only 4 per cent for high-income parents (Asscher, 2015). In England, the costs to parents of early years care that are not covered by tax credits are high. The fee paid for 25 hours of early years care for a child aged 2+ rose 69 per cent over the period 2005–2015, while inflation measured by the Consumer Price Index rose only 28 per cent (DfE, 2015). In addition, the burden of fees does not fall evenly. Alakeson and Hurrell (2012) found that couples who work full-time and have two pre-school children were likely to spend more than 10 per cent of their net income on childcare, with the proportion peaking at around 30 per cent for those earning slightly more than median household income.

Public funding for childcare suggests a measure of acceptance of ECEC as a 'public good' in both countries. But given its labour-intensive character and the need for qualified staff, good-quality childcare is expensive (Folbre, 2008; Paull, 2014). In practice, many lower- and middle-income families struggle to pay for early years care out of their own pockets. In the Dutch system, parents are sensitive to fluctuations and insecure about how much they will be able to afford to spend on childcare. This affects low-income families above all and therefore hinders equal access to childcare. In England, too, access remains a problem, especially for lower-income parents, but other issues are also important, in particular the quality of care.

Childcare as a Matter for State Intervention: Quality and Regulation

Following the argument of the 'Introduction' to this volume, childcare might be defined as a matter for state intervention, which on moral grounds should not be treated as a market commodity. In consequence, the state should engage in activities that purposely limit the risks of the market. This view is only partly in line with what the European Council agreed on at the Barcelona Summit by setting targets for childcare provision and making member states responsible for meeting these targets. The OECD (2015) has also recommended investment in quality childcare in order to secure child development and avoid child poverty, primarily by encouraging mothers' employment. From that perspective, childcare can be seen as a matter requiring state intervention. In the 'Introduction' to this book, the authors argue that the free-market exchange of a good should be blocked if its commodification is not morally permissible. However, neither the European Council at the Barcelona Summit nor the OECD have drawn the conclusion that childcare should be provided as a public service; their only concern is the coverage of ECEC provision. So far, the UK and the Netherlands are the only EU member states in which ECEC is state regulated but mainly (England) or completely (the Netherlands) delivered by the market. This exceptional position also leads to a focus on the quality of the service and policies to regulate market provision in order to guarantee good-quality care for young children, a vulnerable group of the population. In most evaluations of the quality of childcare three criteria are central: health and safety, staff-to-child ratios and staff qualifications.

Comparing the two countries, it appears that the Netherlands performs less well than England in all matters but the crucial one of staff qualifications. Interestingly, in both countries it is public providers – playgroups in the Netherlands and nursery schools in England – which offer the highest quality of ECEC (Akgündüz and Plantenga, 2014a; Sylva et al., 2004).

Regulation in the Netherlands is the responsibility of local authorities and enforced by local public health offices, while in England this responsibility has been transferred from the local authorities to the national Office for Standards in Education, Children's Services and Skills (Ofsted). Evaluation studies conducted by the Dutch Consortium on Childcare Research (Nederlands Consortium Kinderopvang Onderzoek, NCKO) concluded that the quality of childcare fell far below international standards on all criteria as the supply of childcare places increased rapidly in the period from 1995 to 2008. According to the researchers, this might be explained by the rapid growth of childcare provision and, after the 2005 Childcare Act, the childcare market, combined with shortages of qualified personnel and greater work pressures. The same consortium found that average quality ratings increased after 2008, although only a few centres were rated good (compared with none in 2008) (Fukkink et al., 2013; de Kruif et al., 2009; Vermeer et al., 2005). However, Akgündüz and Plantenga (2014b) questioned whether the decline observed between 2005 and 2008 was a direct result of privatization, and pointed out that the market has been able to provide the number of places needed since the 2005 legislation.

In England, places had to be found for the increased numbers of children covered by the free early education entitlement, in and of itself difficult in poor areas, and additionally so in respect of the quality necessary to improve their opportunities. Indeed, many commentators expressed concern about the quality of the large number of early years places that became available in a relatively short period of time. In 2014, a report called for a delay in the expansion of the entitlement until good-quality places could be guaranteed (Mathers et al., 2014). A majority of both two- and three-year-olds were in the (mainly) private for-profit and not-for-profit sector, where staff tended to have lower qualifications (House of Lords, 2015; Family and Childcare Trust, 2014). Commenting in 2013 on the proposed extension of funded places for two-year-olds, the House of Commons' Education Committee said, 'We have concerns about the funding, the quality of providers, the availability of places in effective settings and the impact on places for other age groups' (House of Commons Education Committee, 2013, p. 4). Data from the regulator, Ofsted, on the standards reached by ECEC providers lend some support to concerns about the quality of provision being created. The proportion of two-year-olds in provision ranked by Ofsted as 'outstanding' in 2015 was 17 per cent, and 21 per cent for three- and four-year-olds. But 12–13 per cent of two-, three- and four-year-olds were in provision deemed only satisfactory or requiring improvement, and 2–3 per cent were in 'inadequate' provision (DfE, 2015).

In both the Netherlands and England, availability seems to have been prioritized over quality in the rapid expansion of childcare provision, and there has been little effort to strengthen state regulation. In the Netherlands the problem was not so much staff qualifications but a lack of regulation, control and inspections. Reliance on the market to secure quality seemed to be successful at first, but a dramatic incident caused a national scandal that led to stricter regulations and inspections. The discovery of large-scale sexual abuse of about 80 babies and young children and the distribution of child pornography by a male childcare worker in an Amsterdam childcare centre in 2010 brought to the fore the failings of both regulation and inspection of the childcare market. The 2005 Childcare Act set out the qualifications needed for childcare workers (but not the owners) of private childcare centres. In addition, too much confidence had been placed in parents' ability as consumers to distinguish between high- and low-quality provision. Lack of both information and alternative provision made consumerist behaviour difficult, particularly before 2012. Finally, regulation of childcare workers' daily work practices fell short when it came to safeguarding children. In reaction, the responsible minister, in cooperation with interested organizations (employers' organization MOgroep, parents' organization BOinK, and the Netherlands Youth Institute, NJi), developed additional guidelines for childcare centres, such as the Open Door policy (under which no childcare worker is allowed to be alone with a child), the requirement of all childcare workers to obtain a municipal 'Declaration of Good Behaviour', and the obligation to respond to any sign or suggestion of child abuse.

In England, the government was faced first with the problem of securing early education places for two-year-olds, and later, in 2015, with the prospect of another major expansion in the entitlement of three- and four-year-olds to a funded place for 30 (rather than 15) hours a week. In response, the decision was taken to try to expand the numbers and role of childminders, who had historically provided the most flexible and cheapest care, but whose numbers had decreased steadily since the introduction of funded places for early years education and the early years curriculum in the late 2000s. Despite the fact that childminders had long been the least-qualified group of private providers, the government sought to remove barriers to entry for them by setting up childminder agencies (see above). The qualifications of childcare workers are a major aspect of the quality of childcare; only highly qualified staff can guarantee the development and protection of young children. Comparative studies have shown the extent to which the early years workforce in the UK remains low paid and low qualified (EC et al., 2014). In England in 2013, 87 per cent of staff in formal settings were qualified to level 3 (gained at age 18), although the figure for childminders was only 66 per cent (Brind et al., 2014). The funding provided by the Labour governments in the 2000s to improve workforce training and graduate leadership was abolished by the coalition after 2010. However, the idea of early years teachers was promoted in 2013, albeit without granting crucial parity with school teachers. Thus, since 2010, there has been only moderate government support for intervention to improve the qualifications and hence the pay of the early years workforce. The first major coalition document on the early years stated that 'employers have primary responsibility for the quality and effectiveness of their staff' (DfE and DH, 2011, p. 64), a position in line with the 'hands-off' approach to regulation. However, the 2012 survey of provider finances noted that 'there is a sense amongst most providers that there is some need for staff training, but it isn't generally seen as a massively pressing concern' (Brind et al., 2012, p. 4). Private sector providers tend to employ lower-qualified staff than publicly funded institutions, which usually hire qualified teachers, and non-supervisory early years staff still earn only a little above the minimum wage.

Given the difficulties, current and anticipated, of funding the extension of the early years free hours, neither the government nor employers have much incentive to raise pay. The debate over deregulation and quality came to a head over the issue of staff-to-child ratios, which were clearly set out by Labour in 2008. In 2013, the Coalition government announced its wish to relax the ratios for all ages of pre-school children while also encouraging providers to hire a qualified teacher (DfE, 2013). The government suggested that the existing ratios led to both higher costs for parents and lower pay for staff. But relaxing ratios in a country with a low-qualified and low-paid workforce posed considerable difficulties and aroused intense opposition from private sector provider organizations as well as campaigners such as Mumsnet and Netmums (House of Commons Debates, 11.6.13, col. 231). Most damagingly, the Liberal coalition partners withdrew their support (ibid., cols 236–237), and this deregulation plan was dropped. The main reason why the debate over ratios had been so intense was because it was seen as a particularly important opportunity to tackle affordability, availability and quality: the higher ratio permitted by the presence of a teacher would make it possible to take more children, which in turn would financially benefit providers and hence, it was hoped, bring down costs for parents and increase pay for staff, while also securing better-quality childcare (DfE, 2013). The ratio issue encapsulates the complicated tensions at the heart of ECEC provision in a childcare market. The different policy dimensions lacked consistency in relation to promoting quality: for example, increasing the number of childminders received as much encouragement as, and more practical support than, increasing the proportion of graduates in the workforce. Deregulation has been key to Conservative thinking on quality, which has centred on the promotion of the childcare market first and foremost and, as the means to that, the restriction of government regulation at both central and local level.

Qualifications in the Netherlands are less problematic: childcare workers need at minimum a three-year qualification. Working without such a qualification is not allowed, and one-third of the childcare workers have a higher qualification (a four-year higher vocational degree in social pedagogy). In addition, volunteers and interns work in childcare centres under the supervision of paid staff. But while qualifications are not a concern, continuity of staff is. As large childcare companies reorganized and merged in order to achieve greater efficiency, they also moved from permanent to flexible contracts, towards more agency workers, and away from (almost) full-time jobs to short-hour part-time jobs. This might be a wise market policy given the fluctuation in demand and public subsidies, but it is problematic for both the children and the workforce. Brancheorganisatie Kinderopvang (2015) shows that in the large childcare companies about one-third of the staff left their jobs, and half of them were replaced mainly by agency workers, who were offered worse working conditions (as casual employees). This development has been mentioned by parents as one of the reasons for withdrawing their children, who experience care by too many different people during a week.

9.4 CONCLUSION

England and the Netherlands are exceptional cases in the EU because they make such extensive use of private childcare providers. This raises the question whether, for what reasons, and how state intervention is legitimized. Arguments for the marketization of childcare have been made in both countries in the name of achieving greater efficiency and effectiveness in supply, as well as increasing parental choice of the kind of childcare they prefer. Arguments for state intervention, as outlined in the 'Introduction' to this book, include the guarantee this gives in terms of accessibility by redistributing the costs of childcare and the protection of what is deemed to be a moral good, and that it helps to regulate the quality of care and performance. In addition, it is argued that public services are legitimate if they outperform market provision; however we were unable to analyse this aspect in our chapter because both the Netherlands and England have only a few public ECEC services left above and beyond the pre-school education offered to four-year-olds by schools (playgroups in the Netherlands and nursery schools in England). These services have been shown to deliver better quality, but their coverage is limited.

Our analysis of the childcare market found it to be fragile, fragmented and not very transparent, as well as dependent to a large extent on public financial support and regulation. Both countries have invested a lot of money in childcare in order to stimulate mothers' employment and children's development, especially for those from disadvantaged families, and so promote equal opportunities. In the Netherlands in particular, we have shown that without stable and continuous government support, the market is susceptible to downturns in times of crisis, when parents are likely to feel that the rising costs of childcare are too high in relation to the quality of care offered.

The accessibility of childcare remains a sensitive issue. Childcare is costly if quality of care is to be assured. In spite of government efforts in both countries to redistribute the costs of childcare through access to free part-time early years education (in England) and through tax allowances, tax credits and vouchers for early years care, these policies, as well as parents' own preferences, erect barriers to participation. Eligibility for state-subsidized childcare is restricted in the Netherlands in that tax allowances are confined to working parents, who must also find the money to pay for full daycare (12 hours). While offering only full-day care serves to stabilize the income of providers, not many parents would actively choose such long days of childcare. The English approach of tax credits and vouchers for working parents also risks excluding the poorest children with unemployed parents.

Market restrictions to accessibility result in different patterns of demand, which means that fewer providers offer childcare in poorer neighbourhoods than in better-off ones. This limits poor parents' free choice of a childcare provider. In the Netherlands, better-off parents have limited free choice too, because a few large childcare chains dominate the market; a fact which is hidden by the offer of various services under different names. In England, restrictions arise from the high fees charged to parents beyond the free early education entitlement and the subsidized hours of early years care, together with the often poor quality of provision, which is related to low staff qualifications. Nor does poor-quality childcare contribute much to children's development. All in all, we come to the conclusion that market imperfections call for state intervention, and that a clear, coherent and stable childcare policy is necessary to guarantee accessible and high quality care.

Regulation of the childcare market is, finally, a much-debated policy issue. Quality and accessibility tend to conflict with affordability. Improving childcare quality by increasing staff qualifications and pay, and ensuring equal access, will require higher public expenditure given that private providers must make a profit.

NOTES

1. ECEC policy is devolved in the UK, however some policies and some data sets refer to the UK.
2. The compulsory school age is five in both countries.
3. Playgroups (*peuterspeelzalen* in Dutch) are intended to contribute to the social and cognitive development of pre-school children.
4. Notably, Berkhout et al. (2009) were unable to establish with certainty which childcare centres belonged to the four largest providers because they are registered under various names in the Chamber of Commerce register. Berkhout et al. therefore warn that the share of the big four is probably underestimated.

REFERENCES

Akgündüz, Y.E. and J. Plantenga (2014a). Equal access to high-quality childcare in the Netherlands. In L. Gambaro, K. Stewart and J. Waldfogel (eds), *An Equal Start? Providing Quality Early Education and Care for Disadvantaged Children*, Bristol: Policy Press, pp. 101–121.

Akgündüz, Y.E. and J. Plantenga (2014b). Childcare in the Netherlands: lessons in privatization. *European Early Childhood Education Research Journal*, 22(3), 379–385.

Alakeson, V. and A. Hurrell (2012). *Counting the Costs of Childcare*, London: Resolution Foundation.

Asscher, L. (2015). Cijfers Kinderopvang 2014, Brief aan de Voorzitter van de Tweede Kamer der Staten-Generaal. Den Haag: Ministerie van Sociale Zaken en Werkgelegenheid.

Berkhout, A., P.E.F. Poel, L. Heuts and M. Gemmeke (2009). Marktwerking in de Kinderopvang. Amsterdam: Regioplan.

Bonoli, G. and D. Natali (2012). *The Politics of the New Welfare State*, Oxford: Oxford University Press.

Boogaard, M. and I. Bollen (2014). Gastouders in beeld. Een inventarisatiestudie onder gastouders in Nederland. Rapport 928, Amsterdam: Kohnstamm Instituut & NCKO.

Brancheorganisatie Kinderopvang (2015). Brancherapport 2015, Sector Kinderopvang 2015: feiten, cijfers & ontwikkelingen.

Brind, R., S. McGinigal, J. Lewis and S. Ghezelayagh (2014). Childcare and Early Years Providers Survey 2013. TNS BMRB Report JN 117328, London: DfE.

Brind, R., O. Norden and D. Oseman (2012). Childcare provider finances survey. Research Report DFE-RR213, London: DfE.

Centraal Bureau voor de Statistiek (CBS) (2016). Statline. http://statline.cbs.nl/Statweb.

Centraal Planbureau (CPB) (2011). Kinderopvang in kaart. Op verzoek van het Ministerie van Sociale Zaken en Werkgelegenheid, Den Haag: Centraal Panbureau.

de Kruif, R.E.L., J.M.A. Riksen-Walraven, M.J.J.M. Gevers Deynoot-Schaub, K.O.W. Helmerhorst, L.W.C. Tavecchio and R.G. Fukkink (2009). Pedagogische kwaliteit van de opvang voor 0- tot 4-jarigen in Nederlandse kinderdagverblijven in 2008. Nederlands Consortium Kinderopvang Onderzoek.

Department for Education (DfE) (2012). Provision for children under five years of age in England: January 2012. Statistical First Release. London: DfE.

Department for Education (DfE) (2013). *More Great Childcare. Raising Quality and Giving Parents more Choice*, London: DfE.

Department for Education (DfE) (2014). *Childminder Agencies and Changes to the Local Authority Role*, London: DfE.

Department for Education (DfE) (2015). Review of childcare costs: the analytical report. DFE-00295-2015. London: DfE.

Department for Education (DfE) and Department of Health (DH) (2011). *Supporting Families in the Foundation Years*, London: DfE.

Esping-Andersen, G. (2009). *Why We Need a New Welfare State*, Oxford: Oxford University Press.

EC/EACEA/Eurydice/Eurostat (2014). Key data on early childhood education and care in Europe. Eurydice and Eurostat Report, Brussels: EACEA.

Family and Childcare Trust (2014). *Where Next for Childcare?*, London: Family & Childcare Trust.

Folbre, N. (2008). *Valuing Children: Rethinking the Economics of the Family*, Cambridge, MA: Harvard University Press.

Fukkink, R.G., M.J.J.M Gevers Deynoot-Schaub, K.O.W. Helmerhorst, I. Bollen and J.M.A. Riksen-Walraven (2013). Pedagogische kwaliteit van de opvang voor 0- tot 4- jarigen in Nederlandse kinderdagverblijven 2008. Nederlands Consortium Kinderopvang Onderzoek.

Gaunt, C. (2014). Nursery chains: league tables – all in order. *Nursery World*, 17 November.

Heckman, J. (2006). Skill formation and the economics of investing in disadvantaged children. *Science*, 312(5782), 1900–1902.
Hemerijck, A. (2013). *Changing Welfare States*, Oxford: Oxford University Press.
HM Treasury (2015). Public expenditure statistical analyses 2015. Accessed 30 March 2016 at https//www.gov.uk/government/statistics/public-expenditure-statistical-analyses-2015.
House of Commons Education Committee (2013). Foundation years: Sure Start children's centres. HC364-I.
House of Lords Select Committee on Affordable Childcare (2015). *Report, HL Paper 117*, London: Stationery Office.
Knijn, T. and C. Saraceno (2010). Family law and family policy reforms in Italy and the Netherlands: different timing, increasingly different focuses. *Journal of European Social Policy*, 20(5), 444–455.
Kvist, J. (2013). The post-crisis European social model: developing or dismantling social investments?. *Journal of International and Comparative Social Policy*, 29(1), 91–107.
Leseman, P. and P. Slot (2014). Breaking the cycle of poverty: challenges for European early childhood education and care. *European Early Childhood Education Research Journal*, 22(93), 314–326. DOI: 10.1080/1350293X.2014.912894.
Lewis, J. (2009). *Work–Family Balance, Gender and Policy*, Cheltenham, UK and Northampton, MA, USA: Edward Elgar Publishing.
Mathers, S., K. Sylva and N. Eisenstadt (2014). *Sound Foundations*, London: Sutton Trust.
Morgan, T. (2014). *There's a Cost of Living Crisis*, London: Centre for Policy Studies.
Musgrave, R.A. and P.B. Musgrave (1989). *Public Finance in Theory and Practice*, New York: McGraw-Hill.
National Audit Office (NAO) (2016). Entitlement to free early education and childcare. HC 853. London: Department for Education.
Noailly, J. and S. Visser (2009). The impact of market forces on child care provision: insights from the 2005 Child Care Act in the Netherlands. *Journal of Social Policy*, 38(3), 477–498.
OECD (2009). OECD Family database. Accessed 30 March 2016 at http://www.oecd.org/els/soc/PF3_2_Enrolment_in_childcare_and_preschools.pdf.
OECD (2015). Starting Strong IV: monitoring quality in early childhood education and care. DOI: 10.1787/9789264233515-en.
Paull, G. (2014). Can government intervention in childcare be justified?. *Economic Affairs*, 34(1), 14–34.
Penn, H. (2007). Childcare market management: how the United Kingdom government has reshaped its role in developing early childhood education and care. *Contemporary Issues in Early Childhood*, 8(3), 192–207.
Plantenga, J. (2012). Local providers and loyal parents: competition and consumer choice in the Dutch childcare sector. In E. Lloyd and H. Penn (eds), *Childcare Markets: Can They Deliver an Equitable Service?*, Bristol: Policy Press, pp. 63–77.
Portegijs, W., M. Cloin and A. Merens (2014). Krimp in de kinderopvang. Ouders over kinderopvang en werk. Den Haag: Sociaal en Cultureel Planbureau.
Rekenkamer (2014). Bezuinigingen op de Kinderopvangtoeslag. Realisatie en Effect. Den Haag: Rekenkamer.
Saraceno, C. and W. Keck (2010). Can we identify intergenerational policy regimes in Europe?. *European Societies, iFirst*, 25 June, 1–22.

Schäfer, A. and W. Streeck (2013). *Politics in the Age of Austerity*, Cambridge: Polity Press.

Simon, A., C. Owen and K. Hollingworth (2015). Provision and use of preschool childcare in Britain. London: Thomas Coram Research Unit, Institute of Education, UCL.

Skocpol, T. and M. Somers (1980). The use of comparative history in macrosocial inquiry. *Comparative Studies in Society and History*, 22(2), 174–197.

Speight, S., R. Maisey, J. Chanfreau, S. Lord Haywoor and D. Hussey (2015). *Study of Early Education and Development: Baseline Survey of Families*, London: DfE.

Stewart, K. (2013). Labour and the under fives: policy, spending and outcomes 1997–2010. Social Policy in a Cold Climate, Working Paper 4. London: CASE, LSE.

Stewart, K. and P. Obolenskaya (2015). The coalition's record on the under fives: policy, spending and outcomes 2010–2015. Social Policy in a Cold Climate, Working Paper 12. London: CASE, LSE.

Sylva, K., E. Mewlhuish, P. Sammons, I. Siraj-Blatchford and B. Taggart (2004). The Effective Provision of Pre-school Education (EPPE) Project: effective pre-school education, Final Report 1997–2004. London: DfES.

Vermeer, H.J., M.H. Van IJzendoorn, R.E.L. de Kruif, R.G. Fukkink, L.W.C. Tavecchio, J.M.A. Riksen-Walraven and J. Van Zeijl (2005). Kwaliteit van Nederlandse kinderdagverblijven: Trends in kwaliteit in de jaren 1995–2005. Amsterdam: NCKO.

Wincott, D. (2006). Paradoxes of New Labour social policy: toward universal child care in Europe's 'most liberal' welfare regime?. *Social Politics*, 13(2), 286–312.

Yerkes, M. (2014). Collective protection for new social risks: childcare and the Dutch welfare state. *Journal of Social Policy*. DOI: 10.1017/S0047279414000385.

PART III

Public goods

10. Housing policy and spatial inequality: recent insights from Vienna and Amsterdam

Gerlinde Gutheil-Knopp-Kirchwald and Justin Kadi

10.1 INTRODUCTION: HOUSING MARKETS, PUBLIC POLICY AND SPATIAL INEQUALITY

While pension systems, unemployment benefits and health care have received ample attention in the welfare state literature, housing arguably has not. Indeed, housing has for a long time been strikingly missing from most studies of the welfare state, not least from Esping-Andersen's (1990) seminal 'worlds of welfare' typology. For Torgersen (1987), this lack of coverage is related to the relatively low degree of de-commodification in post-war housing systems compared to other welfare spheres in Europe. In fact, even in the countries with the most de-commodified housing systems, such as Sweden or the Netherlands, private markets have continued to play a key role in the provision of housing even in the heyday of the welfare state, making housing – to borrow Torgersen's term – a potentially 'wobbly' pillar of the welfare state (ibid.; Malpass, 2008). Nonetheless, there is a broad consensus on the significance of housing policy interventions as part of the wider welfare state, with social housing in particular being a material manifestation of de-commodification efforts (Kemeny, 1995; Harloe, 1995).

Although early experiments with social housing date back to the late nineteenth century, it was certainly in the decades following World War II that more comprehensive programmes were established (Harloe, 1995). Whereas in Anglo-Saxon societies such as the United States of America (USA) political support for, and the provision of, social housing has remained marginal compared with the large homeownership sectors, a number of Western European societies have taken political measures to promote public rental housing on a more significant scale. This is also reflected in the structure of housing markets today: in the Anglo-Saxon context, the social rental sector has developed into a residual sector reserved for the very poor; it is clearly set apart from the private rental sector and the dominating homeownership sector ('dual rental system'). In the Western European context, by contrast, social housing sectors have become large and differentiated. The sector competes with the private rental and ownership sectors in terms of price level, quality and target group ('unitary' or 'integrated rental system'). Contrary to the Anglo-Saxon context, social housing has historically become a socially mixed sector (Kemeny, 1995).

Integrated rental markets with large social housing sectors and supply-side subsidies have had obvious redistributive effects and have boosted housing quality, while simultaneously lowering average housing costs (for a European comparison, see Czasny, 2004). Urban geography studies have furthermore highlighted that housing de-commodification policies lead to spatial redistribution. Building on the notion that 'where you live affects how you live', this strand of research emphasizes the nature of space as a resource and the benefits that people who live in attractive locations can accrue. Conversely, people who live in less attractive locations are excluded from accessing these resources and therefore experience various forms of spatial inequality (Musterd, 2005; Soja, 2010). By taking housing out of the private market, at least partially, social housing sectors have dampened these spatial inequalities to some extent and enabled also less affluent people to live in more attractive locations.

Arbaci (2007) examined the relationship between welfare regimes and ethnic segregation in 16 European countries and described four ideal clusters that largely correspond to Esping-Andersen's welfare models, but are additionally characterized by their resulting degrees of socio-spatial segregation (Arbaci, 2007, p. 420). According to her results, ethnic spatial concentration is relatively low in cities of the corporatist welfare cluster (for example, Vienna), moderately higher in cities of the social democratic cluster (for example, Amsterdam), and highest in cities of the liberal welfare cluster (Arbaci, 2007, p. 409). This is in line with earlier findings on the relationship between housing systems and segregation patterns that have underlined the decisive influence of housing de-commodification measures on socio-spatial patterns (see e.g. Musterd and Ostendorf, 1998).

The relationship between housing de-commodification and segregation is not linear, however. High degrees of segregation and spatial exclusion can exist in a highly decommodified environment: for Vienna, Giffinger (1998) points out that migrants used to be excluded from social housing and were therefore forced to live in run-down private rental homes, leading to ethnic segregation in a context where social housing traditionally dampened socio-economic segregation. After the opening of the municipal housing stock to migrants in 2006, many migrant households moved into social housing, leading to a de-concentration of migrants in some traditional rental areas and an increase within the municipal stock (SORA, 2010; Hatz et al., 2015, p. 97f). Musterd and Deurloo (1997) describe a similar development for Amsterdam. After the immigrant population gained access to public housing, a trend of concentration within the public housing sector was observed, paired with an increase in low-income households in this sector.

Coming back to public policy theory, Heath's article on the 'Three normative models of the welfare state' deserves attention (Heath, 2011). He distinguishes welfare state regimes by their normative justification: the redistributive model has the main purpose of reducing inequality, the communitarian model justifies state intervention in cases where market transaction is seen as immoral,[1] and the public goods model stipulates that the state should act wherever it performs more efficiently than the market. According to the last, the primary task of the state is to overcome market failure, since it is 'the only organization in society that has the ability to impose its authority on anyone found within the scope of its territory' (Heath, 2011, p. 25). Heath clearly favours the public goods model and argues that 'it alone is able to explain why, in Western democracies, state spending rose almost continuously over the course of the 20th century as a fraction of GDP [gross domestic product]' (ibid., p. 13).[2] Although his three-model typology has strong similarities to the state function theory in classical public finance (allocation/efficiency, redistribution/equality and merit goods; see Musgrave, 1957, and Chapter 1, the 'Introduction' to this book), it differs in two aspects. First, Heath's communitarian model defines moral limits of the market, whereas in the merit goods concept the state sets incentives in cases where market demand would be too low (or too high) from a long-term macroeconomic (but not necessarily moral) perspective. Second, according to the public finance literature, the different state functions are complementing each other, whereas Heath emphasizes the tension or even contradiction between the models.

This chapter looks at the influence of housing policy regimes on socio-spatial patterns in urban areas, empirically focusing on two somewhat extreme cases, namely Vienna and Amsterdam. Historically, both cities have arguably been at the forefront in de-commodifying housing in Europe. Housing policy interventions have shaped the socio-spatial layout and the social geography of the city in important ways. Our research questions are: how can we understand and describe interrelations between specific housing market structures and socio-spatial inequalities in cities like Vienna and Amsterdam? What role does the social housing sector play in creating social mix? What is the core public task in urban housing policy?

In order to capture the notion of 'spatial inequality' in empirical terms, we use three indicators, all at the level of administrative city districts: median per capita income as a measure of the local income level, the Gini coefficient as an indicator of the district's social mix,[3] and the share of social housing in each district. In our definition, a city's socio-spatial inequality is low if the difference in income levels between districts is low and the Gini coefficient within a district is high.

We summarize the traditional pillars of, and recent changes in, housing policy, study socio-spatial inequalities and try to link them to the local housing market in Vienna (section 10.2) and Amsterdam (section 10.3). Finally, in section 10.4, we draw our conclusions of the case studies and relate our findings back to the theoretical approaches.

10.2 VIENNA

Pillars of Housing Policy and Recent Changes

The most important instruments of housing policy in Vienna are the following:

- Direct provision of housing by the local government (council housing).
- Regulation of rents of the private rental stock built before 1945; due to several liberalization steps, however, (most) new rental contracts are now comparable to those for units without rent regulation (Wieser and Blaas, 2004, p. 18; Rosifka and Postler, 2010).
- Active land policy through a municipal fund that buys and develops building land and re-sells it (mainly) to housing associations.
- Supply-side subsidies for building projects, complemented with demand-side subsidies for households with high housing cost overburden rates.
- Fiscal incentives for limited-profit housing associations.[4]

Housing policy in Vienna addresses large parts of society, not only low-income groups, which can be explained by several political factors: there was a political consensus to raise living standards (also) for middle-income families and young households, who may face difficulties on the housing market and at the same time are an important group of voters. Another goal was to promote socially mixed communities and to prevent spatial concentration of the poor. Maybe the most important factor, however, was the Keynesian economic policy that shaped the post-war period in Austria.

Average housing costs, especially in cities, were supposed to be kept low to allow low wage agreements and, in turn, foster economic competitiveness (see Lugger and Amann, 2013, p. 34). Municipal housing projects in Vienna were historically built throughout the whole city, even in the most expensive districts, promoting forms of socio-spatial integration.

Another essential element of social housing in Vienna is the housing stock of limited-profit housing associations, which mainly targets middle-income households. Rents are calculated on a cost basis and are usually higher than in municipal housing but lower than in the private sector.

Despite the broad consensus for state intervention in the housing market in Austria and, even more so, in Vienna, policies have changed significantly from the 1990s onwards (Kadi, 2015; Gutheil-Knopp-Kirchwald and Kadi, 2014):

- The amendment of the rental law in 1994 led to a partial deregulation of the private rental market. The strict 'category rent system' was replaced by a close-to-market 'benchmark rent system' in new rental contracts for flats built before 1945.
- The council housing programme (new construction) was discontinued in 2004.[5] In the 1990s, municipal housing construction was already very low due to a shift to limited-profit housing associations, whose homes are, however, less accessible for low-income households.
- A 'right to buy' was introduced for the majority of new subsidized rental flats after ten years of tenure.
- Municipal housing flats were opened up to non-European Union (EU) foreigners in 2006.

With the exception of the last, all these changes point to a (partial) re-commodification of the housing system, meaning that non-market allocation and non-market prices have lost importance in the housing sector during the last two decades.

Nevertheless, Vienna is known for its long tradition of social housing: its share of municipal housing is the highest in Europe, with 24 per cent of the Viennese housing stock owned by the municipality or another public body. Together with dwellings provided by limited-profit housing associations, the social housing sector accounts for around 42 per cent of the total stock (Statistics Austria, 2011). The pre-1945 private rental stock, which is regulated as described above, accounts for 26 per cent of the building stock. Unregulated private rental units make up some 9 per cent, and owner-occupied units and other legal positions make up 24 per cent of the total stock. The social housing sector and the regulated private rental

Table 10.1 Tenure structure in Vienna by income quartiles, 2004 and 2011

	Owner (%)	Tenant, council housing (%)	Tenant, limited-profit housing (%)	Tenant, private landlord (%)	Other tenure (%)	Total (%)
2004						
1st quartile	6.9	31.6	6.8	52.4	2.3	100.0
2nd quartile	11.5	32.7	18.2	33.9	3.6	100.0
3rd quartile	16.7	22.9	19.5	40.1	0.8	100.0
4th quartile	30.2	12.4	18.7	37.9	0.8	100.0
Total	16.0	25.1	15.2	41.8	1.9	100.0
2011						
1st quartile	10.8	34.8	10.0	41.4	3.0	100.0
2nd quartile	17.1	29.1	16.8	33.6	3.4	100.0
3rd quartile	19.2	19.1	25.7	34.0	2.0	100.0
4th quartile	39.3	9.1	18.7	31.2	1.7	100.0
Total	21.5	23.6	16.8	35.6	2.5	100.0

Source: Statistics Austria (2004 and 2011), EU Statistics on Income and Living Conditions (EU-SILC). The 2011 data differ from the Statistics Austria census data for 2011 (sampling error).

sector together represent almost two-thirds of the housing stock (Statistics Austria, 2011).

The comparison of the tenure composition in 2004 and 2011 (Table 10.1) reveals a remarkable increase in the share of homeownership. This can be mainly explained by a decline of the private rental sector: many old rental buildings were converted into or replaced by condominiums, and ownership is overrepresented in new housing production.

Looking at the tenure structure by income quartile, the highest-income group is clearly overrepresented in the ownership sector and the upper middle class is overrepresented in the non-profit housing sector. The lowest-income group is concentrated in municipal housing (and increasingly so), but also in the private rental market (but less and less). For Amann and Mundt (2010) this is a sign that the Austrian housing market has not yet fully reached the status of a 'truly integrated rental market in Kemeny's sense [that] would lead to an equal distribution of poor and vulnerable households across different tenures' (Amann and Mundt, 2010, p. 40). The strongest tenure changes from 2004 to 2011 can be observed in the highest- and the lowest-income quartile, with a shift from private rental to homeownership for the first and to council housing for the latter. The following three factors may be most relevant to this development: investment in homeownership has become increasingly attractive for higher-income groups, prices in the private rental market have risen significantly, and council housing was made accessible to non-EU foreigners, who mainly belong to the low-income strata.

Spatial Inequality in Vienna

Although Vienna has a 'declared political goal of an equal distribution of the socio-economically weak population' (Hatz et al., 2015), significant socio-economic differences exist at the district level. Annual average per capita income (2010 data) in Vienna varies from €17 500 (15th district) to €25 900 (1st district); see Figure 10.1. While looking at the district level hides further small-scale differences within districts, it points to existing economic disparities within the city. Figure 10.1 also shows the Gini coefficient of income per district. The higher the Gini coefficient in a district, the higher is its local income inequality. A district with a high Gini coefficient can also be described as an area in which people of very different income groups live (socio-economic mix), whereas a district with a low Gini coefficient is home to rather homogeneous income groups. We can see that the inner city (1st district) is the most 'mixed', and the southern 11th district is the most 'homogeneous' of all Viennese districts.

With a few exceptions, the more affluent districts seem to be more mixed than the poorer districts. This fact is confirmed by a correlation analysis: a strong positive correlation can be found between average income and inequality in a district ($r^2 = 0.49$), which means that very few high-income households live in poor districts (low inequality at the low-income level), whereas all income groups are represented in more affluent districts (high inequality at the high-income level).

Does the social housing sector reflect the patterns of inequality? In a city with an integrated rental housing sector, one might also expect spatial dispersion of the social housing stock (see Amann and Mundt, 2010, p. 39), which is confirmed to a certain extent: out of 23 city districts, the centrally located 8th district, which is characterized by old (*Gründerzeit* era) buildings, has the lowest share of social housing[6] at 10.4 per cent, while the 11th district in the southeast of Vienna has the highest share at 63.4 per cent. Even if there are strong differences in the presence of social housing, there is no obvious link between income levels and the share of social housing in a district. The correlation analysis also confirms the lack of correlation ($r^2 = 0.02$).

In most of the inner-city districts (districts 1–9) and the densely built-up western outskirts (districts 15–18), private rental is the dominant tenure. The traditional workers' districts (10–12, 20) as well as the modern

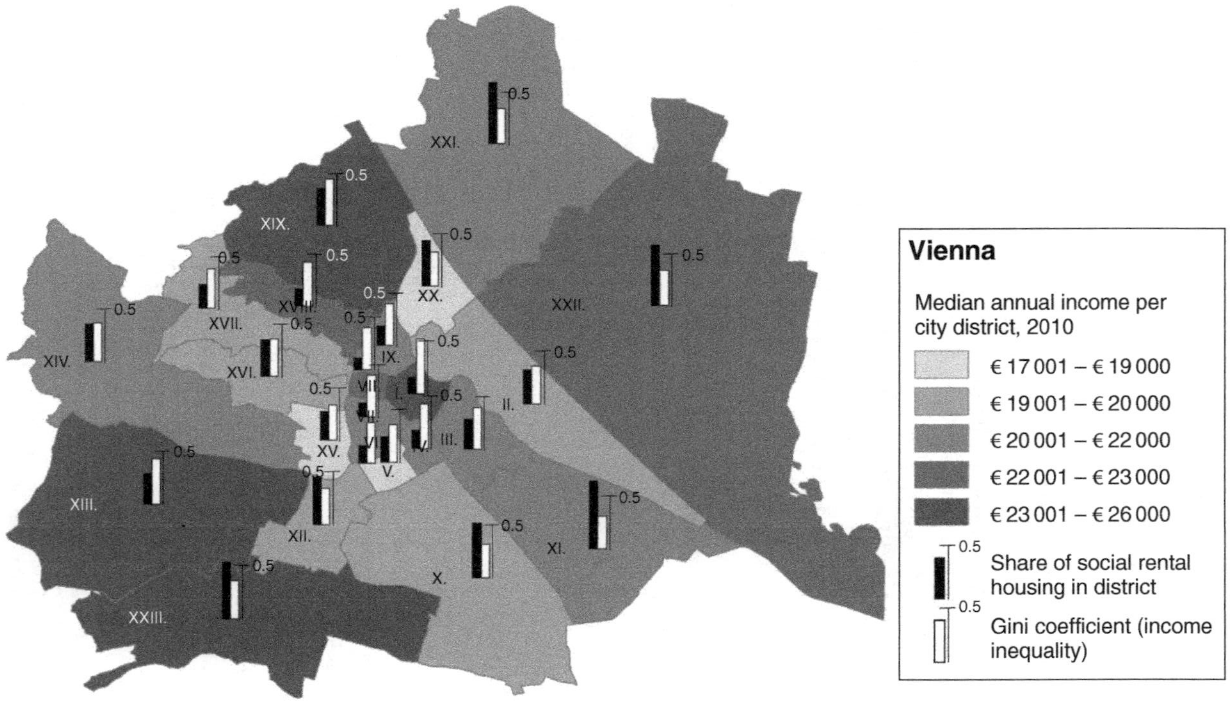

Source: Authors' figure based on Statistics Austria income statistics data for 2010 and census data for 2011. The share of social housing is defined as the share of rental dwellings owned by a public authority or by a limited-profit housing association among all dwellings in the distict. The Gini coefficient data were provided by M. Moser (Vienna University of Economics and Business) and M. Schnetzer (Chamber of Labour, Vienna).

Figure 10.1 Share of social rental housing, income level and income inequality in the city districts of Vienna

Transdanubian districts (21, 22) are dominated by social rental tenure. Only in three rather affluent districts (13, 14, 19) owner occupation is the most common tenure, but it remains below 50 per cent even there.

There seems to be a correlation between income inequality and dominant tenure, which is confirmed by the correlation analysis: it shows a significant (linear) negative correlation between the share of social housing and income inequality in a district ($r^2 = 0.48$). Districts with a high share of subsidized housing have a rather homogeneous income structure. By contrast, districts dominated by private housing tend to be inhabited by households on the edges of the income scale, meaning high inequality or, put differently, a high degree of social mix. These are mainly the inner-city districts that have an old building stock and many old, inexpensive rental contracts, but at the same time are attractive for 'gentrifiers' who live in refurbished, pricey flats. In light of strict rent regulation coupled with the discriminatory access to social housing, private rental was for a long time a vital alternative for many low-income households, particularly people with a migrant background. Lately, however, investment and gentrification have taken off in a number of neighbourhoods, spurred also by urban renewal and the deregulation of the rent law, which has attracted higher-income earners.

10.3 AMSTERDAM

Pillars of the Housing Policy and Recent Changes

Amsterdam's housing market has been shaped by a national policy of de-commodification. The Dutch Housing Act of 1901 created the legal basis for public and non-profit housing organizations. State intervention became even stronger in the 1950s, when the private rental market was more tightly regulated and the focus of housing policy shifted towards the promotion of social rental housing. The political ideal of raising living standards through state service provision played a key role in the establishment of the Dutch post-war housing regime created by post-war reconstruction efforts. These efforts went further than in most other Western European countries, where de-commodification measures as part of the post-war welfare state did not attain such a prominent role as in the Netherlands. State housing provision was supposed to ensure low housing costs and to free up household resources for mass consumption while at the same time establishing housing as a pillar of Keynesian growth management (Boelhouwer et al., 1992). The Dutch post-war housing policy had three main pillars:

- extensive subsidies for the construction of new social housing units;
- strict rent regulation and tenant protection; and
- the establishment of non-profit housing co-operatives, which provide social housing in exchange for public subsidies.

Complementing these national policies, the city of Amsterdam (among other Dutch cities) pursued an active land policy: most of the building land in Amsterdam is publicly owned and handed over for development on the legal basis of a building lease (ground rent), dampening the effect of land price developments on construction costs.

The tenure structure in Amsterdam well reflects the scope of political intervention: in 2009, out of 390 000 dwellings in Amsterdam, 49 per cent were social housing units, 29 per cent were owner-occupied and 22 per cent were private rental units. Additionally, 80 per cent of the private rental sector (approximately 18 per cent of the total housing stock) was under rent regulation and partly allocated through waiting lists. All in all, some two-thirds of the housing stock in Amsterdam is not under direct private market influence but is part of the regulated rental stock, which justifies characterizing the city's housing market as a 'pseudo market' (van der Veer and Schuiling, 2005).

Regulated rental housing in Amsterdam is not reserved for the poor but is quite mixed in terms of the socio-economic profile of its inhabitants. Following from its sheer size and the long-standing deliberate policy intention of promoting a socio-economic mix, the sector houses people with low, medium and high incomes. Low-income households rely the most on the sector, as Table 10.2 demonstrates. Of the 20 per cent poorest households in Amsterdam (first income quintile), some 90 per cent live in a regulated (that is, rent-controlled private rental or social rental) apartment. Very few of them are owner-occupiers and even fewer live in non-regulated rental homes. Among households in the second quintile, the share of those in the regulated sector is almost equally high at almost 80 per cent. However, households in the third, fourth and even fifth income quintiles are also represented in the de-commodified sectors, albeit with lower shares. For them, owner-occupation is clearly of greater significance: more than 60 per cent of the richest 20 per cent in Amsterdam own the home they are living in. Compared to the tenure composition in 1995, the regulated sector in 2009 is targeted more strongly to lower-income groups.

Since the mid-1990s, Amsterdam's housing regime has come under political pressure. National, local and also recent EU policies have promoted a reduction of state intervention and the return to a 'small state' in the housing sphere (see Kadi and Musterd, 2015). In many ways, the Netherlands seem to have followed a standard recipe for neoliberal

Table 10.2 Tenure structure in Amsterdam by income quintiles, 1995 and 2009

%	Owner-occupied housing	Regulated housing	Private rental housing	Total
1995				
1st quintile	3	84	13	100.0
2nd quintile	3	72	24	100.0
3rd quintile	6	70	23	100.0
4th quintile	11	57	31	100.0
5th quintile	35	28	37	100.0
2009				
1st quintile	6	93	1	100.0
2nd quintile	13	86	2	100.0
3rd quintile	32	65	3	100.0
4th quintile	48	41	11	100.0
5th quintile	73	14	13	100.0

Note: Regulated housing refers to social or private rental dwellings with rents below the liberalization limit, private rental housing means private rental dwellings with rents above the liberalization limit. Figures may not add up to 100% due to rounding.

Source: Authors' calculation based on municipal statistics.

welfare restructuring, with the termination of supply-side subsidies, the quasi-privatization of housing associations (Salet, 1999), the liberalization of rent control, and programmes to support homeownership representing key policy changes. Clearly, today, homeownership (rather than social rental housing) is the preferred tenure among policy-makers and support for it has largely replaced programmes to decouple housing from the private market through de-commodification. In 2006, fiscal support for homeowners through mortgage interest payment deduction totalled some €14 billion. By contrast, some €3 billion was spent on the only remaining subsidy for renters, namely housing allowances (Conijn, 2008). Additionally, programmes for the targeted sale of social housing units have been implemented, and sales have recently taken off (AFWC, 2013).

Spatial Inequality in Amsterdam

Although the overall variation in median income between municipal districts in Amsterdam is moderate, median annual income was between €20460 and around €27600 in 2009. Median income was highest in the district of Zeeburg in the eastern part of the city. Adding the Gini index to this picture as a measure of income distribution gives an indication of the social geography within districts. The population is more heterogeneous in terms of income in the inner districts (particularly Binnenstad, Oud-West, Oud-Zuid), whereas it tends to be more homogeneous in the outer districts, particularly in Zuidoost (see also Figure 10.2).

Combining these two dimensions, one can see that there is no clear relationship between the income level of a district and its socio-economic structure. Even though median incomes and also the Gini index tend to be higher in the inner districts – that is, the population is more heterogeneous – there is no direct pattern discernible. Put differently, the highest-income areas are not necessarily more mixed, and vice versa.

Clearly, social housing is spread over the city; even in the districts with the lowest share, almost one-third of all units are made up of social housing. Nonetheless, there is substantial variation: while social housing accounts for almost three-quarters (74 per cent) of all homes in the district with the highest share, it is not even half that (around 31 per cent) in the district with the lowest share. There is a geographical trend discernible that social housing is more represented in the outer districts than in the inner districts.

The picture gets clearer when other housing market segments are taken into account. The owner-occupied stock is spread very evenly over the city, with all districts having at least 23 per cent owner-occupied units and the district with the highest share having only 37 per cent. The differences between the districts in terms of housing stock then mainly relate to whether the social rental sector is dominant or whether there is a balance between the social rental and the private rental sectors. The inner districts of the canal belt and towards the south (Central, Oud-Zuid and Zuideramstel) have a balanced tenure structure, with a relatively higher importance of the private rental market. By contrast, the outer districts are dominated by social rental housing.

What is the relationship of housing sectors with median income? First, the districts with the highest share of social housing also have a comparatively low median income level. This relationship is far from clear, however (non-significant negative correlation between median income and share of social housing per district; $r^2 = 0.24$). The newly built Zeeburg area, for instance, in the east of the city, has the highest median income, but also an average share of social housing. Similarly, Westerpark is a middle-income district, but still has a medium share of social rental housing. From the relatively crude measures applied, there seems to be no direct link between the level of income and the prevalence of social housing. Put differently, social housing can be found in some relatively rich districts of Amsterdam too.

Compared to Vienna, the spatial link between social housing and income

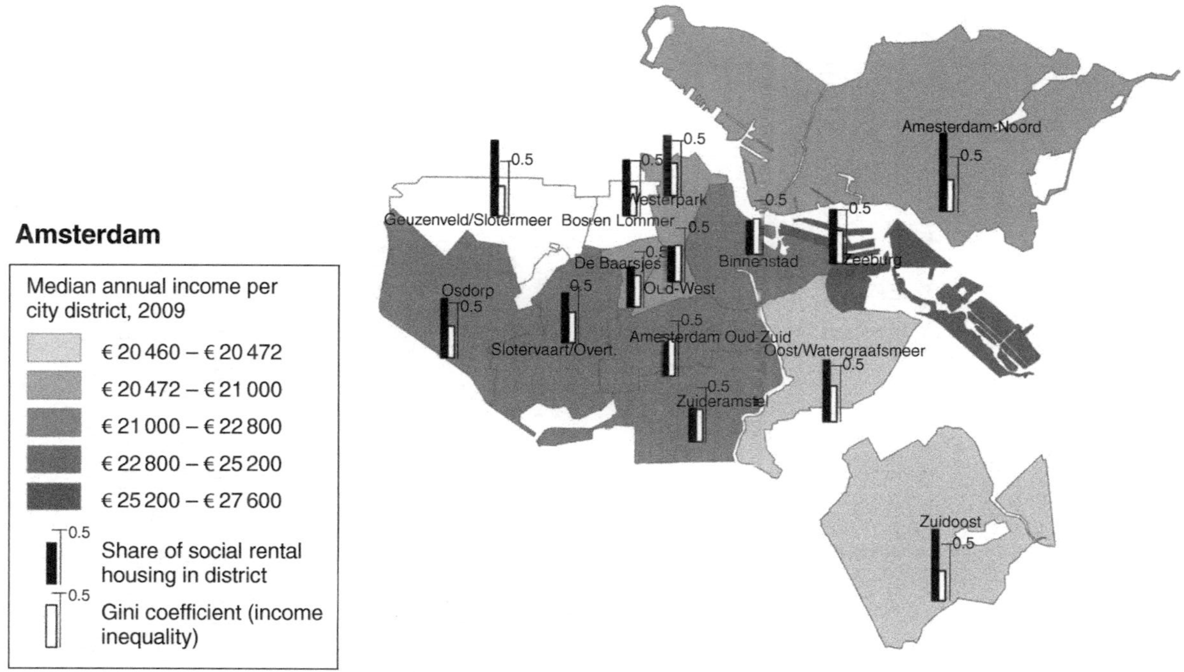

Source: Authors' calculation based on municipal statistics. The figure is based on the 1998 classification of districts to ensure data consistency.

Figure 10.2 Share of social rental housing, income level and income inequality in the city districts of Amsterdam

(in)equality is not so clear. Districts with high social rental shares tend to have a more homogeneous income structure, resulting in a weak negative correlation between Gini coefficient and the share of social housing ($r^2 = 0.33$), but there is no significant correlation as in Vienna.

10.4 SYNTHESIS AND CONCLUSIONS

How can we describe and understand the interrelations between specific housing market structures and socio-spatial inequalities in cities like Amsterdam or Vienna? What role does the social housing sector play in the creation of socio-economically mixed neighbourhoods?

Both cities have a large decommodified housing sector, and the social rental sector addresses broad income groups and competes with the private market. Therefore, the markets can still be characterized as integrated rental markets in Kemeny's sense, but with a trend toward polarization within the social sector, paired with a growing concentration of vulnerable groups within the low-priced subsector. The comparably new subsidized housing stock is inhabited to a great extent by middle-income families, particularly in Vienna.

At the same time, both cities are facing increasing difficulties to ensure access to the social and regulated housing sector for low-income households and new entrants. The problem is exacerbated further by rapidly growing demand in the low-price segment due to immigration; by stable or even shrinking real incomes of low-income households; and by the trend towards smaller households. In Vienna, it is further reinforced by the fact that tenants have the right to transfer social or regulated rental contracts to family members, which reduces the supply for new entrants.

In Vienna, social housing seems to have had an influence on the creation of a locally balanced social structure. However, the social mix – defined as different income groups living close to each other – is more diverse in districts dominated by the private rental sector, which can partly be explained by a differentiated rental regime within the pre-war building stock: while the majority of rental contracts were entered into after the reform of 1994 (approximately 150 000 units in the benchmark rent system), many tenants still benefit from regulated old rental contracts (approximately 60 000 units in Vienna).[7] However, the number of inexpensive private rental contracts in the *Gründerzeit* districts is declining due to gentrification, investment and deregulation, so the social mix may come under pressure: first, demand for ('very') social housing[8] may be expected to rise further, and the waiting lists are already long today.[9] Second, low-income households not (yet) sheltered in the social housing sector may be expected to face overcrowding and/

or drastically rising housing costs in the private rental sector. And finally, there is a risk of rising spatial fragmentation when inner-city districts are no longer accessible to households with low or medium incomes. A recent comparative study (Tammaru et al., 2015) shows that in Vienna, the small-scale spatial segregation of the lowest social group has increased significantly from 2001 to 2011 and is now among the highest among European capital cities (ibid., p. 362f).

In Amsterdam, the reduction of the social housing sector in many inner-city districts with attractive locations is gradually pushing low-income households to the fringes of the city and into less attractive residential neighbourhoods. Tenant protection in existing contracts is relatively strong, but newcomers find it hard to get access to central locations as the social housing stock is shrinking (Uitermark and Bosker, 2014). The low degree of socio-spatial inequality is increasingly threatened by measures to re-commodify the housing stock (Kadi and Musterd, 2015). A growing spatial segregation trend was observed in Amsterdam during the 1990s. This trend was (probably temporarily) interrupted by the economic crisis, which led to reduced residential mobility and a slight desegregation tendency (Tammaru et al., 2015, p. 363).

What is the legitimation of public sector intervention ('public core') in urban housing markets?

To discuss this question, we come back to Heath's typology of welfare states. In a first step, we identify the stakeholders active in urban housing in our case study cities (state, civic society and market) and sum up their activities and instruments (Table 10.3).

In most European countries, all the actors mentioned above (state, civic society and market) play an active role in the housing market, but there are significant differences concerning their size and scope of action. Austria and the Netherlands have traditionally been characterized by strong involvement of the community sector via limited-profit housing associations. In combination with funding and direct provision by the state (supply-side subsidies and housing production by public authorities) this has led to competition between all market suppliers, including the private sector. Competition between the private, non-profit and public sectors is characteristic of unitary or integrated rental systems according to Kemeny (see Amann and Mundt, 2010, p. 36).

However, in the last two decades, a shift between and within the sectors has been observed. Whereas large-scale privatization of public housing has taken place in many countries (the United Kingdom, Germany, and most Central and Eastern European countries; see Murie et al., 2005), the reduction of state involvement in the housing market in Austria and the Netherlands has been more subtle: in Vienna and Amsterdam, the

Table 10.3 Stakeholders and their activities in urban housing, with examples from Vienna and Amsterdam

Description (positive): Who are (and were) the actors?			
	State	Civic society	Market
Provision	Council housing (V), active land policy (A, V)	Limited-profit housing associations (V, A)	Private rental market, private ownership, real estate development
Funding	Demand-side housing subsidies, supply-side subsidies (V; A until the mid-1990s)	Building society savings, community funding of co-housing groups, funding of limited-profit housing associations (V, A)	Private equity, private mortgage market
Regulation	Rent regulation (partially liberalized in A and V), building law, condominium law, law for limited-profit housing (V, Austria)	Compliance rules, professional codes of conduct	

Note: 'V' means a factor is especially valid for Vienna, 'A' that it is especially valid for Amsterdam, and no specification means that it is valid for most European cities or countries.

municipality did not withdraw from the housing sector, but partially shifted from direct provision to subsidiary funding and state guarantees, and within the subsidy schemes from supply-side to demand-side subsidies. This was accompanied by partial deregulation of the private rental market and (especially in Amsterdam) by homeownership programmes. Even if the state's involvement in the housing market is still substantial, there is a risk of losing the integrated character of the housing market as the social housing sector loses importance.

More challenging than the positive description of the actors in urban housing markets is the normative question of why (and how) the state should intervene. Table 10.4 sums up different justifications for state intervention in the housing market according to Heath's distinction.

The simple fact that a broad set of actors and state interventions exist in the housing market does not mean that all of them should exist from a normative point of view. However, it shows a certain awareness

Table 10.4 Arguments to justify state intervention in urban housing markets

Justification (normative): Why should the state intervene?		
Equality	Community/morality	Efficiency
State intervention where markets produce unequal and undesirable results: • Lack of affordable and decent housing for certain groups. • Unequal attractiveness of different districts, leading to cumulative discrimination of residents of deprived areas.	Housing as a social right, 'Right to the city' (Harvey, 2008). • Elements of the housing markets that are seen as immoral (e.g. speculative ground rent) call for alternative forms of provision and regulation (esp. tenants' protection in rental law, land policy).* • State as a guardian of the accessibility of housing markets. • Merit goods in housing (e.g. incentives for energy-saving construction).	Typical housing market failures legitimize state intervention: • Imperfect and asymmetric information. • Externalities, neighbourhood effects. • Submarkets that prevent market clearing. • Slow reaction to changing demand because of high construction costs and long development cycles.

Note: * However, some proponents of this line of argument oppose both market and state intervention, instead calling for bottom-up communitarian solutions.

of the complexity of urban housing markets that becomes even more obvious when looking at the spatial dimension. A monocausal approach to legitimizing public intervention (efficiency or equality alone) does not reflect the multifunctionality of housing policy. We therefore do not share Heath's claim that efficiency is the superior justification of state intervention in the context of housing policy.

Various failures in the housing market (externalities, long production cycles, asymmetric information and more; see Table 10.4) call for efficiency-oriented ('allocative') policies, which is a first justification of state intervention. However, an efficient housing market alone may not be enough to ensure decent housing for low-income groups or other groups that face difficulties in the housing market. This implies a need for distributive housing policies to achieve more equality in housing provision (second justification). Equality is an issue not only at the level of individual households. As we have shown for our case studies Vienna and Amsterdam, the question of spatial inequality, too, needs to be addressed by housing policies (among others). By using a policy mix of public regulation, funding and provision, it is possible to influence the spatial outcome of the housing market, and to ensure accessibility of certain urban areas to people who would otherwise be excluded. Vienna and Amsterdam used to have housing policies in place that were aware of this. A very high degree of spatial inequality in a city can lead to cumulative discrimination of those who live in deprived areas, affecting more dimensions than just their housing conditions (Häußermann et al., 2004).

Jane Jacobs describes the long-term superiority of small-scale economic diversity and mixed land use over 'efficient', specialized and monostructured economies in her concept of 'valuable inefficiencies of cities' (Jacobs, 1969, Chapter 3). Analogous 'valuable inefficiencies' may also exist for urban housing policies, if they contribute to greater social cohesion. Obviously, there is a trade-off between 'efficient' social targeting and the 'less efficient' social mix. However, what is inefficient in the short term (for example, a housing policy that is not targeted only at the poorest) may lead to a more resilient and also more efficient outcome in the long term. Mundt and Wieser (2014) support this thought in their comparative study on housing subsidies and taxation in six EU countries: in countries with 'targeted' housing policies based on housing allowances and tax incentives for homeownership (the United Kingdom, France, and the Netherlands in recent years), the overall level of state subsidies is higher than in countries with a 'broader' housing policy that relies mainly on supply-side subsidies (Austria and the Czech Republic) (Mundt and Wieser, 2014, p. 262).

Vienna and Amsterdam traditionally opted for less socially targeted housing policies by way of supply-side subsidies, rent regulation and a large, spatially dispersed social housing sector that is accessible to broad income groups, resulting in relatively low spatial segregation. However, recent data show that the policy changes made in both cities since the 1990s have led to a residualization of the social housing sector, meaning that it is increasingly dominated by low-income inhabitants. As a consequence, intra-sectoral segregation is on the rise, threatening the already low degree of socio-spatial integration (see Tammaru et al., 2015, p. 358f).

A third possible justification for a public core in urban housing policies is the communitarian aspect (community, morality). It can be linked to the discourse on housing as a civil right and the 'right-to-the-city' movement, where the immorality and ineffectiveness of the market as well as the occurrence of land speculation are seen as the foundation for alternative (albeit not necessarily state-driven) housing provision. The municipalization of urban land, as used to be the case in Amsterdam (and still is to a certain extent), can be interpreted as an instrument in a communitarian philosophy. In our understanding, a land use policy that also ensures the accessibility of attractive urban land for uses (and users) of low ability to pay, and therefore prevents a total separation of land uses according to a land price gradient, is an essential prerequisite both for an effective housing policy and for social coherence in a city. Instruments such as planning gain taxation, land use categories or quotas for social housing, municipal land funds and contractual planning can therefore contribute to a more community-oriented and at the same time more equal urban society.

Obviously, there is a trade-off between the two public policy objectives of socially targeted housing policies (typical of dual rental markets) and housing policies that encourage social mix (typical of unitary rental markets). Vienna and Amsterdam used to prioritize the second approach. With recent policy changes and a growing demand on the lowest price segment, however, this strategy may not work out as intended, though: the spatial socio-economic mix tends to become less diverse, without a notable increase in targeted subsidy allocation.

Without doubt, the primary task of public policy in housing is to ensure decent housing for those who tend to be excluded from or exploited by an unregulated housing market. However, if housing policy is reduced to providing public housing to the poor, trade-offs are to be considered: the risk of rising socio-spatial fragmentation, stigmatization of the social housing sector, and rising average housing costs in the other sectors. Integrated policy approaches that address all three sectors (market, public sector and the civic society) are likely to yield more desirable results in this respect. They require a combination of different policy instruments, which include land policy, market regulation and direct housing provision by the state.

NOTES

1. 'Certain moral and civic goods are diminished or corrupted if bought and sold for money' (Sandel, 1998, p. 94, cited in Heath, 2011, p. 19).
2. Heath (2011, p. 37f) backs his argument by referring to 'Wagner's law of expanding state activity'.
3. Commonly, the Gini coefficient is used as a measure of income inequality. Within a given spatial unit, however, it can also be interpreted as a measure of social mix in terms of income groups.
4. These co-operatives or corporations are subject to the Limited Profit Housing Act (Wohnungsgemeinnützigkeitsgesetz). Profits are not forbidden, but are limited and in large part have to be reinvested in housing production.
5. In reaction to the public discussion of a housing shortage in Vienna, Mayor Michael Häupl announced a restart of the council housing programme in 2016/17.
6. Flats in municipal housing and in buildings of limited-profit housing associations.
7. Estimations for 2014 are based on microcensus data from the Austrian Association of limited-profit housing associations (GBV – Österreichischer Verband gemeinnütziger Wohnbauvereinigungen, 2015).
8. On the concept of 'very social housing' see Levy-Vroelant and Reinprecht (2008, p. 210).

9. From 2005 to 2013, the number of applicants for council flats rose from 15 500 to 27 600, whereas the number of allocations remained stable at approximately 10 000 units per year (Gutheil-Knopp-Kirchwald and Kadi, 2014, p. 23). In Amsterdam, the average waiting time for a two-room apartment rocketed from two to eight years between the 1980s and 2008 (Uitermark, 2009).

REFERENCES

Amann, W. and A. Mundt (2010). Indicators of an integrated rental market in Austria. *Housing Finance International*, Winter, 35–44.

Amsterdamse Federatie van Woningcorporaties (AFWC) (2013). *Jaarboek 2013*. Amsterdam: Amsterdamse Federatie van Woningcorporaties.

Arbaci, S. (2007). Ethnic segregation, housing systems and welfare regimes in Europe. *European Journal of Housing Policy*, 7(4), 401–433.

Boelhouwer, P., H. van der Heijden and O. Papa (1992). *Housing Systems in Europe*, Delft: Delft University Press.

Conijn, J. (2008). Subsidiering Van de Woonconsumptie: Een Zinloos Schip Van Bijleg. In F.J.H. Don (ed.), *Agenda voor de Woningmarkt*, Amsterdam: Koninklijke Vereniging voor de Stathuishoudkunde, pp. 145–177.

Czasny, K. (2004). The importance of housing systems in safeguarding social cohesion in Europe. SOCOHO. Vienna: Facultas.

Esping-Andersen, G. (1990). *The Three Worlds of Welfare Capitalism*, Princeton, NJ: Princeton University Press.

GBV – Österreichischer Verband Gemeinnütziger Bauvereinigungen (2015). Principal residence rental dwellings in Vienna according to their legal basis, 2008 and 2014. Calculations based on Statistics Austria microcensus 2008 data and estimations by Bauer (GBV).

Giffinger, R. (1998). Segregation in Vienna: impacts of market barriers and rent regulations. *Urban Studies*, 35(10), 1791–1812.

Gutheil-Knopp-Kirchwald, G. and J. Kadi (2014). Gerechte Stadt – gerechte Wohnungspolitik? *Der öffentliche Sektor – The Public Sector*, 2014(3–4). Accessed 31 March 2016 at http://oes.tuwien.ac.at.

Harloe, M. (1995). *The People's Home? Social Rented Housing in Europe and America*, Oxford: Blackwell.

Harvey, D. (2008). The right to the city. *New Left Review*, 53, 23–40.

Hatz, G., J. Kohlbacher and U. Reeger (2015). Socio-economic segregation in Vienna: a social-oriented approach to urban planning and housing. In T. Tammaru, S. Marcinczak, M. van Ham and S. Musterd (eds), *Socio-Economic Segregation in European Capital Cities: East meets West*, Regions and Cities series, London, UK and New York, USA: Routledge, pp. 80–108.

Häußermann, H., M. Kronauer and W. Siebel (2004). Stadt am Rand: Armut und Ausgrenzung. In H. Häußermann, M. Kronauer and W. Siebel (eds), *An den Rändern der Städte. Armut und Ausgrenzung*, Frankfurt/Main: Suhrkamp Verlag, pp. 7–42.

Heath, J. (2011). Three normative models of the welfare state. *Public Reason*, 3(2), 13–43.

Jacobs, J. (1969). *The Economy of Cities*, New York: Random House.

Kadi, J. (2015). Recommodifying housing in formerly 'red' Vienna?. *Housing, Theory and Society*, DOI: 10.1080/14036096.2015.1024885.
Kadi, J. and S. Musterd (2015). Housing for the poor in a neo-liberalizing just city: still affordable, but increasingly inaccessible. *Tijdschrift voor Economische en Sociale Geografie*, Online First. DOI:10.1111/tesg.12101.
Kemeny, J. (1995). *From Public Housing to the Social Market. Rental Policy Strategies in Comparative Perspective*. London: Routledge.
Levy-Vroelant, C. and C. Reinprecht (2008). Housing the poor in Paris and Vienna: the changing understanding of 'social'. In K. Scanlon and C. Whitehead (eds), *Social Housing in Europe II*, London: London School of Economics, pp. 209–224.
Lugger, K. and W. Amann (2013). *Österreichisches Wohnhandbuch 2013*, Innsbruck, Wien, Bozen: StudienVerlag.
Malpass, P. (2008). Histories of social housing: a comparative approach. In K. Scanlon and C. Whitehead (eds), *Social Housing in Europe II*, London: London School of Economics, pp. 15–30.
Mundt, A. and R. Wieser (2014). Housing subsidies and taxation in six EU countries: trends, structures and recent measures in the light of the global financial crisis, *Journal of European Real Estate Research*, 7(3), 248–269. DOI 10.1108/JERER-01-2014-0006.
Murie, A., I. Tosics, M. Aalbers, R. Sendi and B. Cernic Mali (2005). Privatisation and after: restructuring large housing estates in European cities. Retrieved 8 March 2013 from http://pdc.ceu.hu/archive/00005315/01/Privatisation_and_after.pdf.
Musgrave, R.A. (1957). A multiple theory of budget determination. *Finanzarchiv*, 17, 333–343.
Musterd, S. (2005). Social and ethnic segregation in Europe: levels, causes, and effects. *Journal of Urban Affairs*, 27(3), 331–348.
Musterd, S. and R. Deurloo (1997). Ethnic segregation and the role of public housing in Amsterdam. *Tijdschrift Voor Economische En Sociale Geografie*, 88(2), 158–168.
Musterd, S. and W. Ostendorf (eds) (1998). *Urban Segregation and the Welfare State: Inequality and Exclusion in Western Cities*, London, UK and New York, USA: Routledge.
Rosifka, W. and R. Postler (2010). Die Praxis des Richtwertmietzinssystems. Ergebnisse einer Untersuchung über Mietvertragsabschlüsse in Wien. Wien: Kammer für Arbeiter und Angestellte für Wien.
Salet, W. (1999). Policy review – regime shifts in Dutch housing policy. *Housing Studies*, 14(4), 547–57. DOI: 10.1080/02673039982777.
Soja, E. (2010). *Seeking Spatial Justice*. Minneapolis, MN: University of Minnesota Press.
SORA Institute for Social Research and Consulting (2010). Wohnqualität und soziale Gerechtigkeit in Wien. Ein Vergleich von Wohnqualität und BewohnerInnenstrukturen zwischen 1995 und 2008. Im Auftrag der MA 50 – Referat Wohnbauforschung.
Statistics Austria (2004 and 2011). EU Statistics on Income and Living Conditions (EU-SILC) for Austria. www.statistik.at.
Statistics Austria (2011). Register-based Census 2011 – Housing Census. www.statistik.at.
Tammaru, T., S. Marcinczak, M. van Ham and S. Musterd (eds) (2015).

Socio-Economic Segregation in European Capital Cities: East meets West, Regions and Cities series, London, UK and New York, USA: Routledge.

Torgersen, U. (1987). Housing: the wobbly pillar under the welfare state. In Bengt Turner, Jim Kemeny and Lennart J. Lundqvist (eds), *Between State and Market: Housing in the Post-Industrial Era*, Stockholm: Almqvist and Wicksell International, pp. 116–126.

Uitermark, J. (2009). An In Memoriam for the just city of Amsterdam. *City*, 13(2–3), 347–361.

Uitermark, J. and T. Bosker (2014). Whither the 'undivided city'? An assessment of state-sponsored gentrification in Amsterdam. *Tijdschrift Voor Economische En Sociale Geografie*, 105(2), 221–230.

van der Veer, J. and D. Schuiling (2005). The Amsterdam housing market and the role of housing associations. *Journal of Housing and the Built Environment*, 20(2), 167–181. DOI:10.1007/s10901-005-9004-7.

Wieser, R. and W. Blaas (2004). Einfluss von Wohnbauförderung und Richtwertsystem auf die Mietenentwicklung. Studie des Instituts für Finanzwissenschaft und Infrastrukturpolitik der TU Wien im Auftrag der Kammer für Arbeiter und Angestellte für Wien. Vienna: Arbeiterkammer Wien.

11. Funding of protected areas: a purely public task?

Grazia Withalm

11.1 INTRODUCTION

Establishment, management and especially funding of protected areas (PAs) have been considered as a core public task ever since their first worldwide appearance in the middle of the nineteenth century (Payer and Zangerl-Weisz, 1997). Recent studies (EEA, 2012; Jones-Walters and Čivić, 2013; Jungmeier, 2014; Payer and Zangerl-Weisz, 1997; Weixlbaumer, 2006) have shown that nature conservation and PAs have been the subject of several paradigm shifts over the past 40 years. In particular, responsibility shifted more to the civil society consisting of local stakeholders, private households, but also non-governmental and non-profit organizations for the establishment and management of PAs (Bertzky et al., 2012). The public sector is still considered to be mainly responsible for nature conservation.

Nevertheless, a study exploring the sustainability of PA funding shows that the public sector reduced its funding of PAs for various reasons (Emerton et al., 2006). Moreover, this study emphasizes the fact that the funding of PAs never has been solely public. The European Environment Agency (EEA) (2012) arrived at the same conclusion and stated that private organizations already have been responsible for funding PAs since their beginning in the early twentieth century in Europe. Today, sources for PA funding range from public funds through revenue from fees (entrance, membership) and sale of merchandise, to funding completely by private sponsors and donors (Emerton et al., 2006, pp. 9–11, 27–74; WCPA and Economics Unit, 2000, pp. 31–46).

As the public sector withdraws its spending for nature conservation, the private (co-)funding of PAs is becoming more formal. With an increasing number of PAs in Austria (EEA, 2012, p. 102) and worldwide (Bertzky et al. 2012), the question arises: who should be responsible for financing PAs – the public or the private sector? This chapter attempts to answer this question using the public goods model (Heath, 2011, pp. 23–8). This model suggests that the public sector sometimes provides certain goods more efficiently than the private sector. The analysis follows a dual approach. First, the current state of PA funding as well as national and international trends are analysed, focusing on funding mechanisms and sources. Second, based on empirical analysis, the chapter examines how funding sources and funding responsibilities match. For this purpose, responsibility is evaluated using characteristics of the bundle of ecosystem services produced in the relevant PA. The second part of the analysis is based on a sample of four Austrian PAs. The results of this analysis allow conclusions to be drawn that are valid not only for Austria but also on a more general level.

11.2 APPROACH

Central Assumptions

According to the official definition of the International Union for Conservation of Nature (IUCN), a PA is 'a clearly defined geographical space, recognized, dedicated and managed, through legal or other effective means, to achieve the long term conservation of nature with associated ecosystem services and cultural values' (Dudley, 2008, p. 8). The actual form of a PA depends on the topographical, economic, political and social surroundings of the area. Hence, every single PA is unique in terms of size, habitat and ecosystems conserved, management and ownership structure, restrictions on human activities within and near its boundaries, as well as acceptance and level of support by local population and politicians (Dudley, 2008; EEA, 2012). The uniqueness of every single PA leads to a large variety in PA categories serving different aims. All PAs, however, have at least one aim in common: effective biodiversity conservation (Emerton et al., 2006). In pursuing this aim, PAs provide benefits for human well-being in the form of ecosystem services (Millennium Ecosystem Assessment, 2005). These ecosystem services arise mostly from natural processes and are widely considered to be consumable for free. Against this background, ecosystem services are often defined from an economic point of view as public goods, differing from other goods because of their non-excludability and non-rivalry in consumption (cf. Costanza, 2008).

From an economic perspective 'a protected area can be seen as a business operation' (WCPA and Economics Unit, 2000, p. 7) or it can be perceived as a commodity which can be consumed by its visitors (Getzner and Jungmeier, 2009). Concentrating on the first option, this chapter assumes that the entity 'protected area' is a productive business operation. Its products are goods and services in the form of ecosystem services.

Ecosystem services thus can be classified according to their (non-)excludability and (non-)rivalry in consumption (Costanza, 2008). Consequently, all ecosystem services can be classified as either private, club, common or public good (ibid.). Based on these assumptions, it is assumed that public funding can be justified if the ecosystem services produced are not excludable from consumption. In this case, according to the public goods model, the market fails to provide ecosystem services in an efficient way (cf. Heath, 2011). Market failure occurs, on the one hand, because of the incompletely defined property rights based on the non-excludability of consumption. On the other hand, the market fails because everyone can consume public ecosystem services to the same extent and consequently there is no rivalry in consumption. Therefore, it is likely that the market price for ecosystem services would be zero and that the services either would not be produced, or if they were, they would be exploited. It is assumed that the public sector is usually more efficient in providing such goods than the private sector (cf. Heath, 2011). The provision of ecosystem services is thus a purely public task.

The responsibility for funding PAs therefore depends on the goods characteristics of the ecosystem services they produce. Nowadays, PAs are multifunctional areas, which do not only aim at conserving nature but also have a positive influence on, for example, the economic development of a region and the social life of its residents. PAs, thus, provide a bundle of various ecosystem services (EEA, 2012; Jones-Walters and Čivić, 2013; Jungmeier, 2014; Payer and Zangerl-Weisz, 1997; Weixlbaumer, 2006). The challenge is to ascertain who should be responsible for funding a PA based on the ecosystem services provided. To deal with this, an indicator of 'publicness' will be introduced. The term 'publicness' is described in the *Oxford Dictionary* as the quality, condition, or fact of being public (Oxford Dictionaries, 2015). For the purpose of this chapter 'publicness' is defined as the share of ecosystem services provided by PAs that can be categorized as public goods. The publicness indicator takes into account the public ecosystem services and evaluates them according to their contribution to the PA's objectives, because funds are mainly spent in these areas. Another reason for evaluation is the fact that public ecosystem services sometimes derive from external effects, while the funding actually aims at producing other non-public goods and services. In a second step the publicness indicator is applied to compare the funding sources with the actual characteristics of ecosystem services provided.

Based on these considerations, it is argued that public responsibility for funding PAs is determined by the publicness of PAs. The degree of publicness depends on the number of goods and services provided by an PA that can be characterized as public goods, and on the extent to which these goods and services contribute to achieve the given objectives of a PA. Consequently, the degree of publicness attributed to an area determines the responsibility of the public sector for funding. However, this does not imply that the public sector funds PAs efficiently or sustainably. It is further assumed that the category of PA and objectives following from this determine the publicness of the PA.

Analysis Methodology

In a first step, funding of PAs is analysed based on a literature review. The research concentrates on identifying different funding mechanisms, their frequency of application and relevant actors. This is supplemented by an overview of international and national trends in funding PAs and comparing the international with the Austrian situation. The case of Austria is especially relevant in this context because in Austria 27 per cent of the total territory is under protection, which is a comparatively high percentage. On the other hand, Austria with its special funding instrument of contractual nature conservation, dividing the funding and the operational responsibilities between the public and the private sector, already has a proven system for funding PAs.

Second, documents and data is empirically analysed, comparing the responsibilities of the different actors, defined by the characteristics of the ecosystem services produced, with the financial resources used. Four Austrian PAs have been chosen as objects of research, based on four main characteristics: PA category, year (period) of establishment, stakeholders involved and size of the PA. The objects of inquiry are the Nature Reserve Rheindelta, the Nature Park Sparbach, the National Park Hohe Tauern and the Biosphere Reserve Großes Walsertal. Analysing the four PAs, in a first step the ecosystem services produced in these areas is identified and in a second step they are classified according to the public goods model. The third step consists of the evaluation of the PAs' publicness. Applying the publicness indicator then makes it possible to determine the principal responsibility for funding the PA. The fourth and last step then evaluates the actual funding schemes of the four PAs and establishes how they correspond to the publicness of these PAs. As a result of the evaluation it becomes possible to define the potential lack of funding and identify the responsible to fill the gap.

11.3 FUNDING OF PROTECTED AREAS

PAs need a certain kind of organizational structure to ensure effective biodiversity conservation. Therefore, many areas have their own PA management. Financial resources are required, on the one hand, to cover expenditure for personnel, public relations, research and education as well as other costs connected to the PA management structure. On the other hand, financial resources are needed to realize biodiversity conservation measures; that is, cultivation projects and compensatory payments for restrictions in land use (Emerton et al., 2006).

The legal framework for funding PA management and biodiversity conservation measures in Austria is rather limited. Exceptions are, for example, charges for landscape and nature conservation to private companies or contracts between the federal government and the states (*Bundesländer*) regarding financing national parks (Tiefenbach et al., 1998, p. 90). More important though is the framework for the implementation of measures relating to PAs and biodiversity conservation established by international and national conventions and policy agreements, for example, Convention on Biological Diversity and Ramsar Convention (Emerton et al., 2006, p. 7). These documents emphasize the need for financial support of PAs and often also define the respective financial responsibilities of the contracting parties (ibid.). The following provides an overview of the current actors financing PAs and shows which financial challenges PAs will face on the international and national level.

Recent International Trends

The IUCN examined the sustainability of PA funding worldwide for the year 2006 and established that public budgets are the main source for funding PAs together with some international funds (Emerton et al., 2006). Over the past two decades, however, public funding increasingly failed to meet the needs of sustainable PA management. This made non-governmental and private sector funding ever more important (ibid.).

The study mentions several reasons for the shortfalls of public funding in PA management. A fundamental fact is that sums spent for PAs are relatively small compared to total government spending (in the United States only 0.1% of the total public budget is spent on PAs, and in developing countries even less) (ibid.). Moreover, the 'funding for PAs has struggled to keep pace with the growth in the number and area of PAs . . . Recent rapid growth in the number and area of PAs has stretched the capacity of PA management authorities to increase their budgets accordingly' (Emerton et al., 2006, p. 12).

In addition, public budgets have been influenced by a mix of austerity policies, connected with policies of liberalization and decentralization, resulting in tighter public expenditure. This led to mergers of budget accounts for similar responsibilities (for example, consolidation of ministries and portfolios). Furthermore, new objectives for PAs emerged, caused by socio-economic developments, for example the increase of social inequality. As a result, public expenditure for PAs suffered, on the one hand, from a tightening of public budgets and, on the other hand, from a growing number of tasks that have to be realized with budgets that have not increased accordingly (Emerton et al., 2006). To conclude:

> although there is a widespread commitment by most countries in the world to allocate funds to PAs, existing financing falls far short of the amount required to manage the world's existing PAs. There is clearly a need to find new financial resources to supplement existing funding for PAs, as well as greater efforts to place PAs firmly onto the development and poverty reduction agendas. (Emerton et al., 2006, p. 14)

The Case of Austria

General information regarding PA funding in Austria

In Austria, responsibility for nature conservation lies with the nine states, according to the distribution of powers in the federal constitution. This means that they are responsible for biodiversity conservation and the establishment of PAs (Penker et al., 2004). Accordingly, the bulk of financial resources for the realization of PAs comes from the state budgets, with some federal funding as well (Tiefenbach et al., 1998). Five states (Burgenland, Lower Austria, Salzburg, Tyrol and Vorarlberg) have introduced special taxes for landscape and nature conservation (so-called *Landschafts- und Naturschutzabgaben*) that apply to the mining of sand, gravel, stones and other similar resources (Penker et al., 2004; Tiefenbach et al., 1998). The revenue from these taxes are invested in special funds (so-called *Landschafts-, Landschaftspflege oder Naturschutzfonds*). However, the use of means from these funds is restricted, in whole or in part, to financing biodiversity conservation measures (Penker et al., 2004; Tiefenbach et al., 1998).

Additionally, international funding instruments are available in Austria. One of these is the European Union's (EU) LIFE programme. Its main focus is to support the contribution of member states to the European network of nature reserves called NATURA 2000[1] (Penker et al., 2004; Tiefenbach et al., 1998). The EU bears half the costs for nature conservation projects within the LIFE programme. National public institutions have to cover the other half of the costs (Penker et al., 2004; Tiefenbach et al., 1998). From 1996 to 2012, 46 nature conservation projects were funded within this programme. In total €154 million has been spent, around €70 million of which was subsidies from the EU (BMLFUW, 2016a). Compared to this, the public sector spent around €75 million each year from 2005 to 2012 for the conservation of species and landscapes (see Statistics Austria, 2015a).

Apart from the LIFE programme, the ÖPUL agri-environmental programme (*Österreichisches Programm zur Förderung einer umweltgerechten, extensiven und den natürlichen Lebensraum schützenden Landwirtschaft*) is the most important funding instrument for biodiversity conservation in Austria. In contrast to the LIFE programme, which concentrates on funding projects, ÖPUL contributes to biodiversity conservation by supporting farmers in realizing environmentally friendly agriculture

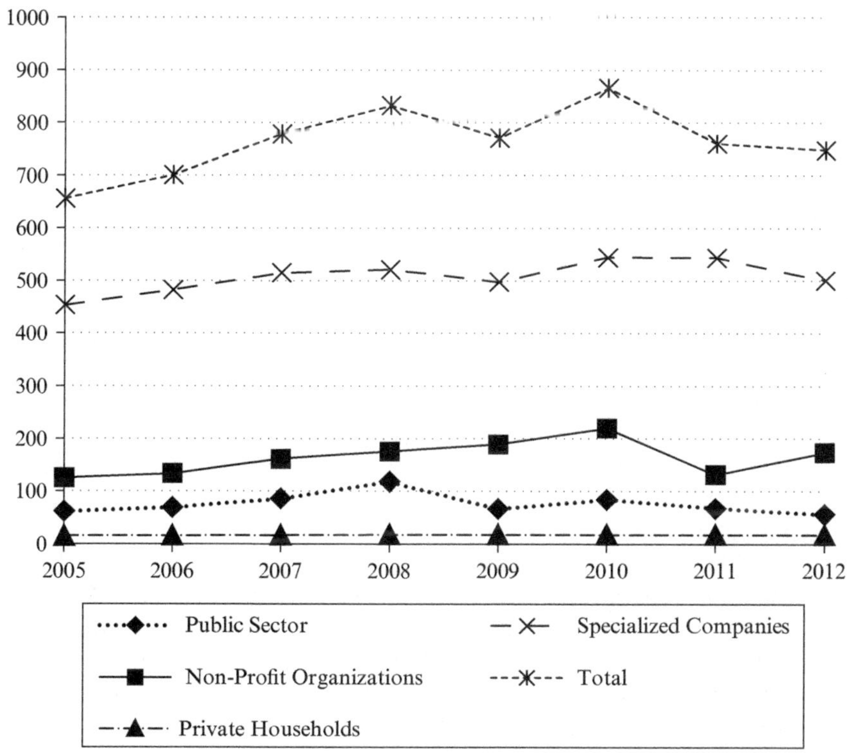

Source: Based on Statistics Austria (2015a).

Figure 11.1 Expenditure for the conservation of species and landscapes in Austria (in € millions)

(Tiefenbach et al., 1998). One of the most important and efficient instruments of ÖPUL is contractual nature conservation (Penker et al., 2004). Another difference between LIFE and ÖPUL is the fact that ÖPUL can also fund measures outside of nature reserves and thus contributes not only to *in situ* but also to *ex situ* nature conservation.[2] The financing structure of ÖPUL is the only similarity between the two programmes. The EU provides around 50 per cent of the financial resources for ÖPUL, and the other 50 per cent stems from national public budgets (BMLFUW, 2016b).

A specific funding programme is in place for national parks. As already mentioned, it is usually the responsibility of the states to establish and fund PAs. For national parks, however, there exists an intra-governmental contract between the federal and the state governments, stipulating that the federal government (Ministry of the Environment) carries the sole responsibility for establishing, funding and maintaining national parks that would otherwise be a shared responsibility (Maier, 2012).

Expenditure for PAs by actors

Expenditure for PAs is not usually monitored statistically because the PA managements are frequently organized as private societies and associations. Consequently, there is no detailed information on the amount of money spent, for which PA and by whom. Especially in the case of ÖPUL funding, it is not possible to assign public expenditure exactly to a specific PA, for various reasons. First, the data provide only total funding sums; and second, the funding sums have no geographic reference. However, general information on the total expenditure for the conservation of species and landscapes has been collected in preparation of the establishment of Environmental Protection Expenditure Accounts (EPEAs).[3] Therein expenditure for conservation of species and landscapes constitutes a separate category of expenditure referring to activities such as 'the acquisition of land for nature protection purposes, afforestation, restoration of landscapes, the establishment of green belts and the displacements of technical infrastructure' (Statistics Austria, 2012, p. 28, author's translation). In the official definition of this category of expenditure it is assumed that the activities mentioned have to be carried out mainly by the public sector and non-profit organizations. The private sector is assumed to be present only in the form of specialized companies (for example, farms) and is attributed only a supporting role for the conservation of species and landscapes (Statistics Austria, 2012).

Public sector expenditure for the conservation of species and landscapes increased slightly from 2005 to 2008, according to the data collected within the EPEA. In 2009, expenditure decreased significantly and since then has been declining slightly. Non-profit organizations reduced their expenditure in the period from 2010 to 2011, but are the only actors increasing expenditure from 2011 to 2012. In contrast to the official description of the category (Statistics Austria, 2012), it is specialized companies from the private sector that spent the highest amount of money compared to the public sector, non-profit organizations and private households. The reason is that the term 'specialized companies' subsumes not only manufacturing and service companies but also the agricultural sector. Almost 91 per cent of the expenditure in the category 'Conservation of Species and Landscapes' can be assigned to the agricultural sector (Aichinger, 2016). As farmers receive public subsidies for environmentally friendly farming (for example, over the ÖPUL programme) it can be questioned whether the results of the EPEA are accurate and whether private spending really is private. It seems that much of the seemingly private expenditure rests on public funds.

Recent trends in funding PAs

Public expenditure for environment conservation is only a small fraction of the Austrian total public sector expenditure. On average, 1 per cent of the total public sector expenditure is spent on environment conservation from 2011 to 2014 (Statistics Austria, 2016a). Of this only 6.4 per cent is funds assigned especially to the conservation of species and landscapes (Statistics Austria, 2015b). Thus, the funding situation of PAs in Austria is similar to the international one (see Statistics Austria, 2015b, p. 5).

The Austrian economy and thus the public budgets have also been influenced by austerity policies, institutional changes and increasing social inequality, in particular since the worldwide financial crisis in 2007. These developments resulted in a noticeable cutback of total public sector expenditure after 2007 (Statistics Austria, 2016a). As a consequence, expenditure for conservation of species and landscapes also declined. Although the total public sector expenditure increased again in 2009, public sector expenditure for the conservation of species and landscapes is still declining (see Statistics Austria, 2016b). At the same time, the number of PAs and their size have developed in the opposite direction: they are increasing (EEA, 2012, p. 102). Consequently, there is a growing gap in public sector funding.

Moreover, PAs are increasingly perceived as instruments for regional development, recreation, tourism and education (Getzner et al., 2010). They are no longer considered as areas strictly protected from human activities, but as '"landscapes of hope" [in particular] for underdeveloped regions' (Mose, 2006). The increasing number of biosphere reserves, focusing on the development of coexistence between humans and nature, underlines this trend (Großes Walsertal in 2000, Wienerwald in 2005 and

Nockberge in 2012; UNESCO, 2016). Furthermore, the multifunctional benefits PAs are able to distribute are also reflected in the new strategy for Austrian nature parks (Handel, 2010). This strategy is based on four pillars: protection, recreation, education and regional development. Other studies even go one step further, stating that PAs are able to contribute 'to human welfare, poverty alleviation and sustainable development' (Getzner et al., 2010).

During the past 20 years, one nature conservation instrument in particular has played an important role for the funding of PAs in Austria (Penker et al., 2004): the instrument of contractual nature conservation, receiving its financial resources primarily from the ÖPUL programme. Contractual nature conservation emphasizes, on the one hand, the essential role of farmers as local stakeholders for achieving effective biodiversity conservation. On the other hand, it demonstrates the high degree of funding responsibility by the public sector. Contractual nature conservation illustrates the development of task distribution between the public sector, civil society and private companies over the past 40 years. While citizen and stakeholder participation is one of the key instruments for efficient and sustainable establishment and management of PAs today, the funding is still seen as a public task.

11.4 PUBLICNESS OF PROTECTED AREAS

The question of who is responsible for funding PAs can be determined by applying the characteristics of the ecosystem services produced in these areas. More precisely, the responsibility for funding is connected to the publicness of the PAs. Publicness in this context subsumes the goods characteristics of the produced ecosystem services weighted by their agreement with the PA objectives. The produced ecosystem services will be defined by their legal regulations, management plans, guiding principles, or descriptions in official documents (for example, on their homepages) and accomplished projects.

To compare the four PAs, a common evaluation framework is required. As already mentioned in the subsection on 'Central Assumptions', every PA is unique, but they all have at least one goal in common: the effective conservation of biodiversity. Since it is difficult to determine biodiversity conservation the argumentation is based on the assumption that PAs share another feature: they are all multifunctional (cf. Weixlbaumer, 2010). This means that a PA never has only one objective, but serves various functions to which ecosystem services can be assigned. These functions are: (1) regulation functions (for example, climate and soil regulation, flood and disease control); (2) provisioning functions (for example, provision of food and raw materials or ingredients for medical purposes); (3) habitat and support functions (for example, assurance of livelihood for indigenous species, maintenance of genetic diversity); (4) cultural and scientific functions (for example, protection of natural and cultural heritage, recreation, mental and physical health, environmental education, research); and (5) regional development functions (for example, basis for sustainable development, reduction of economic inequalities, tourism) (Weixlbaumer, 2010, p. 19; TEEB, 2016).

The aim of the following paragraphs is thus to identify the ecosystem services produced in the four PAs chosen as representative of the Austrian situation according to their management plans, to assign the ecosystem services to the PA functions and based on this to classify them as public, common, club or private good. A further aim is to investigate whether funding responsibility (given by the indicator of publicness) and funding sources match. Based on the result of this investigation conclusions can be drawn regarding the funding situation, leading to the possible identification of responsible actors (agency), who should increase their spending for PAs.

Nature Reserve Rheindelta

This nature reserve is situated on the south-east coast of Lake Constance and covers an area of around 2000 ha (Tiefenbach et al., 1998; State of Vorarlberg, 2016). It is one of the oldest nature reserves in Austria and was first established in 1942 by legal regulation based on the Reich Nature Protection Act (EEA, 2012). However, the legal regulation was lost after World War II. In 1976 a new regulation came into force and the nature reserve became legally accepted again (Aschauer et al., 2007). Already in 1962, the area was included on the international list for water bodies and wetlands. With the accession of Austria to the RAMSAR Convention in 1982 (Convention for Wetlands), the area was one of the first Austrian wetlands to be protected under this international convention (Tiefenbach et al., 1998). Since 2003 the Rheindelta has also been a Natura 2000 area based on the Wild Birds Directive and the Habitats Directive (Aschauer et al., 2007, p. 103).

The area is managed by the Rhine Delta Nature Conservation Association, which was established by and is still supported by the Nature and Environmental Conservation Department of the state of Vorarlberg and the four affected municipalities (Grabher et al., 1990, p. 15). Private households, private companies and other associations (non-governmental organizations, NGOs) can also become members of the Rhine Delta

Nature Conservation Association and support the PA by paying membership fees (Rhine Delta Nature Conservation Association, 2016). Apart from membership fees, the association is funded by the state nature conservation fund (Grabher et al., 1990, p. 15) and by project funding through the LIFE programme (LIFE project Wasserhaushalt Naturschutzgebiet Rheindelta; BMLFUW, 2016c). Additionally, affected farmers can apply for compensation payments for environmentally friendly agriculture primarily within the ÖPUL programme, and in some cases also within the nature conservation fund (see the subsection on 'General information regarding PA funding in Austria') (Aschauer et al., 2007; State of Vorarlberg, 2015).

The publicness analysis of the Nature Reserve Rheindelta shows that the ecosystem services provided in the PA are mostly public ones. In particular, the main objective of the PA – conserving a natural habitat for various birds – is public by its characteristics, because it is non-rival and non-excludable in consumption. Private and club goods are only rarely provided in the form of provisioning services, under which material or energy outputs from ecosystems such as fish or timber are subsumed, or cultural services such as special guided field trips. The comparison of the PA's publicness and its funding shows that the share of actual public funding (90 per cent) is higher than that suggested by the publicness indicator (65 per cent) of the area, and that private funding resources could be extended.

Nature Park Sparbach

The Nature Park Sparbach was the first nature park to be established in Austria in 1962. It is situated in the district of Mödling in Lower Austria, 16 kilometres southwest of Vienna (Nature Park Sparbach, 2015) and covers an area of around 355 ha (Regional Court of Audit of Lower Austria, 2013). The main objective of the nature park has always been the provision of recreation opportunities for (urban) citizens. Nature conservation and protection measures seem to play a side-role only (ibid.; cf. Weixlbaumer, 2006). This impression is supported by the fact that Prince Johann from Liechtenstein designed the area in the early nineteenth century, following the tradition of the English garden (Nature Park Sparbach, 2015).

The nature park receives core funding from the State of Lower Austria as part of the provincial landscape cultivation funds (Regional Court of Audit of Lower Austria, 2013). It is also funded by its visitors, who have to pay entrance fees. Furthermore, the Foundation Prince Liechtenstein, which acts as landowner and is responsible for the Nature Park Sparbach, receives compensatory payments over the ÖPUL programme for environmentally friendly agriculture (ibid.). Consequently, the funding is primarily public. In contrast, the PA provides primarily private or club goods which can be traced back on the PA objectives and on the entrance fee. Thus, there are big differences between the funding responsibility given by the publicness indicator and the actual funding.

National Park Hohe Tauern

The National Park Hohe Tauern occupies the border area of the three Austrian states of Carinthia, Salzburg and Tyrol, and thus consists of three parts, each of them established in different years by the respective states. First, in 1981, the National Park Hohe Tauern in Carinthia was established. Second, in 1984, the regulation for the National Park Hohe Tauern in Salzburg was legislated. Third and last, the protection of the Tyrolian part of the National Park Hohe Tauern was legally established in 1991 (Environment Agency Austria, 2001). Today the National Park Hohe Tauern covers an area of around 180 000 ha and is thus the biggest PA in the Alps (Kremser, 2003).

Most of the territory in the National Park Hohe Tauern is owned by local farmers, farming communities and the Alpenverein (Austrian Alpine Association) (ibid.). This specific ownership structure is primarily based on the efforts of Albert Wirth, landowner and timber merchant of the early twentieth century. In 1918, Mr Wirth purchased a big part of the Carinthian Nockberg area and donated the area to the Austrian Alpine Association, stipulating that the Association put the area under conservation (Aichhorn et al., 2011; Payer and Zangerl-Weisz, 1997). The conservation efforts of the Alpine Association have been confronted by the extension of touristic attractions and plans of hydroelectric power stations. The big breakthrough for the conservation of the area was the signing of an agreement between the three states of Carinthia, Salzburg and Tyrol in Heiligenblut in 1971. The main aim of the agreement was the funding and enforcement of the development of the National Park Hohe Tauern (ibid.).

The funding of the National Park Hohe Tauern consists mainly of state funds for the national park and federal resources (see Figure 11.2). Additional funds are obtained through project financing by the EU, the Association of Friends of Upper Tauern, other private sponsors and by economic activities (National Park Hohe Tauern, 2015). Over the past ten years the average share of private funding for the national park was around 10 per cent (see Figure 11.2). Which means, the public sector covered the remaining 90 per cent of the financial support. The predominant role of the public is also reflected by the publicness of the National Park Hohe

Table 11.1 Publicness analysis of representative PAs and comparison with the funding situation

	PA Function	Good Class.	Rheindelta		Sparbach		Hohe Tauern		Großes Walsertal	
			ES[1]	Impor-tance	ES[1]	Impor-tance	ES[1]	Impor-tance	ES[1]	Impor-tance
Regula-tion	Climate regulation	Public								
	Natural hazard mitigation	Public	flood protec-tion	medium					protective function of woods	high
	Water regulation	Public	hydro-logical balance	medium					ecological function of waterbodies	high
	Erosion protection	Public								
	Soil formation	Public								
	Nutrient regulation	Public								
	Waste treatment	Public								
	Pollination	Public								
	Biological control	Public								

Provisioning	Food & water	Private	fish, prey	low	prey	medium	agricultural products	medium	agricultural products (hunting, fishing & alpine farming)	medium
	Raw materials	Private			timber	medium				
	Genetic resources	Commons								
	Medicinal & Bio-chemical resources	Commons								
	Ornamental resources	Private								
Habitat & Supporting	Refugium function	Public	special birds habitat	high	wildlife reserve	high	wildlife reserve, habitat management	high	wildlife reserve	medium
	Genepool protection	Public	protection of litter meadow & natural grasslands	high			protection of genetic diversity	high	protection of genetic diversity and litter meadow	medium
Cultural Function	Aesthetic Information	Public					conservation of the landscape characteristic	high	natural scenery	low

Table 11.1 (continued)

	PA Function	Good Class.	Rheindelta		Sparbach		Hohe Tauern		Großes Walsertal	
			ES[1]	Importance	ES[1]	Importance	ES[1]	Importance	ES[1]	Importance
Cultural Function	Recreation	Commons or Club	biking, swimming, running, walking,. . .	medium	urban citizens & family attraction	high	cultivation and signage of hiking trails	medium	leisure infrastructure	medium
	Cultural and artistic information	Public								
	Spiritual & historic information, cultural heritage	Public					landscape conservation by sustainable cultivation	high	landscape cultivation, preservation of customs	high
	Science and education	Public or Club	field trips, information centre	medium	information centre, field trips, Nature Park School	high	information centre, National Park Acadamy, field trips, scientific publications	high	information centre, basic research, nature and environmental education in local schools	high

Regional Devel-opment	Sustainable Development	Public			regional marketing	high	regional marketing	medium	regional marketing	high
	Tourism	Club	touristic activities	low			mainte-nance of alpine refuge	medium	tourist activities	medium
	safeguarding of jobs	Private					NP regional employer	medium	common development of operation areas	medium
Public vs. Private (in %)	'Publicness' Funding		65:35 95 :5[2]		50:50 95:5[2]		65:35 90:10[3]		65:35 90:10[3]	

Notes:
1 Ecosystem Services.
2 Estimated values because of lacking data.
3 Average value over the available data.
4 Weighting: high = 1.5; medium = 1.25; low = 1.0.

Sources: Compilation and computation by author based on Costanza (2008), De Groot et al. (2002), De Groot et al. (2010), Rhine Delta Nature Conservation Association (2016), State of Vorarlberg (2016), Naturpark Sparbach (2015), Austrian Association of Nature (2016), Kremser (2003), Nationalparkrat (1995), State of Vorarlberg (2005), Biosphärenparkmanagement (2011).

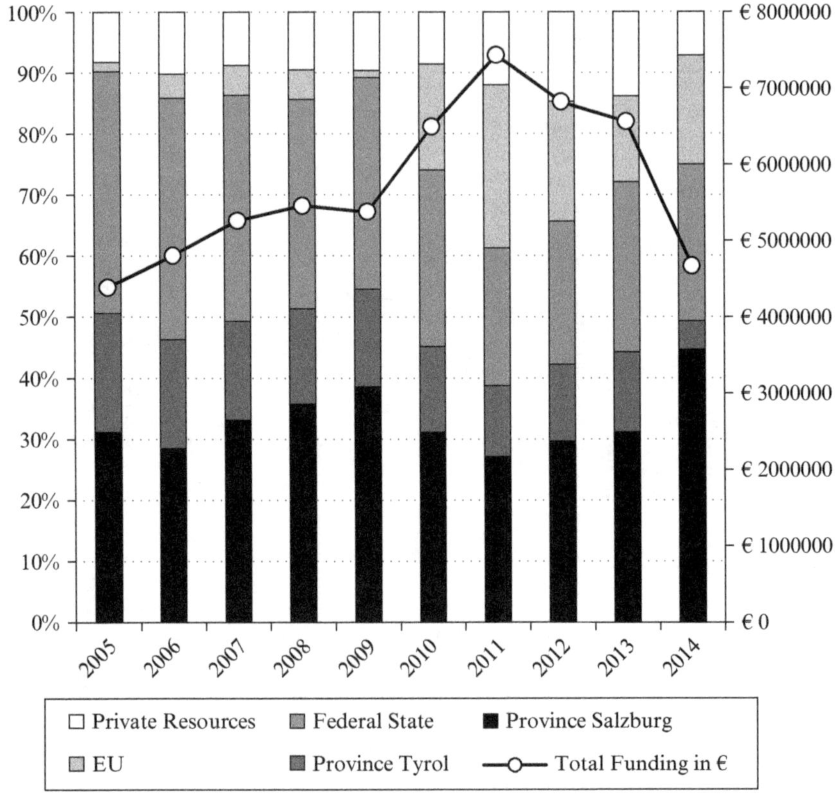

Note: Expenditure refers to the states of Tyrol and Salzburg only. For Carinthia the data are insufficient.

Source: Based on data by National Park Hohe Tauern (2015).

Figure 11.2 Funding of the National Park Hohe Tauern (in % and euros)

Tauern. However, according to the PA's publicness indicator, the share of private funding could be a little higher.

Biosphere Reserve Großes Walsertal

The Biosphere Reserve Großes Walsertal situated in the state of Vorarlberg, was established in the year 2000 and covers an area of around 19 200 ha (Lange, 2006). It is one of six biosphere reserves in Austria, but the first one in to be approved under the 'Man and Biosphere' programme[4] of UNESCO (Aschauer et al., 2007). The primary focus is less on the conservation of nature, and more on the coexistence of human society, economy and nature (ibid.).

The Biosphere Reserve Großes Walsertal differs from other PAs regarding its establishment process. In 1998 a non-profit organization laid the foundation for the biosphere reserve. The guiding principle was to develop the area together with 60 inhabitants so that an impetus for a positive regional development could be achieved (Lange, 2006). The Austrian Federal Ministry of Agriculture, Forestry, Environment and Water Management (BMLFUW) and the state of Vorarlberg supported this private initiative with initial (start-up) financing. Today, the biosphere reserve is financed by 'membership' fees from the municipalities within the biosphere reserve (proportional to the number of residents in each municipality), basic financing from the state of Vorarlberg, sponsoring and project financing by the EU and the federal government's budget (CIPRA, 2016).

The publicness analysis and indicator show that the Biosphere Reserve Großes Walsertal provides a large amount of public goods, such as the protective function of forests, and the conservation of genetic biodiversity. Additionally, there are also private or club goods produced, especially in the form of agricultural products (see Table 11.1). However, the respective shares of public and private funding do not correspond with the publicness indicator (see Table 11.1). Private actors' expenditures are disproportionally low, while public funding is disproportionally large (Figure 11.3).

11.5 RESULTS

The literature on funding PAs shows that private households, non-governmental and non-profit organizations and particularly local stakeholders (that is, the civil society) have always been driving forces in establishing, managing and funding PAs, even though the public sector (governments) has been responsible generally for the legal implementation and establishment of PAs. Funding by civil society sources has always represented only a small share in comparison to public expenditure. The chapter has shown that public expenditure for PAs is declining over time. Declining public expenditure, however, does not reduce the principal public responsibility to fund PAs. This is shown by the results of the empirical analysis in this chapter. The public responsibility derives from the fact that the business operation of the 'protected area' provides ecosystem services as its main output. These services are predominantly public goods in the sense that clear property rights are missing (no excludability) and everyone can consume these services to the same extent (no rivalry). Nevertheless,

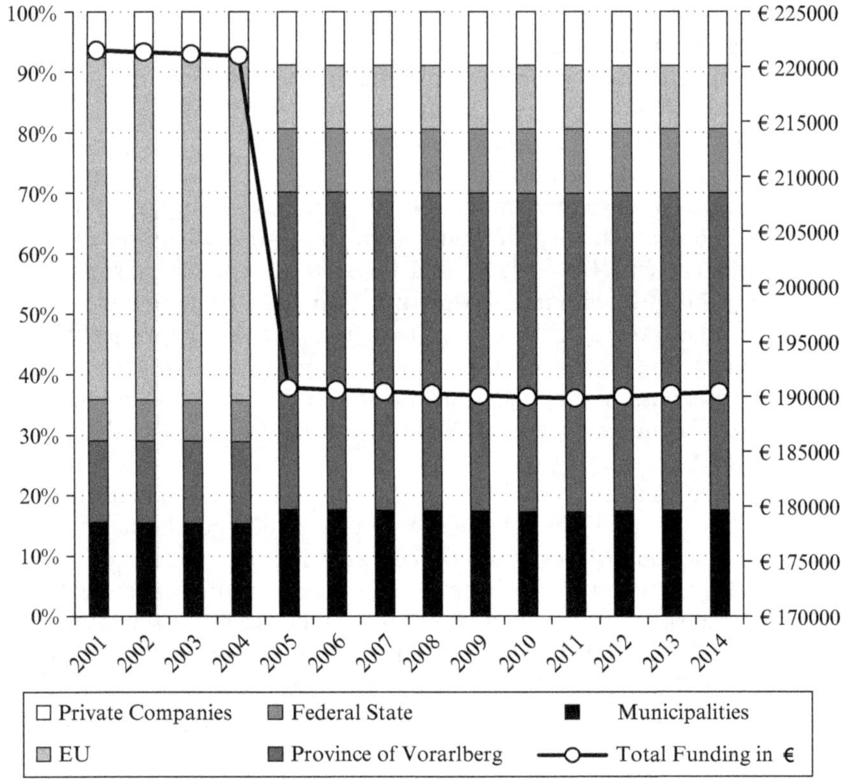

Source: Estimation based on CIPRA (2016).

Figure 11.3 Funding of the Biosphere Reserve Großes Walsertal

there are ecosystem services such as the provision of food and raw materials which are clearly private services and goods. Even though PAs provide a mixture of public and private goods, common and club goods, the funding of PAs is a core public task because the provision of private ecosystem services – for example, timber – is strongly determined by the provision of basic public ecosystem services, such as maintaining the nutrient cycle. For example, a tree cannot grow when the basic functions of the ecosystem, such as maintaining the nutrient cycle, are not sufficiently sustained. The difficulty is that these basic functions are generally not named in the PA management plans or their legal regulation. Because of this lack of information the publicness analysis could not consider all ecosystem services produced in the PAs. As a result, the publicness indicator seems to suggest exactness where it does not exist, and the results should therefore be interpreted with caution.

Furthermore, the assumption that the PA category determines the publicness of the area cannot be justified. The relation between public and private goods is more or less similar for all four PAs. The Nature Park Sparbach is the only PA for which a small difference in the public and private funding relation has been identified. It seems, however, that this difference has not been influenced by the PA category itself; the reason for the difference in funding seems to be the entrance fee and the historical background of the area. The other three PAs have a similar relation between public and private goods. Here too the topographical, economic, political and social surroundings, and in particular the historical background, determined the PAs' publicness.

11.6 SUMMARY AND CONCLUSIONS

Nowadays PAs – manifold areas set aside for nature conservation – are established based increasingly on private initiatives, or at least with intensive citizen participation. The PA management is also increasingly supported by local non-profit organizations, stakeholders and private households. The common goal of all PAs is, however, the conservation of biodiversity and the maintenance of ecosystem services, which can be classified to a large extent as (impure) public goods. Taking a closer look at PAs, it becomes clear that they provide diverse goods and services which are not only public goods, but can be classified additionally as club goods, private goods or common pool resources (commons). Against this background, this chapter aims to: (1) analyse the different sources of PA funding (public, private, donations, sponsoring) and their development; and (2) investigate empirically the sources of PA funding and their correlation to a publicness indicator of PAs. This indicator has been developed on the basis of ecosystem goods and services provided by the respective PAs.

The results of the analysis show that the funding of PAs is a core task of the public sector according to the public goods model (see Table 11.2). At the same time the results also show that the public sector spending has been negatively influenced by international economic developments. Seen from an international perspective, it seems likely that particularly private funding mechanisms could potentially grow in importance, especially if the actual willingness of private households and companies to pay for private and club goods provided by the PAs could be harnessed. The expenditure of civil society and private companies will probably never reach the amount

Table 11.2 Res publica table to jointly compare the chapters of this volume

	Description (positive) Who are and were the actors?			Justification (normative) Why should the state intervene?		
	State	Civil society	Market	Equality	Morality	Efficiency
Provision	Takes care of transaction costs	Citizen commitment		Poverty alleviation	Regulative ES are necessary to provide for basic human needs	ES are mostly public goods
Funding	Special subsidies	Supports public funding				Free-rider problem, information failure
Regulation	Nature conservation laws, international commitments				Public sector sets limit, for the commodification of nature	Property rights missing

of public expenditure, but could supplement the public sector funding and thus contribute to a generally more sustainable funding for PAs.

Nevertheless, from a moral point of view, it can be argued that the funding of PAs has to be public (see Table 11.2). As the publicness analysis showed, PAs provide a lot of services that are not visible and also not tangible. These so-called regulation services, however, are basic ecological processes and thus form the basis for all other services and goods produced in PAs. If these basic services were treated like commodities, it is likely that market activities could lead to the exploitation of natural resources and thus endanger the satisfaction of basic human needs. Public sector intervention is necessary in this case to prevent the exploitation of natural resources by limiting the scope of the market. In conclusion, whoever takes over the funding responsibility – the public, the private or the autonomous sector – should be assessed regularly, based on the sustainability of their expenditure, to make sure that the money spent really contributes to effective biodiversity conservation.

NOTES

1. 'Natura 2000 is a network of core breeding and resting sites for rare and threatened species, and some rare natural habitat types which are protected in their own right. It stretches across all 28 EU countries, both on land and at sea. The aim of the network is to ensure the long-term survival of Europe's most valuable and threatened species and habitats, listed under both the Birds Directive and the Habitats Directive' (EU, 2016).
2. *Ex situ* nature conservation contains the protection of species outside their natural habitat while measures of *in situ* nature conservation are limited to natural habitats.
3. The EPEA aims at describing the expenditure for environmental protection within the Austrian economy (Statistics Austria, 2012).
4. The 'Man and Biosphere' programme is oriented towards an international cooperation in the field of environmental research. The aim is to conserve natural habitats and protect biodiversity by combining results of natural science research in nature and social sciences (UNESCO, 2016).

REFERENCES

Aichhorn, K., K. Eisank, G. Hofer, H. Keuschnig, G. Mussnig, P. Rupitsch, A. Staats, E. Stüber and T. Suntinger (2011). 30 Jahre Nationalpark Hohe Tauern. Band 13 der Kärntner Nationalparkschriften, Kärntner Nationalparkfonds Hohe Tauern, Großkirchheim, Austria.

Aichinger, A. (2016). Environmental Protection Expenditure Accounts (EPEA), correspondence, 13 January.

Aschauer, M., M. Grabher and I. Loacker (2007). Geschichte des Naturschutzes in Vorarlberg - Eine Betrachtung aus ökologischer Sicht. Bregenz, Austria.

Austrian Association of Nature (2016). 50 years of nature parks in Austria. Accessed 8 January at http://www.naturparke.at/.

Austrian Federal Ministry of Agriculture, Forestry, Environment and Water Management (BMLFUW) (2016a). 20 years of LIFE. Accessed 3 January 2016 at https://www.bmlfuw.gv.at/.

Austrian Federal Ministry of Agriculture, Forestry, Environment and Water Management (BMLFUW) (2016b). ÖPUL 2015 the Agri-environmental Programme until 2020. Accessed 3 January 2016 at http://www.bmlfuw.gv.at/.

Austrian Federal Ministry of Agriculture, Forestry, Environment and Water Management (BMLFUW) (2016c). Wasserhaushalt Naturschutzgebiet Rheindelta. Accessed 8 January 2016 at http://www.bmlfuw.gv.at/.

Bertzky, B., C. Corrigan, J. Kemsey, S. Kenney, C. Ravilious, C. Besançon and N. Burgess (2012). Protected Planet Report 2012: Tracking progress towards global targets for protected areas. Gland, Switzerland: IUCN and Cambridge, UK: UNEP-WCMC.

Biosphärenparkmanagement (2011). Leitbild. Thüringerberg, Austria. http://www.grosseswalsertal.at.

CIPRA (2016). Ein Tal blüht auf – Regionalentwicklung im Biosphärenpark Großes Walsertal. Accessed 15 January 2016 at www.cipra.org.

Costanza, R. (2008). Ecosystem services: multiple classification systems are needed. *Biological Conservation*, 1(141),350–352.

De Groot, R.S., R. Alkemade, L. Braat, L. Hein and L. Willemen (2010). Challenges in integrating the concept of ecosystem services and values in

landscape planning, management and decision making. *Ecological Complexity*, 7, 260–272.
De Groot, R.S., M.A. Wilson and R.M.J. Boumans (2002). A typology for the classification, description and valuation of ecosystem functions, goods and services. *Ecological Economics*, 41, 393–408.
Dudley, N. (ed.) (2008). *Guidelines for Applying Protected Area Management Categories*, Gland: International Union for Conservation of Nature (IUCN).
Emerton, L., J. Bishop and L. Thomas (2006). *Sustainable Financing of Protected Areas: A Global Review of Challenges and Options*, Gland, Switzerland and Cambridge, UK: IUCN.
Environment Agency Austria (2001). *State of the Environment in Austria*, Vol. 6, Vienna.
European Environment Agency (EEA) (2012). Protected areas in Europe – an overview. EEA Report, No. 5/2012, Copenhagen, Denmark.
European Union (EU) (2016). Natura 2000. Accessed 15 January at http://ec.europa.eu/.
Getzner, M. and M. Jungmeier (2009). Integrative management of protected areas – a new scientific discipline?. In M. Getzner and M. Jungmeier (eds), *Improving Protected Areas*,: Proceeding in the Management of Protected Areas series, Vol. 1, Klagenfurt, Austria: Verlag Johannes Heyn, pp. 11–19.
Getzner, M., M. Jungmeier and S. Lange (2010). *People, Parks and Money – Stakeholder Involvement and Regional Development: A Manual for Protected Areas*, Proceedings in the Management of Protected Areas series, Vol. 2, Klagenfurt, Austria: Verlag Johannes Heyn.
Grabher, M., V. Blum, K. Farasin and W. Lazowski (1990). *RAMSAR-Bericht 1 Rheindelta/Marchauen – Bestandsaufnahme österreichischer Schutzgebiete*, Umweltbundesamt Monographien Nr. 18, Wien, Austria: Environment Agency Austria.
Handel, F. (2010). Einleitung. In Verband der Naturparke Österreichs (ed.), *Neue Modelle des Natur- und Kulturlandschaftsschutzes in den Österreichischen Naturparken*, Graz, Austria: Verband der Naturparke Österreichs, pp. 6–14.
Heath, J. (2011). Three normative models of the welfare state. *Public Reason*, 3(2), 13–43.
Jones-Walters, L. and K. Čivić (2013). European protected areas: past, present and future. *Journal for Nature Conservation*, 21(2), 122–124.
Jungmeier, M. (2014). In transit towards a third generation of protected areas? Analysis of disciplines, forming principles and fields of activities by example of recent projects in protected areas in Austria. *International Journal of Sustainability*, 6(1–2), 47–59.
Kremser, H. (2003). *Nationalpark Managementplan – Kernzone*. Salzburg, Austria: National Park Hohe Tauern.
Lange, S. (2006). Leben in Vielfalt, Biosphärenparks in Österreich – Modellregionen für nachhaltige Entwicklung. Broschüre, Vienna, Austria: Österreichische Akademie der Wissenschaften.
Maier, F. (2012). Österreichs Nationalparke – Zwischenbilanz und Herausforderungen. In P. Haßlacher and Österreichischer Alpenverein (ÖAV), *Alpenverein und Österreichische Nationalparke – Heute und Morgen, Tagungsband*, Alpine Raumordnung Nr. 37, Innsbruck, Austria: Österreichischer Alpenverein, pp. 16–26.
Millennium Ecosystem Assessment (2005). *Ecosystems and Human Well-Being: Synthesis*, Washington, DC: Island Press.

Mose, I. (2006). Personal communication. Oldenburg/Klagenfurt. In M. Getzner and M. Jungmeier (eds), *Improving Protected Areas*, Proceedings in the Management of Protected Areas series, Vol. 1, Klagenfurt, Austria: Verlag Johannes Heyn, p. 55.

National Park Hohe Tauern (2015). Activity reports. Accessed 20 October at http://www.hohetauern.at/.

Nationalparkrat (1995). *Nationalpark Hohe Tauern Leitbild*, Salzburg, Austria. www.hohetauern.at.

Nature Park Sparbach (2015). Our philosophy. Accessed 22 September at http://www.naturpark-sparbach.at/.

Oxford Dictionaries (2015). Definition of 'publicness'. In *British and World English*, Oxford Dictionaries. Accessed 3 January 2016 at http://www.oxforddictionaries.com/.

Payer, H. and H. Zangerl-Weisz (1997). Paradigmenwechsel im Naturschutz. In H. Zangerl-Weisz, V. Winiwarter, H. Schandl, H. Payer, H. Walter and M. Fischer-Kowalski (edss), *Gesellschaftlicher Stoffwechsel und Kolonisierung von Natur: Ein Versuch in Sozialer Ökologie*. Amsterdam, Netherlands: G+B Verlag Fakultas, pp. 223–240.

Penker, M., H.K. Wytrzens and B. Kornfeld (2004). *Natur unter Vertrag – Naturschutz für das 21. Jahrhundert*,Vienna, Austria: Faculatas Vertrags- und Buchhandlungs AG.

Regional Court of Audit of Lower Austria (2013). Funding of nature parks in Lower Austria. Report 3/2013, St Pölten, Austria.

Rhine Delta Nature Conservation Association (2016). Nature Reserve Rhine Delta. Accessed 4 January at http://rheindelta.org/.

State of Vorarlberg (2005). Regulation by the Province Government over the 'Biosphere Reserve Großes Walsertal', LGBl.Nr. 33/2000, 46/2005.

State of Vorarlberg (2015). Statement of nature and environmental protection accounts. Accessed 20 October at http://www.vorarlberg.at/.

State of Vorarlberg (2016). Protected areas in Vorarlberg. Natura 2000. Accessed 7 January at http://www.vorarlberg.at/.

Statistics Austria (2012). *Standard-Dokumentation Metainformationen (Definitionen, Erläuterungen, Methoden, Qualität) zur Umweltschutzausgabenrechnung*, Vienna, Austria.

Statistics Austria (2015a). Environmental Protection Expenditure Accounts (EPEA), on behalf of BMLFUW, tables 21 February 2008 to 27 February 2015. Accessed 25 July 2015 at http://www.statistik.at/.

Statistics Austria (2015b). Environmental Protection Expenditure Accounts (EPEA), explanation. Accessed 25 July 2015 at http://www.statistik.at/.

Statistics Austria (2016a). Expenditure of general government by function (COFOG) 2011–2014. Accessed 2 January 2016 at http://www.statistik.at/.

Statistics Austria (2016b). General Government Revenue and Expenditure, annual figures. Accessed 2 January 2016 at http://www.statistik.at/.

The Economics of Ecosystems and Biodiversity (TEEB) (2016). Ecosystem services. http://www.teebweb.org/.

Tiefenbach, M., G. Larndorfer and E. Weigand (1998). *Naturschutz in Österreich*, Vienna, Austria: Environment Agency Austria.

UNESCO (2016). Man and biosphere. Accessed 3 January 2016 at http://www.unesco.at/.

Weixlbaumer, N. (2006). Auf dem Weg zu innovativen Naturschutz-Landschaften-Naturverständnis und Paradigmen im Wandel. In K.H. Erdmann, H.R. Bork

and T. Hopf (eds), *Naturschutz im gesellschaftlichen Kontext*, Naturschutz und biologische Vielfalt, Issue 38, Bonn-Bad Godesberg, Germany: Bundesamt für Naturschutz, pp. 7–27.
Weixlbaumer, N. (2010). Großschutzgebiete in Europa – Ansprüche, Entwicklungen und Erfolgsfaktoren. In Verband der Naturparke Österreichs (ed.), *Neue Modelle des Natur- und Kulturlandschaftsschutzes in den Österreichischen Naturparken*, Graz, Austria: Verband der Naturparke Österreichs, pp. 14–23.
World Commission on Protected Areas (WCPA) Financing Protected Areas Task Force, IUCN and Economics Unit, IUCN (2000). *Financing Protected Areas*, Gland, Switzerland and Cambridge, UK: IUCN.

12. The role of governments in conserving and funding cultural institutions

Michael Getzner

12.1 INTRODUCTION AND BACKGROUND

A significant part of government funds, on the central as well as on regional and local levels, is devoted to research, conservation, and the operation and management of cultural institutions such as historical buildings, monuments, museums and theatres. In some countries, public spending in the cultural area has increased compared to other areas of public spending, above gross domestic product (GDP) growth rates. This was the case even in times of financial and economic crises (see for Austria, Getzner, 2015; see Benhamou, 1996).[1] Compared to other countries such as the United States (US) and United Kingdom, public spending for cultural institutions seems to be substantially higher in continental European countries. The involvement of the private sector (private households, companies, non-governmental organizations) in form of sponsoring and donations remains much stronger in the US and United Kingdom, despite the fact that a stronger commitment of the civil society (third-sector organizations) in cultural policies has long been discussed and promoted in Europe (Ilczuk, 2001). The main question of this book can thus be applied to cultural institutions as well: is there a core of public responsibilities and activities with respect to conserving and funding cultural institutions which cannot be transferred to the private sector?

Against this background, this chapter aims to identify public functions, roles, tasks and activities in conserving and managing cultural institutions. In particular, this chapter addresses the following questions:

- How can goods and services connected to cultural institutions such as national museums and theatres be classified:
  - along the lines of the 'traditional' public finance literature (as public, private, club goods, and/or as commons); and

  - by means of the structured and detailed *res publica* approach for classification?
- How may indicators or units of measure for the 'publicness' of goods and services look like with respect to the following approaches:
  - analytical; that is, classification of cultural goods and services based on economic criteria (rivalry, excludability, meritory character);
  - positive; that is, based on statistics (for example, expenditure, revenues); and
  - normative; that is, defining indicators of 'publicness' and identifying a set of core indicators?
- Finally, how is a public good or service produced, and what is the role of private households and the civil society in producing and funding public services, and achieving the desired outcomes of public activities?

With respect to the large variety of questions to be considered, the scope of the study (cultural institutions as part of cultural heritage) must be clearly defined so as to ensure an operational and empirically manageable degree of detail. What the concept of cultural heritage comprises is a question broadly debated in cultural studies, and more generally in the social sciences. Since the concept of cultural heritage has changed significantly over the past few decades this chapter follows a pragmatic approach. The dimensions and elements of the debate and the theoretical foundations of the concept will therefore not be discussed in detail. Change becomes evident, for instance, in the meaning and use of the term 'cultural heritage' in national and international law and agreements on the conservation and management of cultural institutions. Up until the 1950s the physical contents and characteristics of cultural heritage were considered to be valuable historical cultural capital (for example, the existence of historically important and/or aesthetically valuable buildings). Since then the understanding of the concept has broadened to include immaterial (intangible), perceptual, contextual (place and time) and democratic elements. Cultural heritage thus is understood as a primary basis for and at the same time an important expression of societal development. This includes developing society identities, and accounts for the diverse processes of producing, perceiving and using cultural heritage. The concept of cultural heritage has also moved from a static, protective understanding (for example, including a historical building on a list of valuable cultural or historical assets) to managing and actually 'using' cultural heritage in the widest sense, and deciding in public and political discourses on the values associated with artefacts (see Vecco, 2010; Montella, 2015). Based on this broad understanding of cultural heritage, the current chapter deals with cultural institutions such as national theatres and museums.

While defining cultural heritage could be normative, as can be shown in the development of its definition, Cheng (2006) distinguishes several basic notions of cultural economics, that is, goods, services, capital and 'cultural atmosphere'. Cultural goods are 'tangible or intangible items of cultural significance' (Cheng, 2006, p. 264) such as buildings, sites and artefacts (for example, paintings, scores). The stock of cultural goods taken together forms the existing cultural capital. Cultural capital provides 'a flow of services that may be consumed as private and/or public goods entering final consumption immediately, and/or they may contribute to the production of future goods and services, including new cultural goods' (Throsby, 1999, p. 7; see Barile, 2014, concerning the 'service logic' of cultural institutions). Services which emerge (not necessarily exclusively) from cultural capital are called 'cultural services' (Cheng, 2006). Finally, the consumption of cultural services accumulates – in the sense of positive consumption externalities – to the 'cultural atmosphere' which may be thought of as a public good. As this chapter will show, the cultural atmosphere can form a part of social capital together with other social benefits of cultural institutions.

In the following sections the economic analysis will focus regionally on Austria, and on national museums and theatres as important parts of (national) cultural heritage, and on further cultural institutions constituted under public law and funded by the central government. More specifically the chapter deals with the following national cultural institutions:

- National museums:
  - Kunsthistorisches Museum Wien (KHM), combined with further museums such as Weltmuseum Wien and Theatermuseum;
  - Naturhistorisches Museum (NHM);
  - Albertina, Belvedere, Museum für angewandte Kunst (MAK).
- National theatres and important (internationally renowned) festivals, including:
  - Staatsoper, Volksoper;
  - Burgtheater;
  - Salzburger and Bregenzer Festspiele.

Criteria for selecting the above-mentioned cultural institutions are: (1) the perceived (assumed) importance with respect to national (society-wide) interests (for example, conservation, documentation, research, national pride and cultural atmosphere, identification); (2) economic interests (for example, cultural institutions as important factors for quality of life, tourism and recreation); and (3) their constitution and financing being based on national, public law (for example, cultural spending by the Austrian federal government). Owing to the lack of data, some major cultural institutions, such as the Schönbrunn Palace, could not be included.

The structure of this chapter is as follows. Section 12.2 gives a brief overview of important theoretical aspects for discussing the research questions of this chapter with emphasis on the several dimensions of values attributed to cultural goods, the public goods model, the co-production of goods and services (complementary public and private activities), and the differentiation between inputs, outputs and outcomes. Based on these aspects indicators of 'publicness' are analysed empirically and discussed. In section 12.3 the '*res publica*' classification table (see Chapter 1, the 'Introduction' of this book) is adapted to cultural institutions, and discussed with regard to the eminently important differences between normative and positive analyses. Section 12.4 provides a discussion of the empirical results of the study, as well as indicators of 'publicness' of goods and services provided by cultural institutions. Finally, section 12.5 summarizes the results, and details the conclusions.

12.2 THEORIES AND CONCEPTS CONCERNING THE ROLE OF THE PUBLIC AND THE PRIVATE SECTOR IN CULTURAL POLICIES

Individual Values Attributed to Cultural Institutions

Cultural economics, of course, investigates the arts market, production, demand, prices and values connected with artefacts. However, a classification of the diverse economic values citizens attribute to cultural goods may also include perspectives based on environmental valuation methodologies. The perceived value of public goods and their financing was formulated for the first time by Tiebout in his concept of 'voting by foot'. More recent environmental valuation methods focus on attributing monetary values to non-market goods and services,[2] especially public goods. These concepts of economic valuation distinguish between values depending on whether public goods are used by the individual in a consumptive or non-consumptive manner. The personal values (based on preferences) are usually summed up as total economic value (TEV) (e.g., Ferretti et al., 2014) (see Table 12.1 regarding cultural institutions). Similar classifications can be found for environmental goods and services. Ready and Navrud (2002) describe use and non-use values with special emphasis

Table 12.1 Classification of values attributed to cultural institutions (national museums and theatres) according to use (consumptive) and non-use (passive, non-consumptive)

Use values Associated with a direct (personal, individual) benefit (i.e., utility) of using the good (or resource):	Non-use values (passive use values) Associated with individual, personal utility without using the good (or resource)
1. Direct use values, stemming from consumption (extractive use); e.g. buying and reading an exhibition catalogue as a private (exclusive) good; (illegal) taking of a souvenir.	1. Existence values, associated with the mere existence of cultural heritage; e.g., preferences for the conservation of paintings or buildings as part of cultural heritage, without actually using it, including aesthetic values (e.g., historical buildings contributing to a historic urban landscape).
2. Indirect use values, stemming from using the good in a non-consumptive way (non-extractive use); e.g. visiting a museum and enjoying painting, watching a theatre or opera show.	2. Altruistic values, expressed by one's preferences for heritage access or use of others (existence and altruistic values may also include preferences for the conservation of cultural heritage with respect to social identity, cohesion and the cultural atmosphere)
3. Option values (option demand); e.g. individual willingness-to-pay for the conservation and operation of cultural heritage for one's own (potential) use in the future.	3. Bequest values, attributed to cultural heritage in order to conserve goods for future generations; e.g., preferences for storing, conserving, archiving artefacts.

on historical buildings and landmarks. They classify cultural goods in a straightforward approach basically as public goods which need government action to be preserved on the grounds of non-excludability and non-rivalry of consumption. However, they also add some caveats with respect to excludability (for example, excludability could be technically feasible yet associated with prohibitively high cost), and rivalry (for example, congestion could make a non-rival consumption impossible). In addition, they also refer to local public goods (for example, a historical building in a small town with only limited recognition by outsiders) versus landmarks famous nationwide.

Serageldin (1999) adds a further component labelled 'aesthetic value'. This is basically non-consumptive in character, and does not require direct recreational efforts, but is perceived through some (personal) sensory experience. Other authors stress the mixed and combined values associated with cultural goods, for example combinations of historic and recent urban design. For instance, Forte and Girard (2009) demonstrate that values associated with urban beauty are complex, relating to tangible as well as intangible (immaterial) components such as symbols, meaning and originality. Similarly, Choi et al. (2010) argue that cultural institutions provide a wide range of values such as 'symbolic cultural items, historical value, social value, aesthetic value, spiritual value, educational value and shared experience' (see also Armbrecht, 2014).

Table 12.1 highlights several important dimensions of preferences for the conservation of cultural heritage expressed through individual values in favour of the conservation of cultural institutions based on diverse goods and services 'produced'. While a simplified model of cultural institutions may basically relate only to the public goods character of cultural institutions, and thus provide a general argument for government intervention, a differentiated approach leads to a more refined perspective on the role, functions and financing instruments of different actors.

With respect to the role of the public and the private sector in conserving and funding cultural institutions, the literature generally suggests that values not traded on markets, for which societal preferences exist, should be provided for by the public sector. Cultural institutions, goods and services can be irreducibly social, and 'have made us what we are, and . . . we have an obligation to maintain them' (Rushton, 1999, p. 143). In this sense, the merit goods argument does not derive from paternalism or external effects, but from the very essence and quality of culture – the values of which are not merely individual ones according to Table 12.1, but are social ones not directly connected to individual preferences or perceptions, and thus economic valuation methods should not be applied (see the discussion in Provins et al., 2008).

The Double Public Good Model

How a public cultural good is produced by efforts from both the public as well as the private sector is one of the central questions mentioned in the introduction. When it comes to cultural institutions, one might argue that national museums and historic buildings are public goods by their mere existence. Citizens 'consume' cultural heritage as a public good by knowing that these institutions exist, and they attribute some values – most often passive (existence) values – to them. Benhamou (1996) concedes that historic monuments can be owned publicly or privately, yet they are connected both with external effects (pride, prestige, preservation for future generations), making them public goods, and with private effects in the form of consumption capital (human capital formation), as well as recreation, entertainment and tourism. Even the 'consumption' of the most distant passive use values, the mere existence of a historical building, only carries any value if citizens perceive the historical building as part of the cultural heritage, thus associating and attributing values to it. Therefore – even in the broadest sense – some effort of private households (citizens) is connected to the public good which only becomes this very (public) good if it is 'co-produced' by citizens as such. On the other hand, if citizens do not know about a historical building, and do not obtain any benefits (utility) in terms of existence or bequest values from it, it can still be classified as a public good on the basis of Musgrave's classification of goods in the sense of non-rivalry of consumption, and non-excludability.

Sable and Kling (2001) present a simple analytical model to describe the concept of citizens willing to bear some costs (efforts) in order to 'produce' public goods and to use these goods to experience historical buildings and museums. In their 'double public goods model', households derive utility from private goods, from the stock of public goods per se, from the 'use' of the public goods for cultural experiences, and from the shared experience of using the good together with other households. This model therefore assumes that the stock of cultural capital does not produce any (public) goods or services per se, but that it always requires private efforts in terms of out-of-pocket expenses, time, opportunity costs of foregone (private and public) consumption alternatives, and attention as well. The individual efforts thus co-produce diverse goods and services; some of them may of course be individual (private) goods such as merchandise (booklets, posters), jointly consumed goods (club goods such as museum visits), and public goods for which non-use (existence) values exist (see section 12.4 of this chapter for a more detailed discussion). The model of Sable and Kling (2001) can be interpreted in a wider context as 'production' of regional or national cultural heritage for which citizens feel (national) pride, and are therefore also willing to pay taxes to finance cultural institutions.

Following this argument, the concept of joint public sector and citizens' production of public goods transcends the commonly assumed conflict between the public and the private sector concerning the use of scarce resources. Gronau (2008) has recently presented a concise overview of the significance and problems of household production regarding consumer goods, highlighting the manifold problems in empirically studying this important phenomenon. However, the idea that public goods are produced jointly by the public and the private sector seems to be a novel approach to public policies. Public and private efforts are no longer seen in conflict. Rather public goods and services are produced collaboratively (for outcomes, see the subsection below) since a separate use of resources is not sufficient to produce the desired good or service (and finally, values). To conclude: efforts (resource use) of both the public and the private sector are inherently complementary factors of production.

The concept of 'citizens' in the current context refers not only to private households in their role as consumers, co-producing public goods for their own benefits, but also comprises the 'autonomous' sector (third sector, civil society) (co-)producing public goods and services for society's benefit and common welfare. Especially in the cultural sector, cultural events, even prominent ones such as festivals, are managed and funded jointly by the public and the private sector, the latter including consumers, citizens and the civil society.[3]

Outputs, Outcomes and the Diffusion of Benefits

Are public goods, such as conserving and managing cultural institutions in the sense of 'producing' national pride and contributing to a nation's self-esteem, outputs or are they perceived as valuable outcomes only? In the strict sense of Musgrave's classification of goods as private, public or mixed, outcomes do not play a role regarding the characteristics of a good (service). If excludability and rivalry in consumption is given, the good (service) is a private good; if the good (service) is non-excludable, and non-rival in consumption, it classifies as a purely public good (Musgrave and Musgrave, 1989). Concerning cultural institutions, this classification seems too narrow. Let us consider the case of a collection of historically unique paintings, documenting certain periods and styles, which are in storage and are forgotten. Their quality as a potential part of cultural heritage could classify them as a public good; benefiting from the mere existence of these artefacts is non-excludable, and non-rival. But in order to benefit from them (private or societal) citizens must perceive (know about the existence of) and positively value these artefacts, and the artefacts must indeed 'produce' (that is, be connected with) the aforementioned self-esteem and national pride. The mere output in form of existing, conserved and stored paintings does not provide benefits; only if a certain outcome is achieved may the artefacts indeed contribute to the development of cultural institutions. For contributing to and developing cultural institutions, these artefacts have to be perceived and valued, and have to actually contribute to the joint production of 'cultural heritage'. Consequently, cultural goods are not produced through proper conservation only, but need to be communicated to citizens, and benefits (concrete as recreation benefits, abstract as non-use values of existence) have to be spread across the population. Therefore, to acknowledge the importance of cultural institutions and thus secure the funding for the conservation and management of artefacts it is a prerequisite to spread the benefits of cultural institutions in the widest sense (see also Girard, 2011).

12.3 POSITIVE AND NORMATIVE APPROACHES TO THE CORE OF *RES PUBLICA* IN THE DOMAIN OF CULTURAL POLICIES

In the 'Introduction' to this book the editors proposed a '*res publica*' table to analyse the role of the private and the public sectors in providing public goods and services. Table 12.2 gives an overview with respect to cultural institutions, with an analogue structure.

The left side of Table 12.2 describes the manifold dimensions of providing cultural goods and services in positive terms. The classification distinguishes three main groups of actors: the state (government policies and interventions, that is, the public sector), the autonomous sector (civil society, non-governmental organizations, non-profit), and the private sector (private households, profit-oriented companies). These three groups of actors play different roles in providing, funding and regulating cultural goods and services. With respect to all three dimensions, the public sector certainly plays an eminent role since the national museums and theatres are in most cases organized and funded on the basis of public law, and institutionalized as public bodies. However, quite a number of institutions are also supported by non-governmental organizations (NGOs) promoting their aims and objectives, for example through education and information. The extent to which NGOs play a role in cultural policies differs, depending on institutions: for instance, their role is more prominent in connection with large festivals, and regional or local cultural initiatives. The private sector is involved in two ways: on the one hand, private households and companies fund cultural institutions by purchasing tickets and merchandise (and ultimately also by paying taxes). On the other hand, the private sector 'co-produces' the outcomes of cultural policies in terms of, for example, perceiving, learning and enjoying cultural goods and services.

The right side of Table 12.2 addresses the normative perspective on justifications for state intervention in cultural institutions. Based on the three dimensions of equality (socially equitable distribution), community/morality and efficiency, the table presents arguments in favour of government interventions (for example, public provision of cultural institutions for distribution as well as efficiency reasons). From the author's perspective,

Table 12.2 Positive and normative reasons to provide cultural goods and services

	Description (positive)			Justification (normative)		
	Who are/were the actors?			Why should the state intervene?		
	State	Civil Society	Market	Equality	Community/ Morality	Efficiency
Provision	State (central government) is the property owner, and owner of the providing companies; some employees are civil servants	NGOs, civil society provide some shows, exhibitions (e.g. artists' associations such as the Secession); Association of Friends the of the KHM/ NHM	Some types of shows/exhibitions are profitable (e.g. musicals, festivals) and thus produced by the market; private organizational form of public companies	Every citizen should be able to benefit from the cultural heritage incl. access to culture/the arts	Freedom of cultural expressions, new forms of art languages and opinions; participation in cultural/social affairs and future generation	Cultural heritage as a public good (economy-wide non-exclusive. importance); merit character, (positive) external effects of cultural institutions; failure of the market to provide long-term coordination and 'cultural atmosphere'
Funding	Basic funding (public cultural spending), coverage of deficits, provision of funds for conservation, research, documentation (also for not-state-owned institutions)	Sponsoring and donations from art funds, associations, civil society	Revenues from admission fees marketing/ merchandise sponsoring by private companies: funding of specific projects	Reduction of admission fees for senior citizens, school and university students (not for low-income households)	Freedom of cultural opinions should not depend on income / other resources; public funds guarantee innovative, non – market/not – for – profit driven avantgarde	Lack of private funds (public goods) [crowing-out of private funds by public funds?]

Regulating	State regulates and manages cultural institutions (e.g. conservation, operation of theatres and museums)	Membership, regulations regarding exhibitions, principle; codified in by-laws	Business – centred regulations regarding which art forms should be supported / funded; taxes for donations	First come, first served – equal access to tickets; ticket lotteries and waiting lines	Basic human rights – non – discriminatory access to cultural international regulations (UNESCO)	Conservation and further exploration and development of cultural institutions should be regulated centrally (long – term, lack of information, myopia)
	Nature of the good					
Public/ private goods and services	Cultural heritage as a public good: every citizen benefits from the conservation of cultural heritage (and cannot be excluded); option demand (provision of consumption opportunities in the future); public goods: scientific research, conservation/restoration and documentation; private goods: provision of recreation and cultural events entertainment; meritory goods: education and information, build-up, 'consumption capital'; positive externalities: basic provision of services and image for the tourism industry, Austria as a cultural nation and significant tourism destination, 'quality of life'; 'joint production' of goods/services and values by the private and the public sector					
Tangible and intangible goods and services	Conservation of some cultural heritage is tangible (e.g., palaces, antic historic landmarks); most goods/services are intangible (art exhibitions, theatres, opera, other shows); 'Austria is a 'cultural nation': = intangible (international image, self-perception, national pride); visibility of landmarks = contribution to the intangible visual appearance of cities/landscapes; differentiation between outputs and outcomes					
	Type of government intervention					
Visibility	*High* visibility of government in . . . terms of buildings: conservation of heritage and landmarks; . . . public discourse / debate on actors (Anna Netrebko, Klaus-Maria Brandauer), festivals (Salzburger Festspiele), directors (Claus Peymann), authors (Thomas Bernhard, Elfriede Jelinek) / debate on public funding of theatres, museums, opera houses; Low visibility . . . restoration, documentation, scientific research					

Note: Areas shaded dark or light grey indicate the importance of these aspects (dark = high importance, light = medium importance).

the 'public good' is certainly the most important normative argument. If the state does not regulate, provide and fund the basics of cultural institutions – research, conservation, documentation and education – these institutions are not able to produce other (private) goods and services that may also lead to public values.

Nevertheless, at least two caveats remain. First, the normative justification (or recommendation) for government intervention applies to a particular political and societal context. For instance, traditions and the fundamental understanding of government roles and functions are inherently different between countries. Second, even if the arguments in favour of government interventions are accepted, the overall (economic) costs of public policies could be higher than the aggregated benefits (for example, if public cultural spending is administered and financed in a highly distortionary or inefficient way). Also, the form of government intervention (public sector policies) is not a priori fixed. The government may have an important role in cultural policies but can intervene through different instruments and approaches (for example, providing goods directly, subsidies to providers of goods, regulating standards, outsourcing the management and operation of cultural institutions). Thus, the government can have the responsibility for providing certain goods and services, but may decide on various approaches regarding the organization and management in providing them.

The lower part of the table sums up a couple of additional aspects for the discussion of cultural institutions. On the one hand, cultural goods and services can certainly be classified as public goods; however, as will be argued in more detail below, cultural institutions form the basis of a wide range of goods and services, not all of which are purely public goods (services). Some may be more likely private goods, and others may be classified as merit goods. Using the concepts of public goods, externalities, spillover effects and national identity, Hutter (1996) discusses the qualities and goods characteristics in the cultural domain. He talks about a 'degree of publicness' (see below, section 12.4) which is also required for the functioning of some private markets (for example, prices for famous paintings). Mazzanti (2002) considers the merit goods character of cultural goods and services, and emphasizes the wide range of different goods and services (for example, private, public, mixed and collective services; see also Mason, 2005; Choi et al., 2010). On the other hand, cultural institutions are certainly tangible when it comes to hard infrastructure (buildings, artefacts, historical landmarks); however, many outputs and, especially, outcomes are intangible such as national pride, the general quality of life, or the cultural atmosphere.

Finally, the table describes the dimension of 'visibility' of government intervention or public sector activities. Preserving and providing cultural institutions is a highly visible process; cultural policies and the role of the state in organizing and financing cultural institutions are under public scrutiny and intensely discussed.

12.4 DEVELOPING A POSITIVE AND NORMATIVE INDEX ON THE DEGREE OF PUBLICNESS OF A GOOD OR SERVICE

Description and Classification of Goods and Services Produced by Cultural Institutions

As already emphasized above, cultural institutions provide a wide range of goods and services that cannot be classified simply as either public or private. The question therefore remains whether there is a quantifiable index (or degree) of 'publicness' for goods or services, by which the extent to which the public sector actually is, or should be, involved in providing cultural services can be analysed. The following classification of goods and services describes – not exclusively – the main outputs (some may already be outcomes), and provides main categories (dimensions) of cultural services:

- Hard infrastructure such as buildings, historical landmarks, for example the palaces of Hofburg and Schönbrunn, the inner cities of Salzburg and Vienna:
  - appearance of cities, landscapes, particular places as public goods: national pride, image, self-perception (prestige/symbolic value), quality of life, cultural atmosphere;
  - intended positive external effects, infrastructure, spillover: tourism (for example, Vienna, Salzburg) produces and visitors consume private goods (funded by private revenues); cultural institutions function as cultural infrastructure (that is, as a condition for the production of services in the tourism industry).
- Artefacts, paintings, music scores as important elements of cultural institutions;
  - documentation, restoration, conservation of cultural assets (existence value, bequest value) as public goods.
- Recreation, entertainment, consumption of cultural events:
  - cultural infrastructure and its management/operation produce private goods, some of which are also club goods (theatre shows);

  - and realize social-equity aims (distribution) through reduced admission.
- Education and information, accumulation of 'consumption capital';
  - private goods (for example books, brochures, private interests and benefits such as enhanced knowledge about the arts, merchandise);
  - merit goods (externalities and 'paternalism'), that is, contributions to a 'good, humanistic society' lead to financial support and subsidies;
  - externalities (higher education, productivity).
- Conservation and management of cultural institutions in terms of option demand (option value).
- Scientific research and publications:
  - knowledge as a public good, and as a fundamental precondition for conserving and using cultural heritage.

Based on these broad categories, several indices of publicness will be conceptualized in the following, providing analytical as well as normative (policy-oriented) tools to identify core public tasks. Based on the discussion in sections 12.2 and 12.3 of this chapter, two indices will then be discussed in more detail and applied to various cultural institutions:

1. 'Inputs': that is, funding for different cultural institutions which makes up most of the federal policy concerning national cultural institutions (national theatres, museums, festivals).
2. 'Outputs': that is, measuring different goods and services produced by employees, taking the example of one prominent cultural institution, namely the Kunsthistorisches Museum Wien.

However, these two indicators provide only a limited view on the public value of cultural institutions; the most adequate indicator would measure outcomes in terms of achievement of certain objectives (impacts), for example the level of education attained through a museum's education and information activities, or the extent to which artefacts are conserved and thereby contribute to the cultural atmosphere. While it is rather straightforward to measure the input in terms of (private and public) cultural spending – even if there are also, of course, numerous caveats in terms of accuracy – outputs cannot usually be measured (quantitatively, qualitatively) with the same level of precision. If at all, the impacts of outcomes can only be measured qualitatively. This is also a major practical drawback of public–private partnerships in cultural policies since it is difficult for the public sector to monitor the outputs and outcomes of activities by the private partner (see ter Bogt and Tillema, 2015).

Input as Indicator of Publicness

The 'input' index (indicator) as described above measures the actual funding from different sources (public, private, mixed). This general indicator is used for a descriptive analysis, and could be interpreted – at least in an ideal democratic system – as society's (voters' median) preferences for financing cultural institutions. Thus, it could be assumed that funding figures mirror such preferences not only when it comes to the perceived importance of cultural institutions, but also with respect to different sources, and thus for the role of the different actors (sectors).

Figure 12.1 gives an overview of the development of public cultural spending in Austria in the period from 1967 to 2013. Over the years, the federal (central) government spent approximately EUR350 million annually on leading cultural institutions (national theatres, museums); cultural spending of the federal government taken together (consolidated, including all ministries, including all subsidies and tax credits) amounts to roughly EUR805 million per year (almost EUR90 annually per capita). Additionally, regional governments (nine federal provinces, *Bundesländer*) spent approximately EUR900 million, while expenditure of local authorities (municipalities) amounts to about EUR650 million. Depending on the classification of 'private cultural spending' – that is, including not only ticket prices but other private expenditure connected with the consumption of cultural services – private households spent at least as much as the public sector (all figures taken from Getzner, 2015). It is worth noticing that public cultural spending was not limited during times of fiscal crises (for example, 2002, 2008/09) as shown in an analysis by Getzner (2015); public cultural spending increased above GDP growth, and also above the growth of total public consumption.

Apart from direct funding (for example, basic funding of state-owned cultural institutions, subsidies), the public sector is involved in financing by means of indirect funding. Only recently, the Austrian parliament amended the income tax law to allow for tax credits in case of private donations to cultural institutions funded or subsidized by the central government (see Austrian Income Tax Law, 2015). Cultural institutions eligible for such donations include the National Library (Österreichische Nationalbibliothek), national museums as institutions of public law, and the federal agency for the conservation of monuments (Bundesdenkmalamt). Interestingly enough, documents and commentaries accompanying the bill for a new Austrian 'non-profit/for the common good' law state that

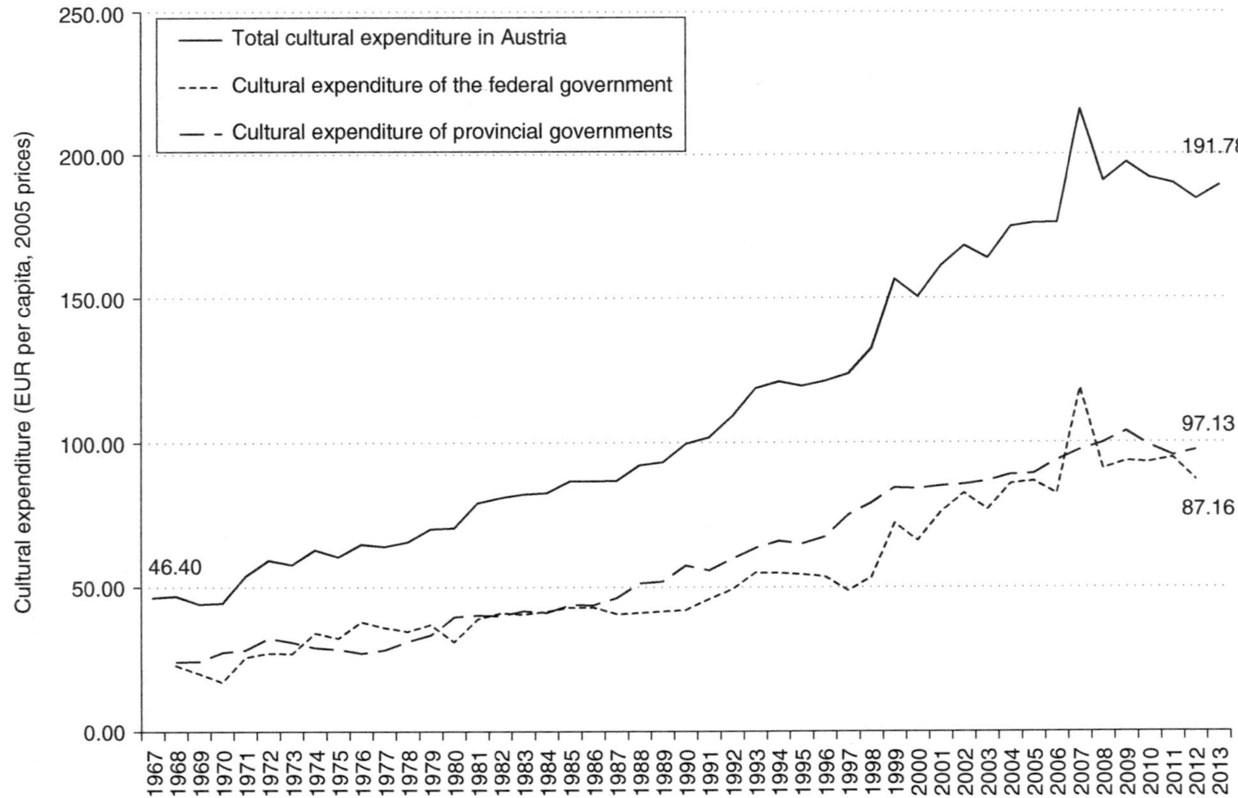

Source: Reproduced from *Poetcis* 49, Michael Getzner, Cultural politics: Exploring determinants of cultural expenditure, p. 65, Copyright (2015), with permission from Elsevier.

Figure 12.1 Public cultural spending in Austria, 1967–2013 (federal and provincial governments; euros per capita, 2005 prices)

in Austria private donations, and generally, the commitment of the civil society to support cultural institutions, are lower compared to neighbouring countries such as Germany and Switzerland. Therefore, the central government aims to provide incentives to strengthen the commitment of the private sector. Given the lengthy debate on the marginal role of the private sector, and the criticism of the 'excessive state involvement in the administration of arts' (Benhamou, 1996, p. 115), it seems important for political decision-makers to promote other forms of funding (for example, attracting private donations, sponsoring, merchandising). However, as will be shown below, the general demand for a stronger involvement of the private sector in financing cultural institutions seems to be restricted to certain outputs (activities), only occasionally comprising basic public goods and services produced by these institutions.

To devise a more detailed 'input indicator (degree) of publicness', this chapter will focus on the main cultural institutions funded by the federal government.[4] Based on a range of legal and institutional arrangements, the national museums and theatres are financed to a large extent by federal funds; however, the extent to which private funds (for example, sponsoring, merchandise and ticket sales) are involved varies significantly.

Figure 12.2 presents the sources of funding for the operation of national theatres, museums and some prominent festivals. Total funding of the Vienna opera house amounts to approximately EUR105 million per year, while the national museums receive total funds in the range from EUR11 million to EUR38 million annually. The total budget for prominent festivals is comparatively high; the figure shows a comparatively smaller share of public funds (especially subsidies from the central government) for festivals, though still significantly high.

While a comparison between these institutions is difficult because the respective aims and objectives differ, it seems that larger and internationally acknowledged museums, being important destinations for tourists, receive more private funds than smaller museums with a focus on more specific topics (for example, Technisches Museum Wien). Figure 12.3 details the sources of funding in the main categories (public, sponsoring and donations, tickets, merchandise, other revenues). For the national museums, at least half the budget is funded by the central government; regarding theatres (including the opera houses), the share of public funding amounts to up to 80 per cent. Festivals, being events limited in time and focus, are mainly funded by ticket sales, yet receive about a quarter of their budget from the public sector.

In developing an index of publicness, it seems that the analysis of the funding sources as 'input' does not lead to a robust indicator that could guide political decisions on finding and measuring a 'public core' of tasks

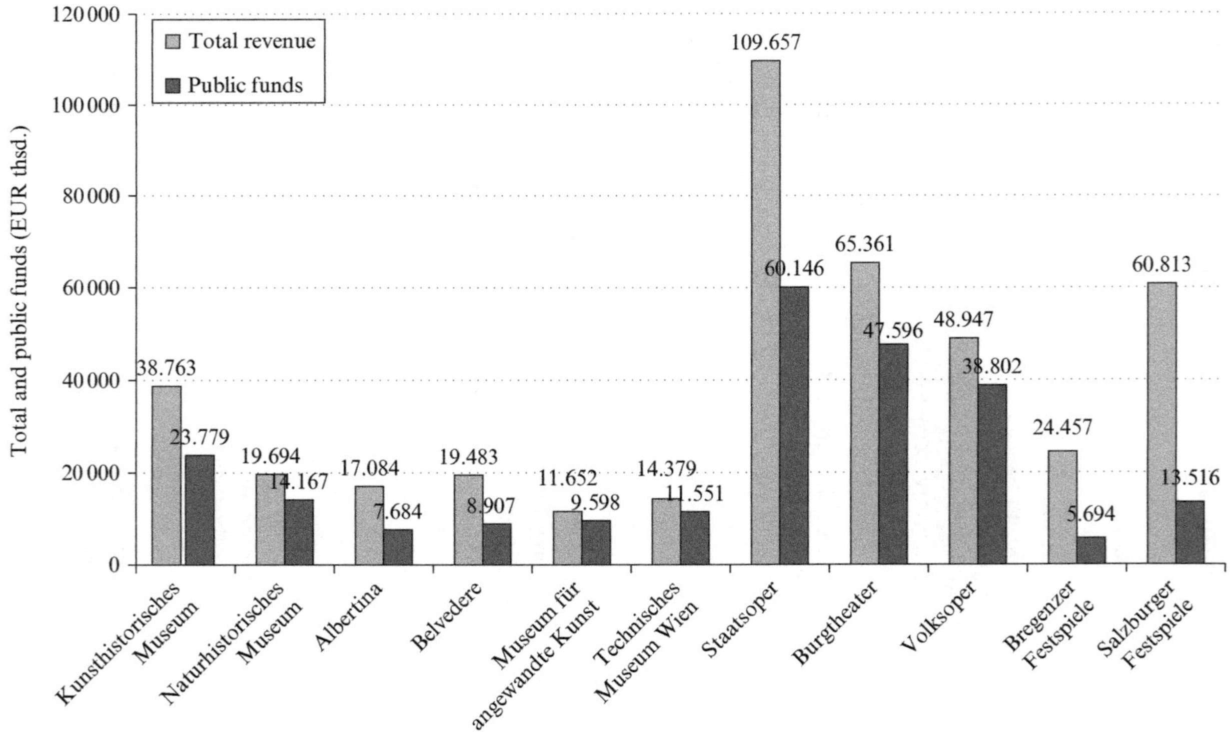

Source: Based on revenue-expenditure statistics and reports by the cultural institutions named.

Figure 12.2 Total funds and public contribution (central government) for the operation of national museums, theatres, and festivals (euros, 2014 or most recent data available)

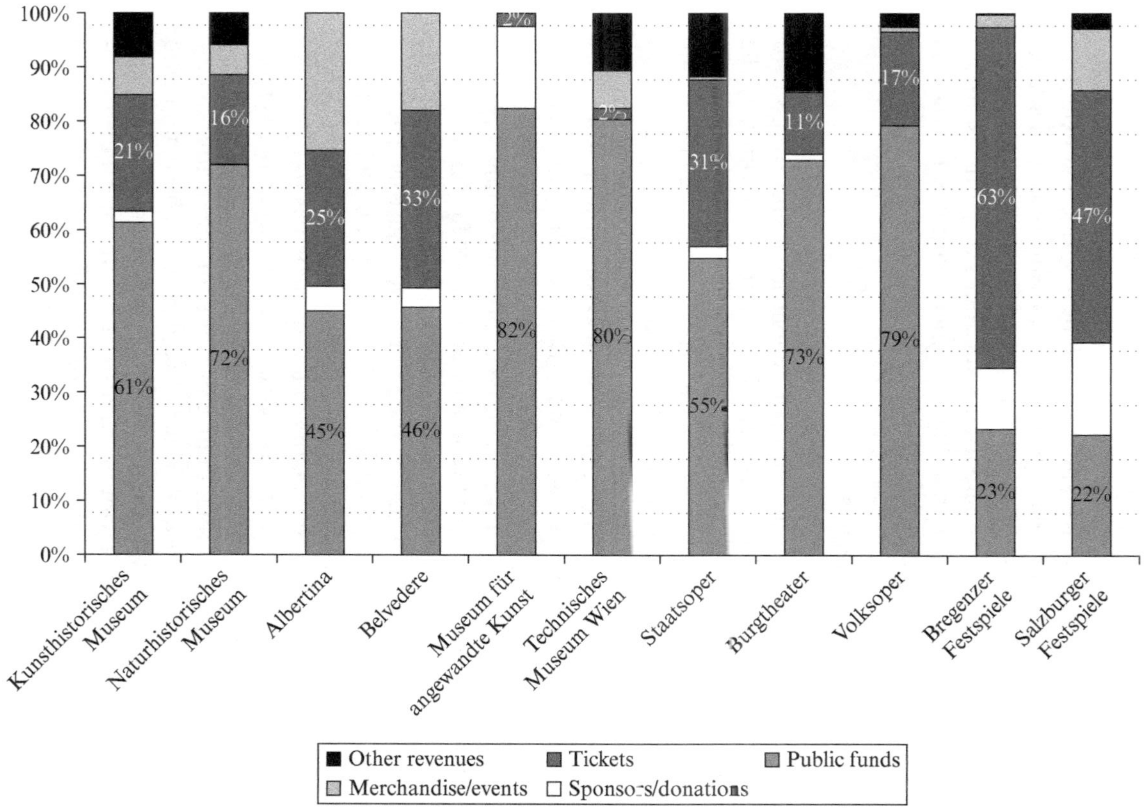

Source: Based on revenue-expenditure statistics and reports by the cultural institutions named.

Figure 12.3 Share of public funds, and sources of funding, for the operation of national museums, theatres and festivals (% of expenditure categories to the total budget; 2014 or most recent data available)

in the fields of conserving and managing cultural institutions. Of course, all institutions contribute to cultural heritage not only regarding personal experience, entertainment, or education, but also with respect to 'cultural atmosphere', and are therefore important elements of Austria's cultural identity (including national pride). Based on this and depending on the level of recognition, acceptance and demand by visitors, the extent to which these institutions provide cultural services can be considered as rather equal. Regarding their financial sources, they vary considerably, especially with respect to their importance for tourism. Festivals attract international audiences no less than highly recognized museums such as the Albertina and the Belvedere.[5]

Output as Indicator for Publicness

In order to construct an indicator of publicness with respect to 'outputs' (goods and services produced by cultural institutions), the Kunsthistorisches Museum Wien serves as example for an institution that combines being a major attraction for tourists, with large departments for research, restoration and conservation. Analysing the goods and services provided, an interesting source of information is the public law institutionalizing the museum not only as a 'mere showroom' displaying artefacts, but also as a public research body.[6] Based on this, the museum's bylaws (*Museumsordnung*) include specific objectives and tasks to be achieved by the museum's management. The most important objective for federal museums in Austria is to enable a comprehensive 'participation of the population in the cultural and social diversity of the artistic and historic . . . collections' owned by the Republic of Austria. The stock of all collections of artefacts, their adequate presentation and scientific research, build the basis for reaching this objective (KHM bylaws, 2009). To achieve the museum's objectives, the following activities (outputs) are listed in the bylaws: collecting artefacts, conserving and restoring artefacts, documentation, research and exhibitions.

It is difficult to establish a quantitative measure for the relative importance of these activities, because of a lack of readily accessible data. Based on the law and their respective bylaws, cultural institutions negotiate and sign performance agreements with the Ministry of Cultural Affairs detailing qualitative and quantitative objectives to be achieved within a fixed period of time (usually 3–5 years). However, the funds and resources are not provided to the cultural institutions according to these objectives but are paid in the form of a lump-sum federal contribution.

This means that it is not possible to value the outputs directly in financial terms. However, the museum's statistics detail the number of employees working in the different departments, producing the desired outputs; analogous to the value of public services in the European System of National and Regional Accounts (ESA), the value of the outputs is measured by a combination of input variable (for example, number of employees) and accumulated costs of personnel which are then imputed in the GDP estimations. Based on this, Figure 12.4 compiles the proportional numbers of personnel working in the different departments of Kunsthistorisches Museum Wien. The figure clearly indicates the importance of research, restoration and documentation, followed by the significant efforts in the departments of communication and education.

To examine whether a task is more likely to be financed by public or private funds, the various activities of the departments are aggregated into three main categories ('output clusters'). The funding of the museum

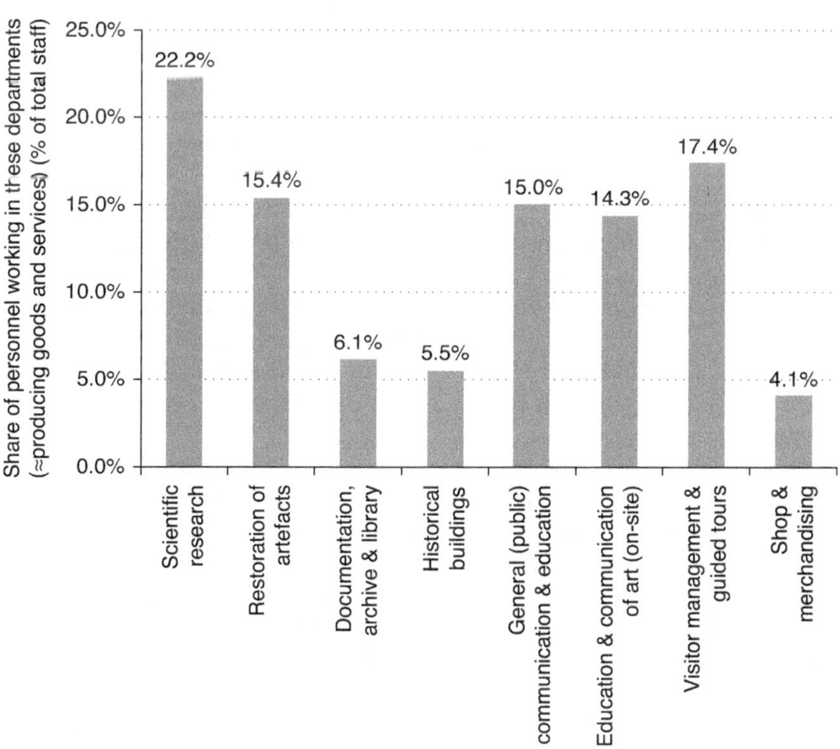

Source: Based on statistics by Kunsthistorisches Museum Wien.

Figure 12.4 Proportion of staff working in the different departments of Kunsthistorisches Museum Wien, 2015

(presented in Figure 12.3) can be related to the respective output categories. To begin with, the departments of scientific research, restoration, documentation and historical buildings are aggregated into one cluster. Concerning this cluster, the business report of the museum, and other documents such as reports on publications, restored artefacts, and so on, indicate that the activities (outputs) are financed predominantly by public funds. However, the museum receives public funds that exceed the accrued expenditure for this cluster of output (see Figure 12.5).[7] This surplus is apparently used to finance activities producing outputs not sufficiently funded from private or other resources (see Figure 12.5). The second output cluster, producing various kinds of information as well as educational products and services for private households and the general public alike, is partly funded by donations and sponsoring, and – at least to a certain extent – by public and project funds. Compared to the cost of managing and operating exhibitions and shows, revenues from ticket and merchandise sales exceed the expenses, again leaving some funds for information and education outputs.

Looking at the funding for the different outputs, we can assume that the first output cluster is considered a fundamental public task by the federal government as well as in the legal framework. However, the business report (KHM, 2015) indicates that some private donations are made with respect to specific activities such as the restoration of single artefacts, or the sponsoring of certain collections and the research required to set them up. It therefore seems reasonable to assume that the first output cluster is also not fully funded by the public sector, and that private financing contributes about 5–10 per cent of the total expenditure. Regarding the second output cluster (education and information), it seems reasonable to assume a mixed funding structure because it provides a broad range of goods and services, including products targeted at specific groups with defined aims and purposes, among them one-off projects. So it seems that sponsoring, donations and, especially, project funds (in which public financing may also play a significant role), combined with some basic public funding and private spending (for example, books, catalogues, lectures), form the financial basis for these activities. Third, for activities connected to personal experiences (exhibitions, visits to the museum by locals and tourists alike), private funds seem to constitute the main source of funding; however, since the legal and managerial frameworks also require reduced ticket prices for specific groups of visitors (for example, students, seniors, artists), public funds could also form part of the financial basis for this branch of activities.

Combining this discussion and the underlying assumptions, Figure 12.6 and Figure 12.7 present rough estimates for the funding of the Kunsthistorisches Museum Wien both in a vertical perspective (sources of funds, that is, public, private, mixed/other), and a horizontal perspective

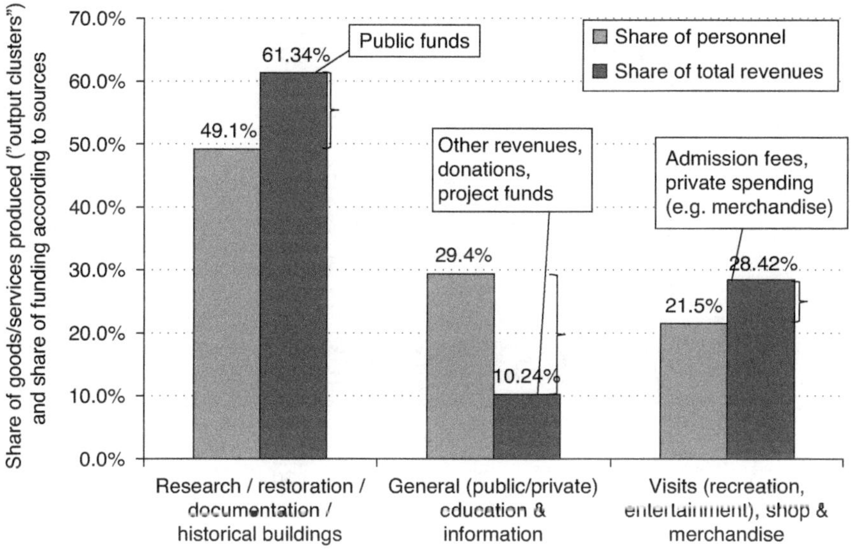

Note: Brackets show the estimated surplus/deficit for each of the three clusters.

Source: Based on statistics by Kunsthistorisches Museum Wien.

Figure 12.5 Percentage of personnel of Kunsthistorisches Museum Wien compared to equivalent shares of funds devoted to core 'output clusters' of the museum

(activities/outputs funded). As described above, the quality of the data, especially concerning the allocation of funds to the different outputs, is limited. However, given the whole range of data, the two figures present a rough operationalization of the output indicator of publicness.

Figure 12.7 presents a roughly estimated assignment of funds to the different output clusters. Public funds are mainly allocated to the fundamental activities enabling the museum to educate, inform and exhibit artefacts, namely research, restoration, and so on. Private funds are in most cases connected to personal experiences. Mixed funding (project money, sponsoring) is assumed to be used for various purposes, for example publications. Figure 12.6 presents these results from the horizontal perspective. Activities connected to the production of public goods and services are mainly financed by public funds, while activities connected with visiting the museum are funded privately.

It has to be emphasized that the presentation and discussion of the output indicator of publicness – besides being based on a rough estimate

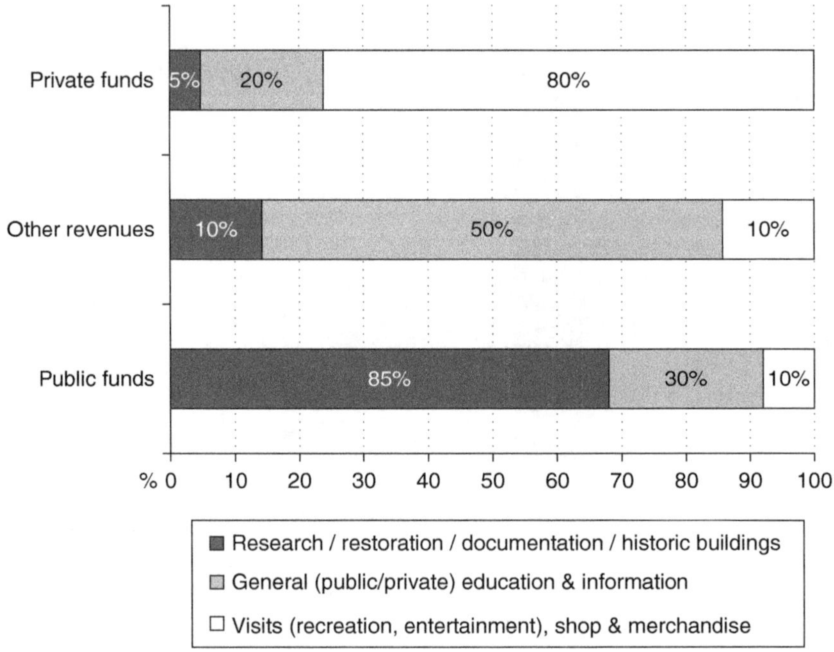

Source: Based on statistics by Kunsthistorisches Museum Wien; own assumptions.

Figure 12.6 Funding of the activities of Kunsthistorisches Museum Wien according to sources of funding (vertical perspective; use of funds, %, rough estimate)

of the allocation of funds – may also change over time. While the basic public funding seems to be rather stable, visitor numbers, project funds and donations may vary substantially. In addition, the museum's management constantly has to adapt to political strategies restricting public funding, and render other sources of funding accessible by applying for project financing, research programmes and specific short-term funding programmes (for example, limited programmes to restore or extend buildings). New organizational frameworks may also be used, such as public–private partnerships (PPPs) in the cultural sector (see Monreal and Al Hassan, 2013). While the problems of monitoring and evaluating the outcomes of cultural activities pose a fundamental hindrance towards such partnerships comprising the full range of cultural activities (outputs), the basic conditions for efficient and effective public–private partnerships in the cultural sector also include, among others, good governance, effective public administration, and risk-sharing. Given the long debate on PPPs, and

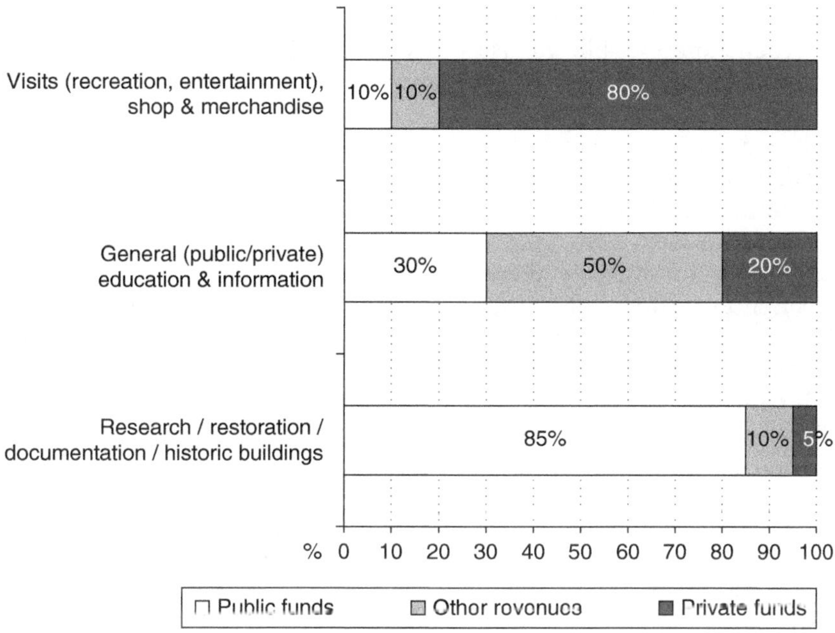

Source: Based on statistics by Kunsthistorisches Museum Wien; own assumptions.

Figure 12.7 Funding of activities of Kunsthistorisches Museum Wien according to activities/outputs (horizontal perspective; source of funding, %, rough estimate)

the lack of institutional and governance structures to achieve efficiency by means of PPPs in the cultural sector, it is not surprising that public funding – at least in many countries in Europe – still forms the financial basis for many cultural institutions.[8] Furthermore, while the basic public financing may have decreased over time, many other sources of funding such as project funds, research funds and programmes provide further forms of (indirect) public funding.

12.5 DISCUSSION, SUMMARY AND CONCLUSIONS

The main research question of the current chapter focuses on identifying possible core public tasks in the conservation and management of cultural institutions; more specifically, major cultural institutions such as national theatres, museums and festivals. The chapter started with theoretical and empirical key concepts of cultural policies, such as economic values connected to cultural institutions, the role of joint experiences and co-production of public goods by private households, and the differentiation between input, outputs and outcomes originating from the new public management literature.

The aim of the theoretical and conceptual discussion was to find clues for defining an index for the publicness of goods and services produced by cultural institutions. It turned out that it is most relevant to differentiate in great detail the goods and services 'produced' by cultural institutions, for example research, conservation, exhibitions and visitors' experiences in museums. From a descriptive and analytical perspective, these goods and services can be classified along the usual dichotomy of public and private goods. However, this chapter has indicated that the differentiation between the two is not at all clear-cut. First, basically all cultural goods and services include both public as well as private elements. For instance, a visitor's experience in a museum may well lead to personal benefits, but may also contribute to general education and information, thus building up cultural consumption capital. Besides, cultural experiences are also frequently thought of as merit goods for which the state provides supporting funds. Second, the discussion emphasized that even the most private cultural goods and services produced by cultural institutions are based on public goods and services, for example on research, restoration and documentation. Third, some public goods and services such as the contributions of cultural institutions, or the provision of education and information services, are ultimately co-produced by private households. This co-production can consist of private learning efforts, private expenses for cultural experiences, and the household's (citizen's) perception and valuation of the contribution of cultural institutions to a society's development, self-esteem, social cohesion and national pride.

It is thus not an easy task to develop an index of publicness with respect to the goods and services produced by cultural institutions. The first step in this chapter was to measure input in terms of sources of funding for selected cultural institutions (theatres, museums, festivals). The chapter finds that the degree of public funding varies substantially across the institutions. The public is, however, significantly involved in funding all sorts of cultural institutions, even in the case of international opera festivals, where an international audience pays high ticket prices for exclusive opera productions. The differences in the funding of cultural institutions can thus be explained basically by the number of visitors (and, of course, by the size of the institution). Museums and theatres that are not as prominent nevertheless produce valuable public goods and services. The measurement of the publicness in terms of input may thus be distorted and may mirror historical developments rather than show economic reasoning and informed policy-making.

A second approach to measure the publicness of goods and services was applied not to all prominent cultural institutions of Austria, but took the Kunsthistorisches Museum Wien as an example. Measuring the outputs is challenging since many goods and services produced are intangible and hard to measure. Outputs were thus valued by personnel costs in the respective departments of the museum. The results were then compared to the museum's financing structure. Conforming to expectations, this differentiated picture underlines the importance of public funds for public goods and services both in terms of cultural infrastructure for other goods and services produced by the museum (for example, exhibitions, shows, presentations), and in providing the basis for co-production of cultural identity, and other social benefits.[9] Private funding can be found mainly for activities related to recreation, entertainment, education and information, while some mixed funding (for example, project funds, sponsoring) can be assumed for a variety of goods and services connected with public information, education and other activities.

The two indicators of publicness – concentrating on inputs or outputs/activities – implicitly acknowledge the meaning of cultural institutions with respect to society's identity and cohesion (Rushton, 1999) as desired outcomes carrying public value. This argument leads directly to a call for public funding because social (instead of individual) values are connected to and produced by cultural institutions.

The chapter also shows that the set-up of the funding basis of cultural institutions may vary over time, and may also vary substantially between countries, based on traditions and historical developments. While research and documentation of artefacts is without doubt a public good, and is funded in Europe by public funds, there might be other, equally efficient institutional or social arrangements where private funds – supported by tax credits – may also form a stable basis of funding for cultural institutions. In the case of Austria, with its emphasis on public funding, the provision of public goods and services in the context of cultural institutions – research, conservation, documentation, education – is, without doubt, a core public task. This does not mean that cultural institutions have to be funded completely by public money, nor are all public goods and services currently produced by them. Even if this chapter has argued for a strong involvement of the public sector in conserving and financing cultural institutions, it also becomes apparent that the answer to the core of *res publica* is not straightforward, and that a differentiated picture of goods and services, actors, activities and outcomes is the necessary basis for a profound public discourse on the involvement of all parts of society in cultural policies.

ACKNOWLEDGEMENTS

I am grateful to the Wirtschafts- und Sozialwissenschaftliches Institut WSI of Hans-Böckler-Stiftung (Germany) for financial support in writing this chapter. The editors and reviewers provided many helpful suggestions for substantial improvements of the chapter. I would like to thank in particular W. Schönbäck, B. Unger, F. van Waarden and the whole Res Publica team for their suggestions and constructive criticism. All errors remain, of course, the responsibility of the author.

NOTES

1. Austria may be somewhat different to other countries with respect to fiscal policy reactions following the financial and economic crisis after 2008. For instance, Cuccia and Rizzo (2015) examine the effects of the recent recessions on public budgets regarding cultural funding and find a tendency towards reducing public expenditure for cultural production, forcing cultural producers to search for new strategies, for example diversification and extension of services (see, for public cultural spending in European countries, Council of Europe/ERICarts, 2015).
2. It should be noted that Boulding (1977) criticized the usual dichotomy between 'goods' and 'services', and the extent and importance of 'cultural economics' in this context. In the inaugural issue of the *Journal of Cultural Economics*, he also emphasized the crucial significance of perceiving and valuing cultural preferences and activities which is also a major argument in this chapter.
3. Of course, not all citizens 'co-produce' public goods, and value cultural institutions equally. The government may provide cultural goods only for a minority (see Heath, 2011, p. 27). However, if the government pursues different minority programmes, all citizens will be in favour of such programmes because they expect that their minority preferences will be covered by some of the government's programmes.
4. Rengers and Plug (2001, p. 2) discussed an index of publicness with respect to art production in the visual arts and measured this index, with the extent of 'government funding [making up] about 43 per cent of the total income earned by all artists in the visual arts. The remaining 57 per cent are earned on the private market'.
5. An economic argument for different levels of public funding also lies in the ticket price elasticity based on the demand for cultural goods and services.
6. According to the Austrian Law on Federal Museums (2002), Kunsthistorisches Museum is a scientific body institutionalized by public law with the aim to realize the aims of cultural policies and scientific research in a not-for-profit manner.
7. Due to lack of data it is impossible to calculate the exact costs for personnel and operation of the museum regarding different activities. Based on the business report of the museum, an average wage rate was computed; the value of the outputs was then calculated by linking the number of employees in the respective departments of the museum with the average wage rate.
8. Zaman (2015) supports this impression by comparing European Union countries as a 'high responsibility belongs to the public sector as the most important custodian of [cultural heritage] assets, interested in the respect of local, regional and national cultural features and the appropriation of cultural values by the population' (Zaman, 2015, p. 6).
9. Equally important is the detailed knowledge about cultural statistics and definitions in order to come up with reliable financial statistics in the cultural sector (Hofecker, 2005).

REFERENCES

Armbrecht, J. (2014). Use value of cultural experiences: a comparison of contingent valuation and travel cost. *Tourism Management*, 42, 141–148.

Austrian Income Tax Law (2015). Bundesgesetz vom 7. Juli 1988 über die Besteuerung des Einkommens natürlicher Personen (Einkommensteuergesetz EStG, 1988), as amended on 28 December 2015, BGBl. I Nr. 163/2015.

Austrian Law on Federal Museums (2002). Bundesmuseen-Gesetz vom 7. Januar 2002, as amended on 14 December 2015, BGBl. I Nr. 144/2015.

Barile, S. (2014). Towards a novel conception of Bene Culturale. In G.M. Golinelli (ed.), *Cultural Heritage and Value Creation*, Cham, Switzerland; Heidelberg, Germany; New York, USA: Springer, pp. 53–70.

Benhamou, F. (1996). Is increased spending for the preservation of historic monuments inevitable? The French case. *Journal of Cultural Economics*, 20, 115–131.

Boulding, K. (1977). Notes on goods, services, and cultural economics. *Journal of Cultural Economics*, 1, 1–12.

Cheng, S.-W. (2006). Cultural goods creation, cultural capital formation, provision of cultural services and cultural atmosphere accumulation. *Journal of Cultural Economics*, 30, 263–286.

Choi, A.S., B.W. Ritchie, F. Papandrea and J. Bennett (2010). Economic valuation of cultural heritage sites: a choice modeling approach. *Tourism Management*, 31, 213–220.

Council of Europe/ERICarts (2015). *Compendium of Cultural Policies and Trends in Europe*, 17th edition, Strasbourg: Council of Europe Culture Committee and Secretariat (www.culturalpolicies.net).

Cuccia, T. and I. Rizzo (2015). Less might be better – Sustainable funding strategies for cultural producers. *City, Culture and Society*, 7, 109–116.

Ferretti, V., M. Bottero and G. Mondini (2014). Decision making and cultural heritage: an application of the multi-attribute value theory for the reuse of historical buildings. *Journal of Cultural Heritage*, 15, 644–655.

Forte, F. and L.F. Girard (2009). Creativity and new architectural assets: the complex value of beauty. *International Journal of Sustainable Development*, 12, 160–191.

Getzner, M. (2015). Cultural politics: exploring determinants of cultural expenditure. *Poetics*, 49, 60–75.

Girard, L.F. (2011). Economics of uniqueness – cultural heritage assets and historic cities as public goods. Paper presented at the World Bank, Washington, DC, 3 May.

Gronau, R. (2008). Household production and public goods. In S.N. Durlauf and L.E. Blume (eds), *The New Palgrave Dictionary of Economics*, Vol. 3, 2nd edition, Basingstoke: Palgrave Macmillan, pp. 84–88.

Heath, J. (2011). Three normative models of the welfare state. *Public Reason*, 3, 13–43.

Hofecker, F.-O. (2005). Aus Vergleichen lernen: Zur Kultur des gegenseitigen Abwägens durch Forschung und Politikkommentierung. In T. Zembylas and P. Tschmuck (eds), *Der Staat als fördernde Instanz*, Vol. 5 of Diskurs Kultur–Wirtschaft–Politik, Vienna: Department of Cultural Management and Cultural Studies (IKM), University of Music and Performing Arts, pp. 143–170.

Hutter, M. (1996). The impact of cultural economics on economic theory. *Journal of Cultural Economics*, 20, 263–268.
Ilczuk, D. (2001). Private action for the public good – regulations, incentives and examples of practice. MOSAIC (Managing an Open and Strategic Approach in Culture), Council of Europe, DGIV/CULT/MOSAIC(2001)9.
KHM bylaws (2009). Museumsordnung für das Kunsthistorische Museum mit Museum für Völkerkunde und Österreichischem Theatermuseum, as amended on 1 December 2009, BGBl. II Nr. 395/2009.
KHM (2015). Geschäftsbericht 2014. Wien: KHM (Kunsthistorisches Museum Wien) Museumsverband.
Mason, R. (2005). Economics and historic preservation: a guide and review of the literature. Brookings Institution Metropolitan Policy Program Discussion Paper, Washington, DC.
Mazzanti, M. (2002). Cultural heritage as multi-dimensional, multi-value and multi-attribute economic good: toward a new framework for economic analysis and valuation. *Journal of Socio-Economics*, 31, 529–558.
Monreal, L. and N. Al Hassan (2013). Public private partnerships in the culture sector. Background paper for the UNESCO conference on Culture: Key to Sustainable Development, Hangzhou, China, 14–17 May. Paris: United Nations Educational, Scientific and Cultural Organisation (UNESCO).
Montella, M. (2015). Cultural value. In Golinelli, G.M. (ed.), *Cultural Heritage and Value Creation*, Cham, Switzerland; Heidelberg, Germany; New York, USA: Springer, pp. 1–51.
Musgrave, R.A. and P.B. Musgrave (1989). *Public Finance in Theory and Practice*, 5th edition, New York: McGraw-Hill.
Provins, A., D. Pearce, E. Ozdemiroglu, S. Mourato and S. Morse-Jones (2008). Valuation of the historic environment: the scope for using economic valuation evidence in the appraisal of heritage-related projects. *Progress in Planning*, 69, 131–175.
Ready, R.C. and S. Navrud (2002). Why value cultural heritage?. In S. Navrud and R.C. Ready (eds), *Valuing Cultural Heritage – Applying Environmental Valuation Techniques to Historic Buildings, Monuments and Artifacts*, Cheltenham, UK and Northampton, MA, USA: Edward Elgar Publishing, pp. 3–9.
Rengers, M. and E. Plug (2001). Private or public? How Dutch visual artists choose between working for the market and the government. *Journal of Cultural Economics*, 25, 1–20.
Rushton, M. (1999). Methodological individualism and cultural economics. *Journal of Cultural Economics*, 23, 137–147.
Sable, K.A. and R.W. Kling (2001). The double public good model: a conceptual framework for 'shared experience' values associated with heritage conservation. *Journal of Cultural Economics*, 25, 77–89.
Serageldin, I. (1999). Cultural heritage as public good – economic analysis applied to historic cities. In I. Kaul, I. Grunberg and M.A. Stern (eds), *Global Public Goods*, New York, USA and Oxford, UK: Oxford University Press, pp. 240–263.
ter Bogt, H. and S. Tillema (2015). Accounting for trust and control: public sector partnerships in the arts. *Critical Perspectives on Accounting*, 37, 5–23.
Throsby, D. (1999). Cultural capital. *Journal of Cultural Economics*, 23, 3–12.
Vecco, M. (2010). A definition of cultural heritage: from the tangible to the intangible. *Journal of Cultural Heritage*, 11, 321–324.
Zaman, G. (2015). Cultural heritage entrepreneurship (CHE) – challenges and difficulties. *Procedia – Social and Behavioral Sciences*, 188, 3–15.

13. Income distribution as a public task: the redistributive preferences of (mis)informed voters

Daan van der Linde

13.1 REDISTRIBUTION OF INCOME AS A PUBLIC TASK

Public concerns over inequality date back to early urbanization and industrialization. Accounts of late nineteenth-century England find many rich Londoners 'slumming', descending into the slums in horse-drawn buses to observe the poor. While some observers suggested that poverty as a tourist attraction merely served for the enjoyment of the spectator, Koven (2004, p. 1) shows that the experience instilled in others a sense of the magnitude of social injustices in society, laying 'tenacious claims over their minds and hearts, drastically altering the course of their lives'. Those who did not dare enter the slums watched magic-lantern shows, shaping their collective understanding of social welfare and poverty. In screenings at various venues, such as auditoriums, music halls and churches, 'visitors could witness orphans freezing to death in the snow, drunkards plunging their families into misery and helpless old people begging for a scrap of bread' (Deutsches Filminstitut, 2011).

In the face of this new understanding of the social realities in many European cities, charities stepped in to address the 'social question' of the time. Notable examples from the Netherlands are the *hofjes*: housing projects offered for free to the poor, usually the elderly or widows and widowers. *Hofjes* were financed by both church organizations and guilds, as well as privately by rich individuals, usually from testamentary dispositions. Today we still observe a wide and divergent range of social programmes in welfare states – programmes 'grown public' (Lindert, 2004) – which took over many such private initiatives in different (national) constellations.

What justifications on normative grounds can be given for such public concern over the distribution of income? Economic theory provides two such justifications, one grounded in equity (see the 'equality model' from the 'Introduction' to this book), another in efficiency (see the 'efficiency model'). The argument for equity suggests that market economies with extensive division of labour generally arrive at unequal distributions of income and wealth; distributions likely to be deemed democratically unacceptable. Collective choice may deem certain distributions of income unjust, for instance when income differences are believed to be grounded in circumstances beyond the individual's control (Roemer, 1998). Streeck (2011, p. 3), among others, refers to a tension between conflicting principles of 'market' and 'democratic' forces, the former 'operating according to marginal productivity', the latter according to 'social need, or entitlement, as certified by the collective choices of democratic politics'. Economic theory, however, has shown (under certain restrictions) that market and democratic forces can operate jointly, as any efficient distribution of resources is attainable after the redistribution of income.[1] In other words, societies – democratically mandated – may seek to achieve more equitable distribution of resources simply by redistributing income, afterwards leaving market forces in place.

Can we depend on charity to achieve such equitable distribution of resources, or do we need a government to intervene? As the distribution of income represents a pure public good, being both non-excludable and non-rival, the equity argument seems unlikely to achieve a sufficiently equitable income distribution without government intervention. All of society faces the same income distribution, and no individual can be deprived of the benefits or harms flowing from any such particular distribution. As 'each individual has a vested interest in disguising his preferences concerning his desired income distribution to avoid paying his optimal share of the necessary transfer payments' (Thurow, 1971, pp. 328–329; see also Warr, 1982), public intervention is warranted. Charity or any other form of self-imposed transfers alone are unlikely to reflect citizens' true preferences, hence underproviding income redistribution.

Governments elicit these (concealed) preferences of individuals through elections. These elections are believed to tap into two general motivations for redistribution. First and foremost – and this forms the starting point of this chapter – voting can be seen to be a mere expression of self-interest. In this view, individuals at the bottom ranks of the income distribution stand to gain from redistributive programmes, and hence vote in favour of more equality; while those in the upper ranks stand to lose, and vote in favour of less income equality. Arguments opposing such a limited self-interested voting model are given in the literature, where preferences are also found to be shaped by other-regarding motives. Voting here is not merely to be a function of a person's possible income after taxation; their welfare may also be dependent on the income of others, or on the entire distribution of income. This could be an expression of taste, by which some simply prefer living in more or less egalitarian societies; or it may be driven by the demand for some intermediary product of the income distribution, as at certain levels it may produce social and political unrest.

A second justification does not arise from (democratic) concerns over equitable distribution of resources, but argues for redistribution of income from the point of view of efficiency. Its main contribution is showing the impossibility of functioning markets for insurance against many (often large) risks, justifying public intervention in the market, for insurance. It furthermore shows that redistribution and insurance actually form two sides of the same coin, as 'ex post, every insurance contract implies redistribution from the lucky to the unlucky' (Sinn, 2003, p. 66), hence implying *ex ante* that many redistributive government activities can be interpreted as insurance policies. Market failures in the market for insurance thus form an argument of efficiency to justify many of the labour market insurance policies we observe around the world, as well as old-age or disability insurance. Taken more broadly, even progressive taxation is suggested to form a publicly provided insurance (Varian, 1980). The market failure argument generally runs as follows: while inborn differences can be very large, the unborn are logically unable to insure themselves privately. Once an individual reaches an insurable age, however, the 'dice have already been cast' (Sinn, 2003, p. 68), and those who belong to the so-called 'good' or low-risk group will not want to participate in an insurance scheme; only the 'bad' risks will want to do so.[2] This drives up the price of insurance, causing a new group of relatively low-risk individuals to opt out of the insurance, ultimately unravelling the entire market. As these inborn differences can thus hinder individuals in sufficiently insuring life and career risks in the market sphere later in life, government fulfils the demand for such insurance services which the market cannot provide, leading Krugman (2011) to describe the state as 'an insurance company with an army'.

How Much Should Be Redistributed as Part of the *Res Publica*?

Figure 13.1 gives empirical estimates of the tax rates used to fund all redistributive expenditures, based on the method presented in Groot and Van der Linde (2016).[3] Of a selected number of countries, these partial tax rates are highest for Germany and Austria, followed by the United Kingdom, Denmark, the Netherlands and the United States. Furthermore, clear diverging time trends are found: transfer tax rates in the Netherlands have declined steeply since the 1980s, whereas they have grown for Germany, the United Kingdom and more recently for the United States. The estimated tax rates amount to roughly 30 per cent for the Netherlands and the United

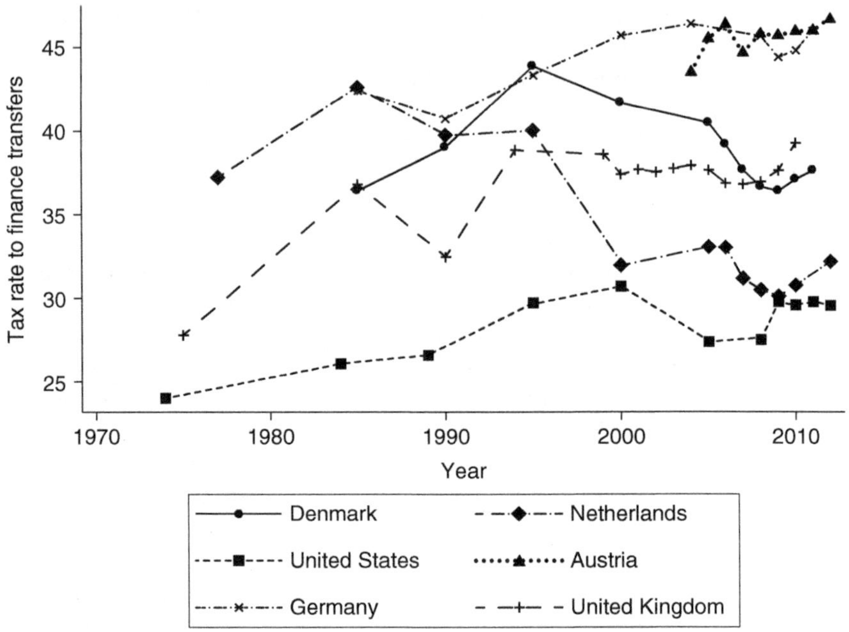

Figure 13.1 Tax rate necessary to finance transfer payments

States, compared with more than 45 per cent for Germany and Austria for the most recent observed years.

Compared with overall expenditures, what is the relative importance of redistribution for governments? Is redistribution a main part of the *res publica*? In order to answer this question, Figure 13.2 gives the ratio of above tax rates to the total income tax rates (consisting of both redistribution and public good provision). Redistribution seems to belong to the 'core' of the *res publica*, as tax revenues necessary for redistribution take out a very large share of overall government expenditures. On average, they represent more than half of government expenditures. The greatest of these shares are found for Austria and Germany, where in both cases the share is around 70 per cent. A second group of countries consists of the United States and the United Kingdom, with a share of around 65 per cent. Finally, the Netherlands and Denmark over time grow closer to roughly 50 per cent shares of public good and transfer components in the total tax rate. Both countries face relatively low income inequality in gross terms, perhaps allowing a greater share of government funds to be used for public good provision.

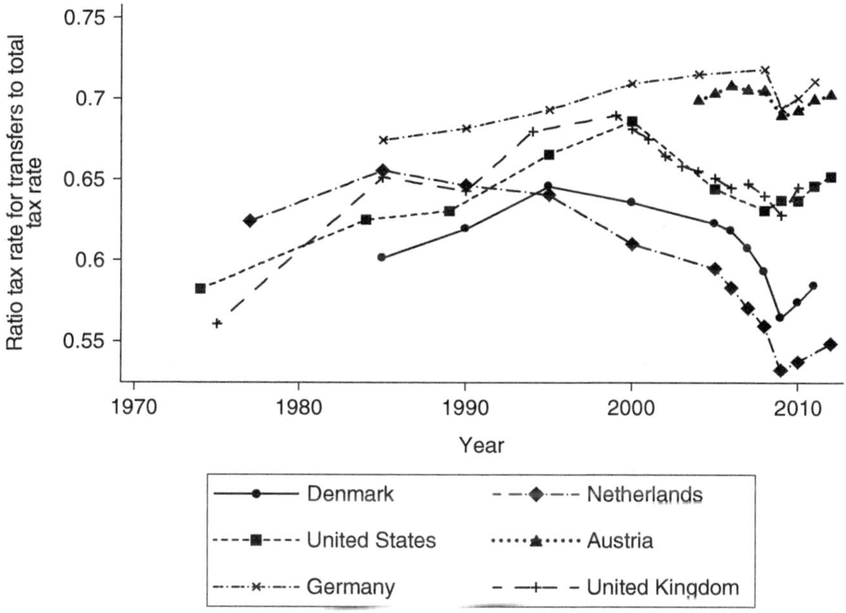

Figure 13.2 *Tax rate necessary to finance transfer payments as a share of the total tax rate*

13.2 EXPLAINING PATTERNS OF REDISTRIBUTION: THE MELTZER–RICHARD MODEL

While redistribution is shown to belong to the 'core' of the *res publica*, Figure 13.2 shows that great heterogeneity between countries persists. While countries such as Germany and Austria devote roughly 70 per cent of their government budgets to their redistributive efforts, others spend roughly half. How to explain this heterogeneity? The main theoretical models predicting the manner in which democratic nations deal with heterogeneous income generally assume self-interested voters, when aggregated, determining the generosity of tax-and-transfer systems. The Meltzer–Richard (MR) model (Meltzer and Richard, 1981) is canonical in this respect, and argues that the extent of redistribution is a function of the relative distance between the median, decisive voter group and mean income earner. This distance grows with increases in the skewness of the income distribution, thus leading to the hypothesis that nations with higher market income inequalities will vote for higher tax rates, dampening

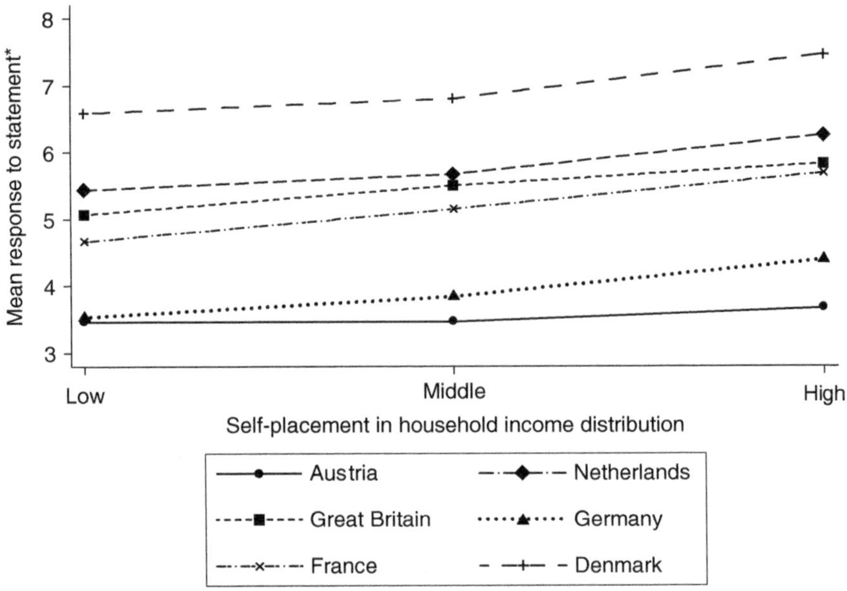

* Place yourself on a scale from 1 (income should be made more equal) to 10 (there should be greater incentives for individual effort)

Figure 13.3 Preferences for redistribution by (perceived) position in the income distribution

the effect of market income inequalities in the distribution of disposable income.

To see whether such a self-interested account of voting generally holds, Figure 13.3 employs data from the World Values Survey (WVS, 2015). It shows average preferences for redistribution (measured on a ten-point scale) by income group. Although significant differences are found in levels (on the vertical axis), entailing structural differences in preferences for redistribution between nations, in all nations, on average, preferences for redistribution decrease as income increases, shown by the upward-sloping lines. In other words, while both in Austria and Denmark higher-income households prefer less equalization of incomes (both with an upward-sloping line), on average Danish respondents are far less in agreement with the statement that incomes should be made more equal compared with Austrian respondents (shown by the difference in intercept). These differences are only partly explained away by other factors, such as education level, union or party affiliation, gender or age.

Thus the assumption of self-interested voting generally does seem to hold. For the hypotheses of MR to hold, however, voters with far greater cognitive capacities would be required. Voters may not be able to correctly specify the income distribution and/or their position in it, affecting the conclusions of MR (see e.g. Bredemeier, 2014). Ultimately, information seems an essential component when proposing a causal link between the distribution of income and the extent to which a nation redistributes. Informational imperfections are abundant, however, and new information may shape opinions, just as the anecdotal evidence above on 'slumming' makes clear. Starting with Downs (1957), a large literature has explored how shortages of information may undermine democracy's promise of 'net equality of influence for each citizen', allowing for unequal distributions of income, position and influence to reign, 'all of which are inevitable in any economy marked by an extensive division of labor' (p. 94).

In order to test the validity of MR, Groot and Van der Linde (2016) calculate the difference between observed net income inequality and predicted net income inequality on the basis of MR's predictions (both in terms of the Gini coefficient). Figure 13.4 shows the difference between observed and predicted levels, and finds inequalities greatly differ from predicted levels. For a first group of countries, Gini coefficients are found far above those which would be predicted on the basis of theory. These countries, including the United States, redistribute too little compared with theoretical predictions. A second group of countries redistributes far more income than would be expected on the basis of theory, including the Scandinavian countries, Slovenia and the Czech Republic, and Belgium. A final group does redistribute around what would be expected, and includes such diverse countries as Australia and Canada on the one hand, and Estonia and Poland on the other.

A large number of plausible explanations can be given for these differences between expected and observed inequality.[4] In the next section, two predictions are put forth and tested, centred on voter information, which when aggregated in the political process may explain the patterns shown in Figure 13.4.

13.3 ALTERNATIVE EXPLANATIONS FOR LEVELS OF REDISTRIBUTION

The MR model is grounded in exogenously formed preferences for redistribution: an individual's (relative) income determines their preferences. Such preferences, however, are not formed in a vacuum, but rather should partly be conceived as a function of existing institutions. Existing institutions impose resources, rules and norms upon citizens (Lowi, 1964), and as Pierson (1996) argues, form 'sources of information for mass publics'

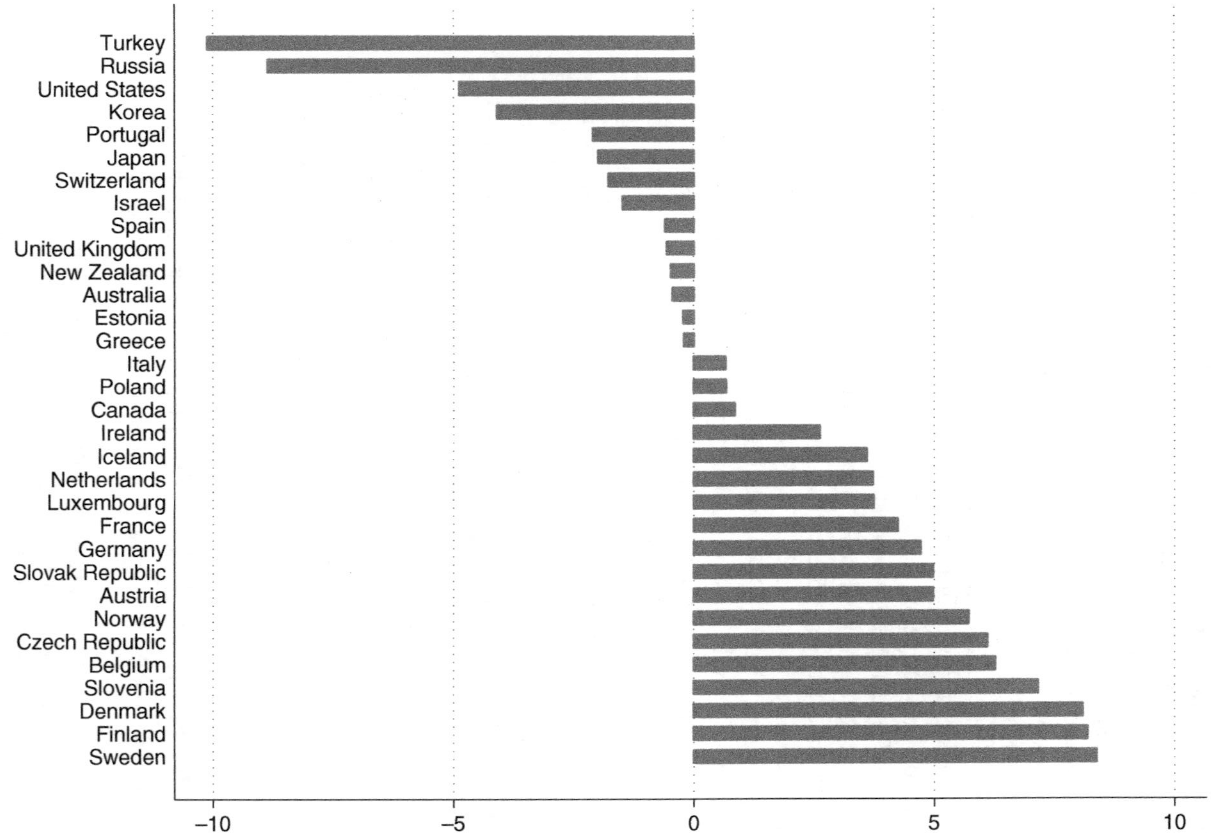

Note: Negative (positive) values entail lower (higher) net Ginis than predicted on the basis of theory.

Source: Based on calculations by Groot and Van der Linde (2016).

Figure 13.4 Difference between predicted and observed net Gini

which produce 'cues that help them [the electorate] develop political identities, goals, and strategies' (p. 619). Policies thus have the capacity to reshape the political realm (Pierson, 2000), and it may hence be the case that 'policy makes politics' (Campbell, 2012).

Research has begun to acknowledge this information dimension of existing policies, and has made a cognitive or behavioural turn, suggesting it is not merely (objective) information on an individual's own income that can explain preferences for redistribution, but underlying beliefs, including those about the causes of inequality, the role of government or the shape of the income distribution, which are important drivers of preferences for redistribution. Individuals may believe that inequalities are the result of differences in effort, or just the result of sheer bad luck, where the latter may make them more likely to support redistributive transfers (Piketty, 1995). Fong (2001) shows that in magnitude, the effects of holding such beliefs by far outweigh the effect income has on redistributive preferences. Beliefs about the role of government in the economy, however, may also shape preferences, where less-visible government policies garner less support (Mettler, 2011), in turn reducing demand for them and for government intervention in general. Finally, beliefs about the distribution of income and the individual's position in it may outweigh objective information on income in determining their preferences (Bredemeier, 2014). The following section contextualizes preferences for redistribution to see whether this can add to our understanding of preferences for redistribution, testing whether, for the Netherlands, perceptions of government or perceptions of the income distribution have explanatory power beyond an individual's position in the income distribution.

Uncertainty over the Role of Government

Could, for instance, beliefs about existing policies spill over into preferences and voting behaviour? Mettler (2011a) argues that they do, and illustrates her argument with a town hall meeting in which a United States congressman is told to keep his 'government hands' off the (government) Medicare programme. This prevailing idea that Medicare is not a government programme, Mettler (2011b) shows, may not be so strange after all, as one in four beneficiaries receive their benefits issued through private insurance companies. These so-called 'submerged' policies through the tax code, or as subsidies to and provision through private companies, largely obscure the role of government and affect the perception of government negatively compared with more visible policies. Asking a sample of Americans whether 'they have ever used a government social program', after which they ask the respondents which from a list of social programmes they have used, Mettler and Koch (2012) demonstrate that a range of policies are in place which are not perceived as government social policies. Respondents claim to have used them, but simultaneously claim never to have used a government social policy. Based on these data, findings show that as policies become more visible, it becomes more likely that citizens view government as beneficial:

> many people fail to recognize government's role in providing for their economic security, health care, and educational opportunities. They may be left under the impression that it is solely through their own efforts or through the largesse of market institutions that they receive various kinds of assistance or lowered financial obligations. (Mettler and Koch, 2012, p. 28)

In order to see whether the findings from Mettler (2011a) reflect an American phenomenon, rather than a general effect, a questionnaire is used from the Dutch Langlopende Internet Studies voor de Sociale wetenschappen (LISS) panel on privatization and corporatization from 2012. Individuals are asked whether they think a number of organizations are: (1) part of the state; (2) non-profit organizations outside the state; or (3) commercial (for-profit) organizations; or (4) can state that they do not know. Figure 13.5 uses the answers to this question regarding the following organizations: Employee Insurance Agency (UWV), which is an administrative body commissioned by the Ministry of Social Affairs and Employment; the Dutch Tax Administration; hospitals; and the national (privatized) Postal Service (PostNL). These variables jointly can capture whether individuals are overestimating the role of government (that is, believe the postal service is still part of the state), or underestimating the role of government (that is, believe the tax and employee insurance administration are not part of the state). Generally, respondents are able to place the organizations, as 90 per cent of respondents recognize the role of government in tax collection, while 78 per cent are aware that the Dutch Postal Service is a commercial organization. Faulty beliefs are largest for the Employee Insurance Agency, where 23 per cent mistakenly believe it to be run either as a non-profit or a commercial organization. Between 4 and 10 per cent of respondents admit to not knowing the answers.

Do these individuals over- or underestimating the role of government hold different opinions to those who can correctly identify its role regarding mail delivery, health care, social programmes or tax collection? In the Dutch case there is no conclusive evidence for this effect: irrespective of their answers to the above question, respondents generally trust government equally, and hold similar opinions about government functioning. This may partly be explained by the fact that – contrary to the example of the United States above – trust in political institutions in the Netherlands is generally very high, and even has been increasing (Van der Brug and Van

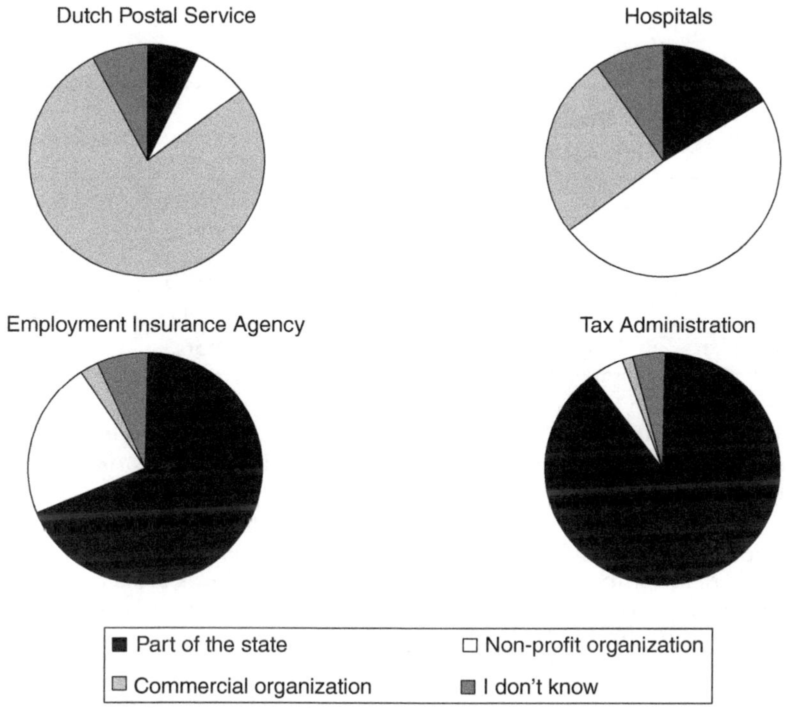

Figure 13.5 Perceived role of four organizations (N = 1904)

Praag, 2007). However, a significant relationship exists between the intent to vote for a certain party and identification of the above organizations. This is largely driven by individuals answering 'I don't know': individuals who also more often report being indecisive or intending not to vote in the coming election. Causality in this case is difficult to establish as it may be (political) knowledge that drives both voting intent and answers to the above questions.

Uncertainty over the Income Distribution

Do individuals over- or underestimating the extent of inequality have different preferences for redistribution to those who can correctly identify the distribution of income? And what is the extent to which individuals over- or underestimate inequality? While MR depart from full information about the shape of and the individual's place in the income distribution, individuals may in reality misperceive the level of inequality in society. Here, individual perceptions of inequality are given by G_i, representing the perceived Gini coefficient of an individual (where 0 is perfect equality and

Table 13.1 Descriptive statistics for the perceived Gini coefficient by income class

Quintile	G_i				N
	Mean	SD	Min	Max	
1	33.4	7.2	15.1	52.3	206
2	31.3	7.5	7.4	51.5	212
3	30.4	7.2	10.6	55.3	280
4	29.9	7.3	9.8	56.3	348
5	29.5	6.5	13.8	48.6	269
Total	30.7	7.2	7.4	56.3	1315

100 is perfect inequality). The Gini measures are constructed using a LISS questionnaire on the effect of perceived social distributions on subjective well-being from 2008. The following question is used:

> The next question is about total net household income of adults in the Netherlands within the last month. Total income includes incomes from payments, pensions, rents, dividends, etc. of all members of the household added up to each other. By 'net' we mean income left after taxation. What percentages of adults living in the Netherlands fall into the following categories?

For which respondents estimate the percentage of people P_j that fall into the following income class j: up to €1000, €1001–€1500, €1501–€2000, €2001–€2500, €2501–€3000, €3001–€5000, and €5001 or more. These responses are aggregated into a Gini coefficient G_i following the method introduced in Chotikapanich and Griffiths (2000). Actual inequality (measured by the Gini) in 2009 is around 28.0 (Caminada et al., 2014).

Table 13.1 gives the average perceived Gini coefficients G_i by income quintile, together with the standard deviations and extreme observations. G_i tends to decrease according to income, yet multiple-comparison tests find significant differences only between the first quintile and the other four quintiles (at a 5 per cent confidence interval). In other words, individuals in the lowest 20 per cent of household income on average believe society is less equal compared with individuals from higher-income households. Middle- to high-income households on average do not differ in their appraisal of income inequality. Respondents generally overestimate the degree of inequality (with an overall mean value of 30.7 compared with the actual level of around 28.0). Within all income classes the standard deviation is large, suggesting that perceptions widely differ.

In order to see whether beliefs regarding the income distribution shape preferences for redistribution, G_i is matched with data on these preferences.

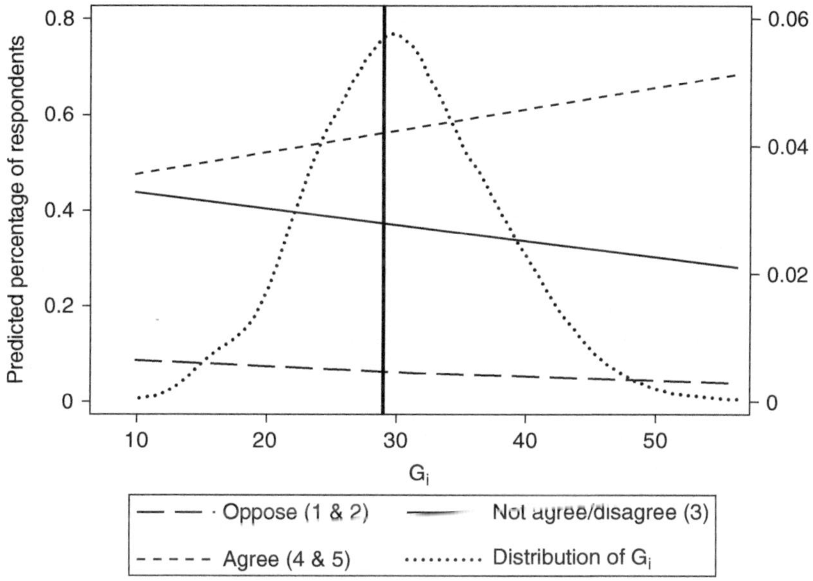

Figure 13.6 Relationship between perceived inequality (measured by the Gini coefficient) and predicted response to the statement, 'differences in income should decrease'

Figure 13.6 gives the predicted percentage of respondents agreeing, disagreeing or being neutral with regard to the statement, 'Differences in income should decrease', for different levels of G_i. In estimating the relationships depicted in the figure, the underlying regression model controls for household income and a number of other control variables (including political trust, education level, age, household size, gender, and a measure for proneness to social desirability when answering).[5]

Those perceiving inequality to be low are on average found to be far more likely to be either neutral or agree with the statement, compared with individuals perceiving society's income distribution to be far more unequal. Agreement increases from around 45 per cent at low perceived inequality to 68 per cent at high perceived inequality. Overall, this generally goes at the expense of neutrality with regard to the statement, as respondents generally disagree with the statement (between 9 per cent of those largely underestimating inequality, and 4 per cent of those largely overestimating inequality). The background density function gives the distribution of the perceived income inequality variable G_i. The vertical line denotes the actual Gini. Ultimately, perceptions of the income distribution thus can partly explain individuals' preferences for redistribution, even after controlling for their income. Furthermore, this section shows that such perceptions widely differ across individuals of all income classes.

13.4 CONCLUSION

Two general arguments on normative grounds can justify public concern for the distribution of income. The first follows from concerns about social welfare, justifying public intervention on grounds of equity. The second views redistribution of income as the outcome of governments seeking to overcome a market failure in a number of insurance markets, justifying public intervention on grounds of efficiency. While historically redistribution sprung from charity, charity alone is not likely to adequately redistribute income, as the distribution of income represents a public good. As redistribution 'grew public', the democratic system took over, whereby states started intervening in the income distribution through tax-and-transfer systems. This, however, puts forth the question of how much states should redistribute. One can observe large national variation in such tax-and-transfer systems, yet note that redistribution is a central part of the *res publica*, as all states are found to devote a substantial share of tax revenues to income transfers.

Dominant theories explaining such variation between nations generally depart from exogenously formed preferences about redistribution, predicting preferences for redistribution to be solely a function of a person's (relative) income position. These theories, however, appear unable to adequately predict different national patterns. Two additional contextual mechanisms are proposed through which preferences may additionally be shaped, suggesting that voter information is an important component in explaining preferences for redistribution. Primarily, evidence is found for uncertainty over the role of government for a sample of Dutch voters, yet contrary to American findings, these beliefs are not found to significantly spill over into preferences or voting behaviour. High and increasing overall levels of political trust in the Netherlands may explain the absence of an effect for the Dutch case. Beliefs about the income distribution, however, are shown to spill over into preferences, and findings show that those who perceive the distribution of income to be more unequal are more likely to prefer more redistribution compared with those who perceive the distribution to be rather equal, even after controlling for income. As cross-national studies have found huge variation in these individual-level inequality perceptions across nations and over time (Kuhn, 2015), this explanation offers a promising additional clarification for patterns of redistribution across countries.

Striking the right balance between the public and private sectors of the economy requires an informed electorate, knowledgeable about the role of government and the income distribution. Galbraith (1958, p. 193) speaks of a social balance: every constellation of realized private demands requires a set of public and common goods. Failure to reach such a balance entails social disorder and harms economic performance. While public production often lags behind, above all, in Galbraith's view, 'forces of advertising and emulation' tilt the balance in favour of private wants, forming a cause for social imbalances.

The public sector generally lacks these tools of advertising that the private sector uses so well, thereby potentially limiting the public's insight into tasks and functioning of government. On the basis of this contribution, one may argue that among the public tasks should be the active provision of accessible information to the public regarding the public sector's impact, following from its regulatory measures as well as from its direct and indirect provision and financing of goods and services. The Dutch organization 'Postbus 51' was an example of such an information provider,[6] which televised information campaigns on government social policies, but also produced information for the public interest on topics such as energy consumption and hygienic measures. The tax authorities – by their nature gatherers of information on incomes – could furthermore provide citizens with information on the distribution of income, as well as on taxpayers' locations within this distribution. Such information is now already provided by the Organisation for Economic Co-operation and Development (OECD) through its 'Compare your Income' web tool, allowing individuals to test whether their perceptions of the income distribution align with reality. National tax authorities, however, would have a far greater reach. Research has found that such information treatments regarding the nature of policies (see Jacobsen et al., 2014; Faricy and Ellis, 2014), and information treatments regarding the income distribution and the individual's position in it (see e.g. Karadja et al., 2015; Cruces et al., 2013), can affect redistributive preferences.

Galbraith feared that the power of emulation and advertising would give rise to 'private opulence and public squalor'. The assertion of this statement is that in order to strike the right balance between the public and private sectors, democracies require voters who are aware of both public squalor and the distribution of private opulence.

NOTES

1. This is the result of the 'second fundamental theorem of welfare economics', under a number of assumptions, including the possibility of lump-sum redistribution of wealth.
2. A similar notion is found in Rawls's (1971) 'original position', where participants reflect on society deprived of information about their characteristics; that is, 'unborn' (a point also made by Barr, 1992).
3. The tax rates are calculated as those able to align observed gross and net distributions of income when assuming a simplified tax and transfer system across countries. With the loss of detail, such assumptions aid the comparability of often very heterogeneous national tax systems. See Groot and Van der Linde (2016) for more details on the method.
4. Groot and Van der Linde (2016) offer a number of explanations for these findings, suggesting differences between welfare state regimes and deviations from the median voter theorem, which could capture logrolling, or unevenly distributed influence in the political process, as explanatory variables.
5. See Van der Linde (forthcoming) for a further analysis.
6. Postbox 51, named after the postal box number to which citizens could send their questions to government. Interestingly, since 2008 a large part of this public information service was privatized to the German Arvato company.

REFERENCES

Barr, N. (1992). Economic theory and the welfare state: a survey and interpretation. *Journal of Economic Literature*, 30, 741–803.

Bredemeier, C. (2014). Imperfect information and the Meltzer–Richard hypothesis. *Public Choice*, 159(3), 1–16.

Caminada, K., K. Goudswaard, J. Been and M. de Graaf-Zijl (2014). Een kwart eeuw inkomensongelijkheid in Nederland. *ESB*, 99(4684), 276–279.

Campbell, A.L. (2012). Policy makes mass politics. *Annual Review of Political Science*, 15, 333–351.

Chotikapanich, D. and W.E. Griffiths (2000). Applications: posterior distributions for the Gini coefficient using grouped data. *Australian and New Zealand Journal of Statistics*, 42(4), 383–392.

Cruces, G., R. Perez-Truglia and M. Tetaz (2013). Biased perceptions of income distribution and preferences for redistribution: evidence from a survey experiment. *Journal of Public Economics*, 98, 100–112.

Deutsches Filminstitut (2011). *Screening the Poor 1888–1914*, DVD, Edition Filmmuseum 64.

Downs, A. (1957). *An Economic Theory of Democracy*, New York: Harper & Row.

Faricy, C. and C. Ellis (2014). Public attitudes toward social spending in the United States: the differences between direct spending and tax expenditures. *Political Behavior*, 36(1), 53–76.

Fong, C. (2001). Social preferences, self-interest, and the demand for redistribution. *Journal of Public Economics*, 82(2), 225–246.

Galbraith, J. (1958). *The Affluent Society*, Boston, MA: Houghton Mifflin.

Groot, L.F.M and D.E. Van der Linde (2016). Income inequality, redistribution and the position of the decisive voter. *Journal of Economic Inequality*. DOI: 10.1007/s10888-016-9333-7.

Jacobsen, R., J.W. Snyder and A. Saultz (2014). Informing or shaping public

opinion? The influence of school accountability data format on public perceptions of school quality. *American Journal of Education*, 121(1), 1–27.
Karadja, M., J. Mollerstrom and D. Seim (2015). Richer (and holier) than thou? The effect of relative income improvements on demand for redistribution (No. 15-10). GMU Working Paper in Economics.
Koven, S. (2004). *Slumming: Sexual and Social Politics in Victorian London*, Princeton, NJ: Princeton University Press.
Krugman, P. (2011). An insurance company with an army. *New York Times*, 22 October. http://krugman.blogs.nytimes.com/2011/10/22/an-insurance-company-with-an-army-2.
Kuhn, A. (2015). The individual perception of wage inequality: a measurement framework and some empirical evidence. IZA Discussion Paper, No. 9579.
Lindert, P. (2004). *Growing Public: Social Spending and Economic Growth since the Eighteenth Century*. Cambridge, UK and New York, USA: Cambridge University Press.
LISS (2008). Effect of perceived social distributions on subjective well-being. CentERdata. http://www.lissdata.nl/dataarchive/study_units/view/55.
LISS (2012). Privatization and corporatization. CentERdata. http://www.lissdata.nl/dataarchive/study_units/view/369.
Lowi, T.J. (1964). American business, public policy, case-studies, and political theory. *World Politics*, 16(4), 677–715.
Meltzer, A. and S. Richard (1981). A rational theory of the size of government. *Journal of Political Economy*, 89(5), 914–927
Mettler, S. (2011a). *The Submerged State: How Invisible Government Policies Undermine American Democracy*, Chicago, IL: University of Chicago Press.
Mettler, S. (2011b). Our hidden government benefits. *New York Times*, 20 September, p. A31.
Mettler, S. and J. Koch (2012). Who perceives government's role in their lives: assessing the impact of social policy on visibility. Working Paper.
Pierson, P. (1996). The new politics of the welfare state. *World Politics*, 48(2), 143–179.
Pierson, P. (2000). Increasing returns, path dependence, and the study of politics. *American Political Science Review*, 94(2), 251–267.
Piketty, T. (1995). Social mobility and redistributive politics. *Quarterly Journal of Economics*, 110(3), 551–584.
Rawls, J. (1971). *A Theory of Justice*, Cambridge, MA: Belknap Press of Harvard University Press.
Roemer, J.E. (1998). *Theories of Distributive Justice*, Cambridge, MA: Harvard University Press.
Sinn, H. (2003). *The New Systems Competition*, Malden, MA: Blackwell.
Streeck, W. (2011). The crises of democratic capitalism. *New Left Review*, 71, 5–29.
Thurow, L.C. (1971). The income distribution as a pure public good. *Quarterly Journal of Economics*, 85(2), 327–336.
Van der Brug, W. and P. Van Praag (2007). Erosion of political trust in the Netherlands: structural or temporarily? A research note. *Acta Politica*, 42(4), 443–458.
Van der Linde, D.E. (forthcoming). More than meets the eye? Demand for redistribution under incomplete information.
Varian, H.R. (1980). Redistributive taxation as social insurance. *Journal of Public Economics*, 14(1), 49–68.

Warr, P.G. (1982). Pareto optimal redistribution and private charity. *Journal of Public Economics*, 19(1), 131–138.
World Bank (2015), World Development Indicators. http://data.worldbank.org/.
World Values Survey (WVS) (2015). Wave 6 2010-2014 OFFICIAL AGGREGATE v.20150418. World Values Survey Association, www.worldvaluessurvey.org. Madrid: Asep/JDS.

14. Conclusions

Brigitte Unger, Michael Getzner and Daan van der Linde

The role of the public sector, the 'public thing' or 'public matter' – the *res publica* as the Ancient Romans called it – as opposed to the role of the private sector, or the *res privata*, has been discussed over centuries. Still today in modern democratic societies, the roles and functions of governments and other actors in society are scrutinized. In this intensive public discourse on the size of government and the public sector, quite often arguments prevail that are driven by ideology, regularly lacking an understanding of the importance of publicly provided goods and services and their complementarity to those provided by the private market. Different perspectives and policy contexts across nations further complicate identification and definition of those public tasks which can be deemed the 'core' of the *res publica*.

As the perceptions, responsibilities and legitimations of public versus private tasks have changed over time, this book has analysed the shifts in governance between the public and the private regarding different policy fields. Which parts of the public tasks have become privatized, which actors took over roles of the state and how were these shifts legitimized in the public debate? Was it in the name of more efficiency, of cost reductions, or less bureaucracy? Or was the argument for more fairness and equality? Or was it motivated by ethical reasons, on moral grounds? The book has limited its regional focus on European countries. Individual contributions investigated a selected range of old and new policy fields. In many cases, new policy fields have not been treated extensively in this context before, such as nature conservation, cultural heritage and protection against natural disasters.

The first part of the book developed the concept for this book. In 'Introduction', Chapter 1, we distinguished between three different actors: the state, civil society actors (such as trade unions or other associations, churches, non-governmental organizations, and so on) and the market. In addition, the family was identified as an important actor. This is why child care policy was included in one of our chapters (Chapter 9). Different roles

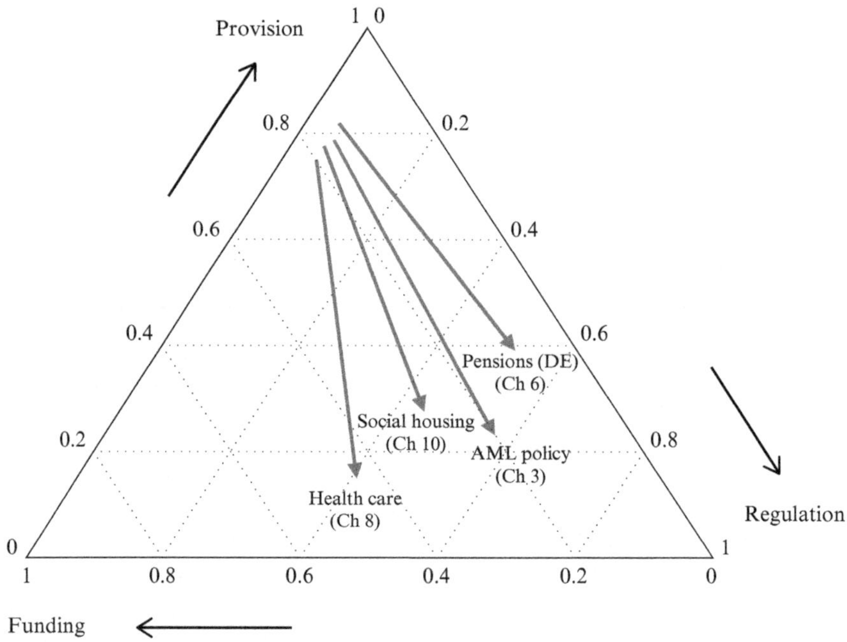

Figure 14.1 Shifts in the state's role described in a number of chapters

could be assigned to each of these actors with respect to three dimensions: the provision of goods and services, their funding and their regulation. Changing roles among these actors and within them were identified along these three dimensions. In this book we have analysed the shifts between the state, the civil society and the market for various policy fields. The general image emerging across the contributions in this book is that of a state retreating from its role as direct provider of goods and services, moving to a role of funder and regulator. The state regulates the economy, supports it financially, especially during crisis, but does not anymore provide goods and services itself.

Figure 14.1 shows the shifts in the state's role described in a number of chapters. The three dimensions are shown along the three axes of the triangle: provision, funding and regulation. For each of the three dimensions, public involvement can range from 0 to 1. Any point in the graph indicates the division of state tasks between these three dimensions, and adds up to 1. Points near the top of the triangle indicate policy fields where the state takes a large role in provision (relative to funding and regulating), the left-hand corner indicates those fields where the public role is stronger in funding (compared to provision and regulation), and the right-hand corner shows policy fields where the public role focuses on regulation (compared to funding and provision). Points more to the centre indicate fields where the state takes on multiple roles, where for example a funding and regulating role is found left of centre, or a funding and provision role is found to the top of the centre.

Throughout the book we could show a shift in the state's role from producer (provider) to financier or regulator. Examples in case are changes in the German pension system (Chapter 6) or in social housing (Chapter 10). Regarding housing policy, the authors described how the policy to provide council housing in Vienna directly through public bodies was terminated. Yet the regulated rental sector still makes up a sizeable stock of the rental market, including a regulated private rental market. In addition, the state plays a funding role in developing building land, which then is resold to housing associations. The public sector hence shifted its role from that of being mainly provider to becoming regulator and financier. There are however also chapters which indicate a more stable role of the state (for example, remaining largely a financier of cultural institutions in Chapter 12), notwithstanding the fact that this role can grow or decline. A decrease in funding for public spaces is noted in Chapter 11.

The starting point of this book was derived from those policy fields deemed a *res publica* in Adam Smith's 'night watch' state: fields considered the bare minimum of public responsibilities. In *An Inquiry into the Nature and Causes of the Wealth of Nations*, Smith (1776) defined three such 'core' functions of the state: firstly, to protect the society from violence and invasion by other societies by means of military force; secondly, 'to protect, as far as possible, every member of the society from the injustice or oppression of every other member of it' (through police and jurisprudence), and thirdly:

> erecting and maintaining those public institutions and those public works, which though they may be in the highest degree advantageous to a great society, are, however, of such a nature, that the profit could never repay the expense to any individual, or small number of individuals; and which it, therefore, cannot be expected that any individual, or small number of individuals, should erect or maintain. (Smith, 1776, Book V, Chap. 1, parts 1, 2 and 3)

Our book does not study the traditional two core tasks mentioned by Adam Smith, though even in these traditional core tasks substantial shifts occurred from the public to the private sector. Increased private military services instead of a state army, privately run prisons instead of state prisons, and private security guards instead of policemen, are some examples of this shift. A modern form of fighting crime is through following the criminal money rather than following the criminals. Depriving criminals of their benefits from crime might deter criminal behaviour. As Ferwerda shows in Chapter 3, the combating of money laundering has largely shifted the responsibility of detecting criminals from the public to the private sector. Private entities such as banks, real estate agents and dealers in large values have to identify criminal transactions and report them to the public authorities. With this they replace some former police tasks of hunting criminals.

'Security' can refer to physical life, to financial security, as well as to a safe and secure environment. The concept of security changed over time and came to include more and more social security. In this sense, many new tasks of the state still refer to providing all sorts of a – newly defined – security. It is in this third category that we note major changes over time. While Smith had mainly physical security, infrastructure and education in mind, over time – and largely coinciding with industrialization – new policy fields required public support, mainly related to social security (comprising old-age, unemployment, health and childcare systems), but also connected to the provision of public goods such as social housing, cultural heritage and natural parks.

The legitimation of such a public role is derived from three general strands of theoretical arguments, concerning equality or efficiency, or following a moral line of reasoning. Justifications for public intervention in economics based on the equality argument suggest that public institutions should serve to redistribute income and wealth to those both inside and outside the labour market. In this vision the market allocates goods and services efficiently, and government steps in only to preserve justice, fairness and/or equality, allowing all members of society to participate in the market economy.

The efficiency model, on the other hand, finds a more encompassing role for governments, exceeding the redistribution of income and wealth. In this view, governments step in to provide those goods and services that markets simply cannot. Market failures hence indicate those areas where the state outperforms markets, that is, in the case of natural monopolies, imperfect markets, externalities, in the production of public goods, or in the case of incomplete markets and information failures. This model attributes a more comprehensive role to the state: direct government funding can be justified, especially when market failures concentrate on the supply side of the market (for example, in the case of natural monopolies). Similarly, a case for the direct provision of certain goods or services by the government can be made most strongly when market failures concentrate on the demand side (for example, in the case of non-excludable goods such as public or common goods).

Finally, moral arguments can provide a justification for an even more encompassing role for the public. Where markets fail, it could be necessary to limit the scope of markets purposefully. From this point of view society has to judge whether the commodification of specific goods and services is morally permissible; or when it is not, the free market exchange of that good that should be blocked. Examples here are public schools or organ donation, not allocated according to market principles, but rather using other mechanisms (for example, equal access or a first come, first served basis).

The structure of this book, following positive, descriptive shifts over time and normative justifications for the distribution of tasks as expressed in the public debate, provoked a number of questions. Firstly, what constitutes the 'core', and do 'core' tasks change over time? Secondly, how do tasks shift over time? Do public tasks diminish, or do they on the contrary grow when income in society increases? Finally, is the changing nature of public involvement the result of public activities that meet the economic needs of the people where the market cannot meet them (that is, the efficiency model), or is the argument underpinning the expansion of the role of the state in certain fields rather a moral one? Is it more welfare and happiness rather than a growth in property and material goods that the state should guarantee?

Figure 14.2 gives an overview of the justifications for public intervention in the policy fields covered by this book. For any point, any combination of justifications adds up to 1, implying that the diagram can show the relative importance of the three arguments. At the top of the triangle are located those policy fields that can be justified mainly on grounds of redistribution. To the right-hand corner moral reasons are indicated, and to the left-hand corner we find efficiency reasons to justify public intervention. In many of the policy fields in our book, the case for public intervention clearly does follow from an efficiency line of reasoning, hence most points are located in the lower left corner. For instance, market failure serves as an argument in the case of unemployment. The same goes for the public goods nature of specific types of public space and cultural heritage. In other cases, however, markets may outperform public provision, yet an argument can still be made for keeping the good or service within the public domain, for example in the case of housing policies in Chapter 10 or health care in Chapter 8. A number of policy issues can be justified on more than one ground, and are located more to the middle. This applies among others to housing policy and health care, which justifies a public role based on all three arguments.

Van Egmond's contribution in the theoretical opening of this book (Chapter 2) discussed the point of separating efficiency and moral concerns, and argued against seemingly value-neutral demarcations between

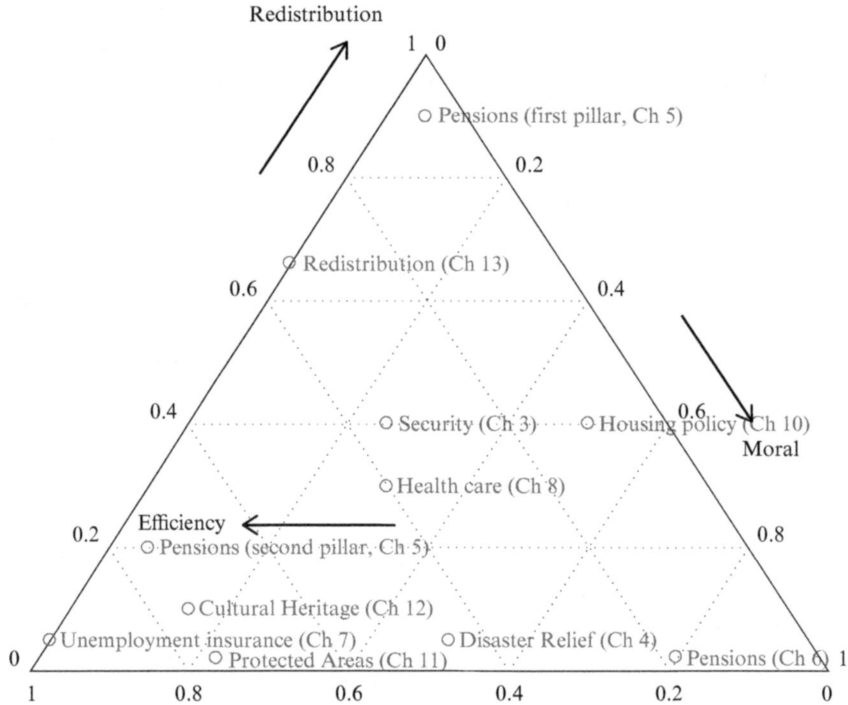

Figure 14.2 Justifications for public intervention in the policy fields covered by this book

private and public domains. The author showed that behind a veil of value-neutrality lie values driving preferences to allocate means either according to market forces or according to a principle of equal access. When in specific cases allocation by both the public sector or through market mechanisms is possible, judgement based on allocative efficiency alone is in itself value-laden, placing a higher value on increased gross domestic product (GDP) than on non-material forms of well-being. He showed that such value orientations are not stable, but change over time. These shifts result basically from increased importance of material values relative to immaterial. Van Egmond's chapter is central to the argumentation of this book because he illustrated how this shift in value orientation implies shifts in the distribution of economic goods, tilting the balance between private and public domains, specifically through the appropriation of public goods and common-pool resources by converting them into excludable private or club goods. This could threaten both our well-being and the democratic functioning of societies. Increasing inequality resulting from too many private goods and material values can cause societies to fall apart.

The contributions of Koetsier (Chapter 5) and of Blank (Chapter 6) on old-age insurance showed that old-age provision always requires involvement of the public or the civil society. Pension systems are institutions that have developed historically and thus differ considerably across countries. In some countries the main institution is a state-financed pension (that is, a one-pillar system, such as in Austria and Germany where the working generation pays for the elderly), while others have multiple pillars (such as the Dutch system, which relies on a minimum state-financed pension and on contributions of employers and employees paid into pension funds). Shifts observed are towards more private pension systems, largely shifting away from provision by the public to more financing and regulation. In Germany, the publicly subsidized *Riester Rente* was promoted; in the Netherlands the 'cappuccino model' urged people to put some mild foam on top of their coffee (the state-financed pension) and their milk (the employee- and employer-funded system) by saving in private pension funds. Confirming the findings of Van Groezen et al. (2009) that people prefer the pension system that they happen to know, both authors pleaded for the pension system existing in their country. Koetsier argued for the Dutch multi-pillar system, while Blank backed the German one-pillar system. Both, however, did agree that old-age insurance should either stay a *res publica*, or be managed by civil society (trade unions and employers' associations), but should in no case become a *res privata*.

Blank discussed the argument for a public role in the German pension system against the backdrop of a recent move from a single- to a multi-pillar system. The ultimate justification of public intervention in old-age pensions according to Blank is moral in nature. He argued that pensions constitute a form of permanent decommodification of labour, making old-age workers independent of market income. Given this overarching argument for public intervention, the question of how to design a system to reach this goal is secondary, and efficiency or redistributive arguments may be brought in to justify mandatory public schemes over private pensions systems.

Koetsier argued that pensions systems fulfil multiple objectives, offering insurance against longevity risk and redistribution (both for individuals over the life cycle, and between individuals). Comparing different constellations of pension provision along the first and second pillar, Koetsier concluded that the public role is prevalent in both pillars, either as an administrator of the pension system in the first pillar and or as an enforcer of rules in the second pillar. In multiple-pillar systems, the justifications for these roles are based on the goals of the respective pillars. The first pillar is redistributive in nature and serves to elevate old-age poverty. The second pillar has an insurance function, and serves to smooth consumption over the lifetime.

Historically it was trade unions who started the first mutual unemployment insurance. As Chapter 7 by Unger showed, unemployment insurance emerged in times of mass unemployment in the 1920s. In some countries the state took over; in other countries the Ghent system of managing unemployment insurance through trade unions persisted. Both systems seem to work, while a private unemployment insurance run by the market would generally fail. The justification for a public role evolves from a clear efficiency argument: market provision of unemployment insurance is likely to fail, as adverse selection would cause the private insurance market to unravel. Furthermore, especially in times of mass unemployment, unemployment risks are mutually dependent, making private insurance impossible. Public insurances fit in with a broader role of government regarding unemployment. Unemployment is a waste of resources, and full employment can be interpreted as a public good which the government can provide through macroeconomic policy or through the right to work. To only insure the unemployed is a very passive role of the state in this case. Large cuts in unemployment insurance indicate a partial withdrawal of the state. However, unemployment insurance is no doubt still a *res publica* or – in some countries – a *res civilita* and cannot be provided by the private sector.

Chapter 10 by Gutheil-Knopp-Kirchwald and Kadi compared housing policies and spatial inequality in the cities of Amsterdam and Vienna. While in many countries (for example, in the United Kingdom, Germany, most Central and Eastern European countries) large-scale privatization of public housing has taken place, in Vienna and Amsterdam, the state (or the municipality) did not withdraw from the housing sector, but shifted partially from direct provision to subsidiary funding and state guarantees. The authors are concerned that the integrated character of the housing market will suffer when the social housing sector becomes less important. The authors hence argued against a mono-causal legitimization of public intervention in housing policy, as policies are multifunctional. Although perhaps government intervention can be warranted from a perspective of efficiency (given, for example, the neighbourhood externalities of private housing choices, or asymmetric information on housing quality), an efficiently functioning housing market alone would not be equipped to reach further goals of housing policy, the authors argued, implying that equality and moral arguments cannot be neglected. Social housing has a clear redistributive function: firstly, between individuals, as it can target groups lacking affordable and decent housing, thus ensuring decent housing for low-income groups or other groups that face difficulties in the housing market. Secondly, there is a spatial redistributive element, as spatial inequality can lead to discrimination of those living in deprived areas, affecting dimensions other than just their housing conditions. Finally, the authors argued along a moral line of reasoning, viewing housing as a civil right, where specific (combinations) of public roles can de-commodify part of the housing market (for example, by introducing rent regulation) and curb undesirable outcomes of a functioning market (for example, speculative behaviour).

Chapter 8 by Van Waarden on health care argued that basic health care has to be publicly provided. It is a *res publica* on efficiency, equality and moral grounds. Market failures due to asymmetric information would endanger the correct treatment of patients; unequal income could lead to parts of the population not being treated, which could have spillover effects especially in the case of infectious diseases and endanger the health of a total population, and furthermore violate moral principles, as everybody has a right to life. However, apart from this basic public core, further health care can be provided by public or by private means. In Europe nowadays there are sectors where we seem to see only the benefit side (such as beer production) and sectors where the cost side seems to be all we consider (such as health care), and this has some odd consequences. We value beer more than health care, although productivity growth in the latter sector can save our lives. Van Waarden explained this paradox through a number of reasons such as forced versus voluntary payment, political short-sightedness and asymmetric information. He called for more transparency regarding costs and benefits so that in a democracy the demos – the people – can decide on their preferred health care package. It is not up to economists, but to politics to decide how much public health care should be provided.

Chapter 9 by Knijn and Lewis on early childhood education and care (ECEC) showed a reversal of roles compared to those found above. Childcare, long considered a family matter, and hence not a market, civil society or state matter, is partly shifted from the family to the public sector and market concern. European Union targets intend to make ECEC available for one-third of all children in a country. Private providers have entered the childcare market, subject to public regulation and monitoring. In the countries studied in this chapter, the Netherlands and England, public funds are channelled to childcare, through either tax allowances and childcare tax credits, or childcare vouchers administered by employers. Comparing ECEC, the authors concluded that in both countries the childcare market is fragile and fragmented, and largely depends on public support, in both financing and regulation. Knijn and Lewis hence came to the conclusion that childcare requires public intervention with respect to finance and regulation, and cannot be left completely to markets alone.

Getzner (Chapter 12) focused on cultural heritage; a largely incommensurable sector producing a range of intangible benefits. Noting a significant and growing role of government spending on cultural institutions, Getzner found that efficiency is the strongest argument to justify the role of the government in the cultural sector. Cultural institutions produce a wide range of goods and services, including research, conservation and documentation, all of which serve as public goods that the market cannot produce. However, Getzner acknowledged that, considering the wide range of goods and services produced in the cultural sector, it is hardly possible to legitimize public intervention based on one single argument alone. There are cases where government intervention may also be justified on moral grounds and for reasons of redistribution. Following this reasoning, it can be argued that access to cultural heritage is a social right, and should not depend on a person's income position. Thus public financing allows every citizen to benefit from the (conservation of) cultural heritage. The chapter furthermore developed an indicator for a 'degree of publicness', applied to the field of cultural heritage protection, in particular for Austrian museums.

Withalm (Chapter 11) examined a field in which the social benefits provided are not easily captured. In her study on the funding role of governments for protected areas, she explicitly assessed four Austrian protected areas. She found the output of protected areas to be broad, offering many so-called ecosystem services such as flood protection, tourism and leisure as well as conservation. Generally, these services are of a public goods nature, justifying public intervention, more specifically public funding, for efficiency reasons. Market actors will not be able to reach sufficient expenditure, while the commodification of natural resources could further endanger its provision.

Koetsier (Chapter 4) looked at the role of governments in preventing natural disasters; a role likely to become more important given global warming. Taking into account this growing necessity of the task, it is difficult to foresee costs and benefits, as states are implicitly indebted, so to speak, and face potential shocks that could even exceed the level of current explicit government debt. While most disaster relief programmes are concerned with rebuilding private goods, Koetsier argued for the provision of natural disaster relief to be a core public task. He called for an active role for governments from a moral point of view, viewing reconstruction as an effort to restore basic material and non-material conditions, such as housing and food, and human dignity. Although seen as a core task, Koetsier questioned why private insurances fail to cover these risks. It is argued that the market is largely absent in this area, or when available it is incomplete due to distorted demand and insufficient supply. This provides a secondary market failure argument for state intervention, given that there are no alternatives to public provision. The author suggested that governments could insure themselves on the cat (catastrophe) bonds market against large future costs, to finance disaster relief due to, for example, climate change, hereby making the private sector participate in its financing.

Van der Linde (Chapter 13) examined the general redistributive role of governments, and showed that justifications can be derived from both an equity argument and an efficiency argument. Collective choice may deem certain distributions of income more favourable than others, and provide an argument for government to intervene and redistribute income to reach a different distribution. The market itself is ill-equipped for realizing these more favourable distributions, as the distribution of income itself is a public good, and realizing any other distribution would face the same problems as the provision of any public good: specifically, free-riding behaviour in providing the required transfer payments. Redistribution, however, may also be argued to be the *ex post* result of what can be interpreted as insurance policies: government in this view is providing a solution to a market failing to provide insurances against, for example, old-age, career or disability risks.

Van der Linde argued that the role of government in redistributive and other public tasks has increasingly become less visible, hampering society in understanding the involvement of the public sector in the economy. When asked what is private and what is public, large segments of the population show a lack of knowledge. Similarly, voters generally know little about income distribution and their position relative to this. Following van der Linde, it is important that the public sector informs the public and is transparent about its role, concerning both redistribution and the provision of goods and services.

The recently published *Oxford Handbook on Transformations of the State*, edited by Stephan Leibfried et al. (2015), makes a compelling case that the state remains a key actor in areas of social and economic life, while shifting its areas and modes of intervention and structures, adapting to various new domestic and international challenges. Our findings confirmed this: case studies on the Netherlands, Austria, Germany and the United Kingdom regarding different public tasks showed in many cases that the role of the state has shifted from being a direct provider to being a financier of public tasks. Still, the ultimate regulatory power generally remains with the state, or has even grown with respect to the increasing role of markets.

These findings, however, raise a dilemma: if the state moves from being a direct provider to a less-visible regulator or financier, perceptions of the state will change. This can challenge the legitimacy of the state. If it is up to the demos to determine what constitutes the *res publica*, how can it form its opinion on issues and policy fields where the role of the government cannot be seen clearly? It therefore seems important to re-establish a clear vision for the *res publica*, making the link between financing, regulation and provision more transparent.

REFERENCES

Leibfried, S., E. Huber, M. Lange, J. Levy, F. Nullmeier and J. Stephens (eds) (2015), *The Oxford Handbook on Transformations of the State*, Oxford: Oxford University Press.

Smith, A. (1776). *An Inquiry into the Nature and Causes of the Wealth of Nations*, London: W. Strahan & T. Cadell.

Van Groezen, B., H. Kiiver and B. Unger (2009). Explaining Europeans' preferences for pension provision. *European Journal of Political Economy*, 25(2), 237–246.

Index